PRENTICE HALL

Language Teaching Methodology Series

Teacher Education
General Editor: Christopher N. Candlin

Language Planning and
English Language Teaching

Other titles in this series include

ALDERSON, Charles
Evaluation

BRUMFIT, Christopher, J.
Problems and principles in English teaching

BRUMFIT, Christopher, J.
Language and literature teaching

CANDLIN, Christopher and MURPHY, Dermot
Language learning tasks

CARROLL, Brendan, J.
Testing communicative performance: an interim study

CARROLL, Brendan, J. and HALL, Patrick
Make your own language tests

COOK, Vivian
Experimental approaches to second language learning

ELLIS, Rod
Classroom second language development

ELLIS, Rod
Classroom language acquisition in context

JOHNSON, Keith
Communicative syllabus design and methodology

KELLERMAN, Eric and SHARWOOD SMITH, Michael
Cross-linguistic influence in second language acquisition

KENNEDY, Chris
Language planning and English language teaching

KRASHEN, Stephen
Second language acquisition and second language learning

KRASHEN, Stephen
Principles and practice in second language acquisition

KRASHEN, Stephen and TERRELL, Tracy
The natural approach

LA FORGE, Paul
Counseling and culture in second language acquisition

LEONTIEV, Alexei
Psychology and the language learning process

LEWIS, E. Glyn
Bilingualism and bilingual education

LOVEDAY, Leo
The sociolinguistics of learning and using a non-native language

MARTON, Waldemar
Methods in English language teaching: frameworks and options

McKAY, Sandra
Teaching grammar

PECK, Antony
Language teachers at work

ROBINSON, Gail
Crosscultural understanding

SWALES, John
Episodes in ESP

TOSI, Arturo
Immigration and bilingual education

WATERS, Alan
Issues in ESP

WENDEN, Anita and RUBIN, Joan
Learner strategies in language learning

YALDEN, Janice
The communicative syllabus

Language Planning and English Language Teaching

Edited by

CHRIS KENNEDY
University of Birmingham, UK

ENGLISH LANGUAGE TEACHING

Prentice Hall

New York London Toronto Sydney Tokyo

First published 1989 by
Prentice Hall International (UK) Ltd,
66 Wood Lane End, Hemel Hempstead,
Hertfordshire, HP2 4RG
A division of
Simon & Schuster International Group

Printed and bound in Great Britain at
the University Press, Cambridge.

Library of Congress Cataloging-in-Publication Data

Language planning and English language teaching/edited by
    Chris Kennedy.
        p.   cm – (Prentice Hall International language teaching
    methodology series. Teacher education)
        Bibliography: p.
        Incudes index.
        ISBN 0-13-523184-1 : $12.00
        1. English language–Study and teaching–Foreign
    speakers. 2. English teachers–Training of–Foreign
    countries. 3. English language–Foreign countries.
    4. Language planning. I. Kennedy, Chris. II. Series.
    PE1128.A2L296   1988
    428′.007–dc19   88–12150

British Library Cataloguing in Publication Data

Language planning and English language teaching.–(Language
    teaching methodology series).
        1. Education. Curriculum subjects: English language.
    Teaching
    I. Kennedy, Chris   II. Series
    420′.7

ISBN   0–13–523184–1

1 2 3 4 5 92 91 90 89 88

Contents

General Editor's Preface

In much of the current literature about language teaching and learning there is an at least implicit assumption that the teacher, and for many authors, the learner stands at the centre of the process, autonomous and free to exercise his or her own particular choices of learning or teaching content, learning or teaching path. Such an assumption, however warranted ideally, finds little reflection in classroom practice. Here teachers and learners find choices of linguistic model, mode of teaching and learning, approved language content, present as predetermined givens, decided so to speak in advance on their behalf.

If this picture has any validity it serves to illustrate how the everyday practices of the classroom in language teaching and learning have been constrained by planning decisions made elsewhere in the organizational structure. Moreover, the organs of such planning and the bases upon which the planning is made are for many teachers and even more so for many learners, entirely opaque. Models are prescribed and texts illustrating them preferred not only without benefit of consumer involvement but often without much if any explicit discussion of the macro issues inevitably involved, be they political, economic or educational. Planning takes place, as it were, in some naturalized context, obeying assumptions that are seen as common-sensical in particular contexts, not open to debate.

If this rings true, it may be worth considering its counterpoint, where teachers and learners do have a measure of autonomy in their actions, opportunities for making their own decisions about curriculum content, methodology and evaluation. Here we see a common narrowing of vision where the individual classroom, or even the individual learner, is regarded as the proper and only possible object of the teacher's focus, deliberately isolated as it were from the social context from which the learner comes. Learning and teaching in such an individualized classroom is an asocial process, as a matter of principle and practice isolated from the linguistic politics of the world outside the institution, entirely a matter of cognitive and pedagogic concern. Here teaching decisions do not rely on data other than those offered by language as a system or those suggested by the learning preferences of individuals.

Both these scenarios are ultimately unquestioning and uncritical acceptances of the perceived autonomy of the classroom, the one *faute de mieux* and the other by personal desire. Neither scenario has much justification if one takes an explanatory and critical perspective on the context of language teaching and learning. Choices of language to be learned, models to be preferred, modes of learning to be fostered, influences and special interests to be taken into account, are never value-free; they always reflect motivated positions and committed ideologies, whether of governments, curriculum development bodies and agencies, or, as here, the syllabus developers and lesson planners among the teachers themselves.

In short, language planning issues are not relevant and of concern at the level of ministries and government only, policy-making matters of little direct concern to the language teacher, they are intimately and acutely local in their classroom significance.

Moreover, the teacher is not only an agent on behalf of these higher powers; in his or her teaching decisions, especially in those systems which actively encourage classroom-based curriculum development, language planning takes place at the coalface of teaching and learning.

Chris Kennedy's new book in the Language Teaching Methodology Series addresses this question of local responsibility and involvement. It does so by concentrating on English Language Teaching and in a world focus. Inevitably, therefore, it reflects the inherent problems of 'world' Englishes, their status and currency, their relationships to indigenous languages, their feasibility and appropriateness in the myriad contexts of language learning and teaching. English offers the classic case for this widened exploration of language planning, allowing all of the macro and micro aspects of the planning process, overt or more often covert, to be opened for debate.

Given this exploratory and questioning perspective, the editor's choice of structure for the book admirably fits the theme. Each contribution both highlights an issue in the debate and provides an international perspective. Each contribution is both prefaced by the editor and followed by a set of tasks. These latter have been specially constructed to encourage the reader, either on his or her own or in a group, to explore the issues of that contribution and cross-reference them to the overall themes of the book.

In sum, this latest addition to the Prentice Hall series not only amply fulfils the objectives of the series as a whole in the way it engages practitioners in the principles and practice of language teaching, it serves to emphasize how any decision in education, whether at the level of the classroom or the system as a whole, must be set in its particular historical and social context if it is to be understood, and more especially if it is to be effective.

CHRISTOPHER N. CANDLIN
Macquarie University
Sydney

Introduction

What is language planning?

Language planning (LP) is the conscious, deliberate attempt to alter the function and/or status of either a language or linguistic variety. Ideally, it should be a problem-solving, future-oriented activity with a number of planning stages from problem identification, to fact-finding (see Olshtain this volume), goalsetting, implementation and evaluation. Many examples of LP or attempts at LP exist (the case studies in Part 3 of this collection providing some examples) especially in the developing world where nations, having inherited the linguistic legacies of colonialism, wish to develop language policies which more accurately reflect the present-day political realities behind the uses of English and the local, or indigenous, languages in their countries.

It is this underlying political reality that makes LP such an interesting, but also a complex, area of study. Any language plan or policy will be linked to broader social, economic or political objectives and decisions about language will always be taken with reference to a particular socio-political and cultural context, perhaps most clearly demonstrated in this collection by the article on Namibia and, from a very different context, by Quinn's article on community languages in Australia. Any language plan that is at odds with the prevailing social or political climate or which runs counter to the feelings and attitudes of interested parties is unlikely to succeed, Gibbons providing the example from Hong Kong of failure of government language policy implementation in the schools because of parental disapproval. Badly managed implementation may indeed lead to violent conflict unless plans are carefully introduced over time and much attention given to the concerns of those whom the plan closely affects. LP inevitably involves change and innovation to a greater or lesser degree, hence the necessity for including in this collection a mention of strategies of change (Horvath) which may be appropriate at all levels whether one is changing the role of a language or introducing a new set of materials into the classroom.

LP is most often regarded as planning by official bodies at government level. What this collection tries to illustrate, however, is that we may legitimately extend this rather narrow notion of LP to include planning carried out at different levels by politicians, officials, curriculum developers, syllabus designers, and language teachers. Tollefson's model, in particular, illustrates the close connection between the different levels from government to classroom and the fact that any decision made at one level has consequences, not always positive, for the levels below.

Is language planning necessary?

Language is an essential tool in a nation's or a group's development, but it is at the same time a basic expression of the identity of a nation, group or individual. The use or nonuse of a language can, therefore, help or hinder both the development of a people's sense of themselves as a nation and that nation's economic and social advance. At the same time, such 'macro' concerns have to be balanced with concern for individual rights at the 'micro' level. The case for LP is that, just as in other aspects of national life a degree of planning may enable objectives to be reached more effectively and perhaps more efficiently, so linguistic aims (whether at the level of government or classroom) may also be accomplished more successfully through a rational problem-solving process.

The argument for LP, of course, applies to many areas of national life: business, administration, law, science and technology, wherever spoken or written languages are influential channels of communication. The focus in this book is on LP and education, specifically the relationships between LP, the different roles and functions of English and other languages in different societies, and the implications for the teaching of English as a subject and as a medium of education.

What curriculum questions can a study of language planning help to answer?

One of the major issues which an LP approach may help to clarify is that of the choice in multilingual societies of which languages should be used for instruction and when, and whether they should be taught subjects or used as 'carriers' for content subjects such as science and history (see Rogers and Abbott this volume). More often than not, the choice is between English and other local languages. Many writers in this collection (for example Emenyonu and Serpell) argue strongly for more attention to be paid to the development of local languages so that they may play a greater part in the life of a nation, including a more significant role in education.

There are many instances of local languages increasing their functions in society in general and in education in particular, and this trend is likely to continue. However, there are many situations where, perhaps for financial reasons, English is likely, in the short term, to remain the language of the classroom, or where, perhaps because there is a multiplicity of local languages and a common language is required, English will have such a role for a long time to come. Those writers in this collection who press for more use of local languages also admit that English will have an important part to play in the educational systems of many multilingual societies for some time.

Where policy is established and subjects are taught through the medium of English, the focus of LP changes (in Tollefson's model we move to lower levels of implementation) and the issue now is to work out ways to make sure that as many learners as possible succeed in the educational system despite the fact that they are learning through the medium of a second language, which is what English will be to the majority. The issue of language in the curriculum is worthy of a book to itself, but many of the articles in this collection deal with the subject from a language planning perspective, and a number of the tasks ask the reader to go deeper into the problem, particularly its linguistic aspects.

We can therefore distinguish two major issues that are developed in this volume: the first is whether language policies themselves should be changed in order to give languages other than English a greater role in education, the second is what to do when an established policy of using English as a medium in the classroom is causing problems for the learners. Answers to the first question will come from philosophy, psycholinguistics and sociolinguistics, (though policy decisions themselves, we should remember, will be primarily political); answers to the second will come from applied linguistics, since we need to study what linguistic problems students are experiencing and how we might design methods and materials to ease those problems.

What are the relationships between language planning and English language teaching (ELT)?

One way of illustrating the connections between LP and ELT is to imagine an English language teacher standing in front of a class in a particular country and to ask what decisions have already been made that influence the teaching. If we use Tollefson's hierarchical model we will be able to place the various influences at different levels of the decision-making process. Several questions might be raised by looking at the teaching situation in this way. For example, 'Who is teaching?' might be one question, raising issues like teacher qualifications, expertise, and command of the language. 'What are the students learning?' and 'How are they being taught?' would focus attention on syllabus design, materials and methods. Who the learners are and their attitudes to English will also be an LP issue, since these aspects are largely determined by the language situation and the language policy arising from it. Many people, from government officals to classroom teachers, will set out reasons for language learning and frequently motivational problems can be traced back to decisions which have been made higher in the system and which conflict with the real needs and wants of students. It is this tracing of decision making and the explicit locating of the causes of problems that is an especially positive aspect of an LP approach to ELT, and in particular it may help the teacher deal more effectively with problems s/he is experiencing in the classroom.

So far, in our discussion of LP, we have distinguished between English and local languages. In many nations, especially those where English is being used as a lingua franca within the country (see Judd this volume for further explanation), English itself is in a very real sense a 'local' language and varieties are emerging ('New Englishes') which are just as much an expression of the speakers' identity as the other local languages. The emergence of the New Englishes is a common theme throughout this collection and its implications for the classroom are discussed by many of the contributors, notably Emenyonu, Serpell, and Abbott. A New English presents a number of problems which will, no doubt, be resolved over time. The English that is used outside the classroom is likely to diverge from the variety presented in the classroom, which may have more in common with an external standard (often British or American). This collection examines the suitability of the target variety which learners are taught and asks whether their needs might not be better served if they were exposed to different varieties of English which they could use in appropriate circumstances. This is not to deny there would still have to be a standard form but this might be more appropriately an internal standard, with an external international norm being necessary only for those who would need to use English in international rather than national settings.

I have tried in this brief introduction to give an idea of the major issues covered in the collection; these include the links between LP and the classroom, questions of choice of medium of instruction, the problems created through learning subjects in a second language, new varieties of English and the role they should have in schools, and the connections between LP and English language teaching in general.

Teachers sensitized to the language planning process and its connections with the classroom may not necessarily become better teachers or be able to solve all their teaching problems. They will however be able to identify more clearly why problems are occurring and where their source lies, a first step towards devising appropriate solutions, and also be able to relate their teaching and their students' learning to a wider social and political context, thus increasing their professionalism.

Organization of the book

This collection is divided into three parts. The first part presents a number of the issues which will be developed in the other articles and puts LP and ELT into a broader social and political framework. This part of the book is intended to be fairly controversial and examines the rationale behind the teaching of English and other languages in national educational systems, especially those in the developing world.

The second part looks at the relationships between LP and language learning from a general viewpoint, not dealing with specific countries. The articles in this section present a number of frameworks suitable for explaining the relationships between LP and language learning and teaching. These frameworks can then be applied to the particular case studies and issues raised in the third part of the book which deals with Namibia, Nigeria, Zambia, Australia, Hong Kong and Malaysia. Issues discussed in this section include the choice of medium of instruction and the linguistic demands placed on students, not only those learning English as a second language, but also those learning content subjects through English. The question of New Englishes and the emergence of new objectives for ELT is also addressed in this part.

Each article is preceded by a brief introduction which summarizes the main issues, and is followed by a number of practical tasks designed to help the reader engage with the issues in the articles and also develop and apply new ideas arising from them. All the tasks are self-contained and can be completed without reference to further reading, but it is hoped that readers will use both the references contained within the task and the recommendations for further reading at the end of the tasks for follow-up work.

The book concludes with a full bibliography for those who would like to extend their study of the subject.

Acknowledgements

I should like to thank both David Haines of Prentice Hall and Chris Candlin for their helpful suggestions and for their unfailing patience and encouragement.

CHRIS KENNEDY

Abbreviations

EAL*	English as an Additional language	JMMD	*Journal of Multilingual and Multicultural Development*
EAP*	English for Academic Purposes		
EFL*	English as a Foreign Language	LP	Language planning
EIL*	English as an International Language	LPLP	*Language Problems and Language Planning*
ELT	English Language Teaching	LWC	Language of Wider Communication
ELTJ	*English Language Teaching Journal*		
ELWC*	English as a Language of Wider Communication	L2	Second Language
		MT	Mother tongue
ESL*	English as a Second Language	NE	New English
ESOL*	English for Speakers of Other Languages	RELC	Regional English Language Centre
		SLA	Second Language Acquisition
ESP	English for Specific Purposes	TL	Target language
ESPJ	ESP Journal	TMT	Taught mother tongue
EST	English for Science and Technology	VMT	Vernacular mother tongue
EWW	*English Worldwide*		
IJSL	*International Journal of the Sociology of Language*		

*'T' with these initials denotes 'Teaching'

Note: The pupils, schoolchildren, students and teachers referred to throughout this book could – unless it is specifically stated to the contrary – equally well be men/boys or women/girls. The form 's/he' has been used in many places, but occasionally 'he' has been used as a universal pronoun.

Part One

THE CONTEXT OF ENGLISH LANGUAGE
TEACHING AND LANGUAGE PLANNING

Chapter 1

'The World for Sick Proper'

JOHN ROGERS

Editor's introduction

It seems appropriate to begin a collection on language planning (LP) and language teaching with an article which highlights some of the important connections between planning or policy decisions and teaching outcomes, and which sets the issues in a wider social and political framework. Many of the questions raised by Rogers we shall see discussed in other contexts in the articles in this collection. Some readers may feel that Rogers overstates the cause–effect relationships between English language teaching (ELT) and the social and economic difficulties experienced by a number of developing countries, and is perhaps ascribing to ELT programmes a degree of influence over people and events which they do not possess. It would make life much easier if we were able to relate problems of poverty and unemployment to the teaching of English, but the issues are obviously more complex and intractable. What is clearly demonstrated, however, is that policy decisions on the role of English in a country's educational system are not made in a vacuum and they will always be related to decision takers' political views. Rogers thinks that in a number of cases those beliefs (perhaps for example that a country's economic development will be closely linked with the degree of access to Western expertise in science and technology) are translated into educational policy that in turn may result in English being taught throughout an educational system to large numbers of students who will never need to use it, and indeed who may mistakenly believe that the learning of English will in some way help their own personal economic advancement.

There are, of course, a number of counterarguments to Rogers' views and we shall be examining some of them in the reply by Abbott (see the following article), but the value of this article lies in the way Rogers focuses our attention on issues of cost-effectiveness and cost/benefit in ELT. Bland statements are often made about learners' needs for English. What Rogers asks us to do is to attempt to assess realistically whether the evidence supports such statements by discovering, for example, just how many learners in a given situation actually do require English for a job, or really do need it for international communication. Rogers argues that the answers to these questions might very well lead to a fundamental rethink in the allocation of resources for ELT, and suggests one possible solution, that of matching actual need and ELT provision more closely by introducing ELT training much later in a learner's education and offering it only to those who really require it. Whether such a solution could always be implemented is another question which Rogers raises but admits he cannot answer. Resistance to such a policy might be considerable from those who felt it was depriving them of an essential part of their education (see Gibbons, this volume). Sceptics might also doubt whether resources saved by cutting back on ELT programmes at lower levels in an educational system would in fact be used to support ELT expansion at higher levels in the way Rogers suggests.

The article, by raising these important issues, both demonstrates the links that exist between language policy and practice and suggests an important role for language planning in assessing outcomes and providing alternative suggestions for action.

IN A SHORT story by Paul Theroux, *The Flower of Malaya*, one of the characters is a young American woman:

She was a teacher... She taught English, most of them do, never asking themselves what happens when a half-starved world is mumbling in heavily-accented English, 'I want –'.

Shortly after I read this, I read the June 1979 issue of the *New Internationalist*, 'Children's voices', in which seventy children from five continents talked about their lives and their hopes for the future. Quite a few of these children, from West and East Africa, West Indies and India, Pakistan and Bangladesh, spoke in their own varieties of English. Here is what some of them said, or 'mumbl[ed] in heavily-accented English':

Kweku (9), Accra, Ghana
My work is that I sell chewing gum around the Orin Circle at cinema time... My mother died before they born me. My father nobody know... I sleep in the far night at 2.00 a.m. sometimes 3.00 a.m. morning time. I no have sleeping house. I sleep at the lorry petrol station... The world for sick proper. I want 1979 to have no war and no children born like I am... I want 1979 to bring house for us and water for village people to drink. Don't take photo of me. I don't want white man see me dirty.

Keshar (9), Nagpur, India
I am looking through all this rubbish every day. It is my work... I look for glass, paper, old iron things, plastic sandals... I don't like this work. You work in sun all day. You get dirty. You get sick easy... I would like to go to school. I like to see small girls going to school with books and slate... I would like to have a house and two sets of clothes...

Vinton (14), Kingston, Jamaica
I want to go back to school and get myself a trade. I learn welding, woodwork, and learn to fix electrics. You have some boys and they get trade, but they follow their friends. They go robbin' and the police kill them. Them idiots. If I get a trade, I cool... In twenty years' time I wish I'm in nice job with my wife and children and house, you know...

Wambgu (12), Nairobi, Kenya
I left school because I failed and I have no money. I want a job nicely. Every day I look for work. Mainly I work with cars. Look at my clothes. I am a dirty boy because I am a mechanic. I am the spanner boy. I only get 5 shillings a day. I try to save it. But I need the money for smoking.

Kenyatta (14), Kenya
The [boy] at school will get to be a manager and have a big car. The [boy] at home will just become a thief and a robber... If you don't know English they will say that you are a useless man and they won't do what you tell them. I want to be a manager and then they will just bring my letters and I will put my signature there. I will give many orders to others, and I will warn those ones who are lazy or drunk. And if they don't agree with me, I will sack them...

Fibi (15), Kenya
At school we used tribal language. When we moved to Nairobi my English is not enough for school. I am sad because I used to do well and now you can see that I am not a person who is educated.

Has English helped these children and the countries they are trying to survive in, or has it in some way been part of the cause of their miserable existence? Is it ethical to go on teaching English to so many children, and so encourage them to believe that it will automatically entitle them to a better job, an office job, a manager's job with a big car, a house and two sets of clothes, a 'better' life? Have we omitted to ask ourselves what happens when this 'half-starved world' mumbles, 'I want –', in English?

The rest of this article attempts a brief examination of what English teaching (and learning) might be responsible for and what some future options might be. It is of course very tentative and, I trust, very provocative. I would very much like to start a discussion of the question and hope that readers will respond, for or against, with feeling.

At the outset I should perhaps make it clear that my attack – for it is an attack – is not directed at the teaching of English to migrants or immigrants who come to live in an English-speaking country and who do not speak English, although even here I would prefer to see facilitation rather than intervention. It is, rather, directed at the often indiscriminate teaching of English in countries where it is a second or a foreign language and where a knowledge of English is regarded as a passport to a 'better' job. In these countries English is also considered essential as a means of international communication and as the means for acquiring access to 'Western' technology, science and, finally, 'Western-style development and progress'. (I make no apologies for the liberal use of quotation marks. These words have been overused to such an extent that they are now almost meaningless and need drastic redefining.)

Several questions are begged. It may well be that in some countries there are a number of attractive, well-paid jobs for which a knowledge of English is essential. How many such jobs are there? How many English learners are there in schools? Do they all want these jobs? Are there enough jobs of this kind for all those who want them? If there are not, and if there are unlikely to be enough, is it not dishonest, even immoral, for the schools and the systems that run them, to pretend that learning English *is* a passport or entry visa to a so-called better future? An example from Kiribati suggests that any secondary school English programme that does not warn its customers about Progress, in the form of the microchip/word processor revolution, is not fulfilling its obligations. One Kiribati commercial company installed an IBM machine that resulted in the redundancy of a number of office workers who, at school, believed that competence in English would guarantee a permanent office job. Perhaps their secondary school English textbook should have included the lexical items, 'redundancy' and 'multinational companies'. Let me quote another young Kenyan office hopeful, Faith (13), from Masailand:

> My best subject is English. I try very hard to learn it well. It is the fashionable language nowadays. You can't work in an office without it. How can you get a job if you just say 'Nintaka Kaze' in Swahili? I will start by sweeping the office and after that I will move up to be a secretary...When I am working I will find jobs for people of my family and tribe. I am the one who studied, the lucky one, so I shall help...

All our Dip.TESL (Diploma in the Teaching of English as a Second Language) course members at the English Language Institute in Wellington tell us that one of the reasons their students learn English is that English is essential as a means of international communication. When we ask these same course members how many of their students can realistically expect ever to meet native speakers of English, or indeed non-native speakers who use English as a second or third or foreign language, or how many of them *will* need English for communication purposes, the replies suggest that only a very small percentage will need English for that purpose.

Related to this, of course, is the necessity for some tertiary level students to be able to read English-language texts and, if they study overseas, to be able to understand the English of lecturers and tutors and to be able to make themselves understood in seminars and tutorials. But what do the figures tell us? In Tonga, to take an example from the South Pacific, only two per cent of secondary school leavers actually need English for higher education overseas. In March 1980, I was told by the then Senior

Education Officer for Curriculum in the Tongan Ministry of Education that the number of Tongans studying overseas was decreasing. Also in March 1980, I was told by the Director of Education in Western Samoa that 0.08 per cent of school leavers need English for higher studies overseas or scholarships. He added that between 15 and 18 per cent of school leavers needed English for government or private company jobs in Western Samoa itself. This need, the need for scholarship students to be able to study through the medium of English, is often quoted as a justification of the learning of English by *all* secondary students. It would be interesting to know the figures for all the countries that continue to insist that *all* secondary students, if not primary pupils, must learn English.

The third question that is begged is the implication that English is the most, or at least one of the most, important means for acquiring access to Western technology, science and, through this, to Western-style development and progress. Apart from the question of the desirability of Western style 'progress', there is the assumption that progress or development can come only through the medium of English. There is now abundant evidence to show that many worthwhile improvements in traditional cultures are being made where local people are consulted, not instructed, that beneficial changes are being implemented without the imposition of Western solutions. The Food and Agricultural Organization bulletins, *Ideas and Action*, are full of examples of successful development programmes that do not rely on the importation of Western ideas and approaches. As Edward F. Douglass says, in 'The discovery of commonness – essential for cross-cultural dialogue' (*Ideas and Action* 112, 1976/5):

> No warnings are offered to the people of the developing countries about the intrinsic problems of Western life: alienation, poverty amidst vast wealth, and the constrictions of urban life. Traditional peoples are not cautioned about the loss of family ties and security, the ulcerous pace of life and the psychological dislocations from the basic truths of traditional life. Yet these changes represent, in part, the price of adopting the Western notion of modernity.

The programmes that took the trouble in the first place to see why African farmers, for example, farmed the way they did have proved to be the most successful.

As an illuminating aside on the role of language in development, in *Ideas and Action* 115, 1977/2, there is an article by Dohol Chandra Soni, 'The spoken and unspoken word in rural communication', which points out that even a country's standard and uniform language may be a barrier to development. In India, particularly in the four states of Bihar, Uttar Pradesh, Rajasthan, and Madhya Pradesh, the standard and uniform type of Hindi is used as the medium of communication between the programme agents and the programme targets. But the programme participants, mostly unschooled adults, have strongly-formed speech habits in the locally spoken dialects. The so-called educators do not 'step down' to the local spoken languages. They expect the programme-target people to change their deeply ingrained adult speech habits and adopt the uniform standard Hindi as a precondition of becoming literate, educated and developed. To quote Mr Soni:

> This is indirectly to discourage the people, to tell them that their speech habits are incapable of literacy, education, and development. As soon as the educator talks and teaches in Hindi, he SILENTLY or in an unspoken manner imprints upon the minds of the people that their own spoken language (which is a part of their personality) is incapable of becoming the medium of education. And since the man cannot make a distinction between himself and his speech habit,

he cannot have the necessary self-confidence for becoming literate, educated, and developed when his spoken language is not made the medium of his literacy, his education and his development.

Similarly, an insistence on the need for English as the vehicle for development and progress might well be counterproductive.

It might be argued that English itself is neutral and does not necessarily bring anything else with it, no alien values, but, like Hindi in the example quoted above, the very fact of using it, relying on it, does have implications. One is reminded of Paulo Freire, in *Pedagogy of the Oppressed*:

> There is no such thing as a neutral educational process. Education either functions as an instrument which is used to facilitate the integration of the younger generation into the logic of the present system and bring about conformity to it or it becomes the 'practice of freedom', the means by which men and women deal critically and creatively with reality and discover how to participate in the transformation of their world.

One reason for my mistrust of the use of English as a means of access to change and improvement is that in the countries of Asia, Africa and the Pacific where I have seen English taught, its function has too often been the first function Freire describes above, and too rarely the second.

Whatever we may think about the advisability or desirability of teaching English to so many learners, a lot of English *is* being taught and a lot of textbook writers (and publishers) are making money out of this English teaching. One wonders, though, how much English is *learnt*. On a recent tour through Polynesia, for example, I was repeatedly told by secondary school teachers that children came to the secondary schools after their primary course 'unable to read English, unable to write English, and unable to understand spoken English'. These teachers complained that they 'had to start all over again'. At the University of the South Pacific, in Suva, Fiji, I was told that average first-year students, some from these same Polynesian secondary schools, know the meanings of about 7,500 common English words. 'Amongst those words known by less than two-thirds of students were "frequent", "anxiously", "explanation", "diligent" and "radical". These Pacific Islands students have an English reading vocabulary comparable to that of New Zealand thirteen-year-olds on the same tests. The results for the Listening Comprehension Tests were even lower' (Elley 1980).

English is, of course, a second language for these students, but they have to study through the medium of English and they are expected to be able to handle textbooks written for native speakers of English. As Elley goes on to say in the same report:

> After six years of primary school instruction, large numbers of pupils are reading with insufficient competence to cope with the expected reading tasks of the classroom. Throughout high school the problem becomes more serious, despite a severe drop-out rate and a series of selective examinations. By the time they reach university, the surviving students are still struggling with what must be largely meaningless English prose in their texts and reading assignments. By their own admission, many students are out of their depth in coping with English as a second language.

Similar situations exist in many other countries. In Ethiopia we found (Rogers, 1969) that after ten years' English learning, including six years with English as the medium of instruction for all secondary school subjects except Amharic, the national language, first-year university students needed to go right back to the beginning again in English.

And these were the persistent, hard-working survivors of a dauntingly flattened educational pyramid-cum-obstacle course. Very few of them could read English passages written within a 2,000 word vocabulary at a speed of 100 words per minute. Very few could write a correct sentence in English. Thai and Indonesian university students often cannot cope with university textbooks written in English. We have found that some of these same students' English teachers, at the English Language Institute in Wellington, through no fault of their own, cannot read university level texts. And their written and spoken English is often poor. What hope have their students? Why go on teaching English if it is taught and learned badly?

Why are attempts made to teach English to so many students who are never going to need it? In Ethiopia's Third Five-Year Plan (1968–73) the projected drop-out figures were astounding. Seventy thousand children were to be in Grade 3 for the year 1968/9 (Grade 3 is where English teaching begins). Ten thousand of these children were expected to drop out after Grade 3. By the time this intake reached Grade 7, in 1972, there were expected to be only 38,100 survivors. In other words, 31,900 children were expected to drop out between Grade 3 and Grade 7. Yet they were all being taught English. What were they going to do with their pathetic scraps of English? English became the medium of instruction at Grade 7; 17,900 children were expected to drop out at the end of Grade 6. They would have been learning English for four years because they would need it for junior secondary classes. Was it fair to give so many children the idea that they would be going on to secondary schools, perhaps even to university?

Quite apart from the dubious ethics of raising so many false hopes, is no concern ever shown about the cost-effectiveness of such language-teaching programmes? I know of only one attempt to encourage cost-effectiveness studies in the teaching of foreign languages, a paper by Peter Strevens, 'Where has all the money gone?' (Strevens 1969). L.A. Hill (in 1978) suggested that English might better be taught at the tertiary level, the way Anglo Saxon, Old Icelandic, Classical Arabic, Persian, Science German, and Science Russian are taught. As Hill says,

> Then [at the tertiary level] the best brains will have been selected out; students will have reached an age when they can make use of reason in their language learning; they will no longer be so afraid of making fools of themselves...

He lists further advantages, related to the points I have been trying to make about student numbers and teacher quality:

> [English] could be taught only to those students who were going to use it, so we would need fewer teachers and could choose the best available; the enormous wastage rate at school level (vast numbers of students failing to reach a level where they could make any meaningful use of the language; or never using the language after they have finished their studies) could be cut down considerably; and both the teachers and the students would be happier because the latter would be learning the language because they really wanted to. The course could concentrate heavily on the reading skill, since that is the most useful one to most students starting at this level.

As far as I can determine, this very sensible proposal provoked no comment or discussion. If it was read, it was ignored or forgotten. But imagine my delight when, in March 1980, the Senior Education Officer for Curriculum in the Tongan Ministry of Education said she would like to see English teaching discontinued in the primary schools, Tongan used as the medium of instruction in secondary schools, and a major effort directed at the teaching of Tongan. She advocated the teaching of English, technical and scientific English principally, to those groups of students, often 'mature' students, who need it for specialized studies overseas. She described one of her department's most successful ESP (English for Specific Purposes) projects, the teaching of English to groups of elderly ladies in Tongan villages who sell their handicrafts to tourists. In other parts of the world also, ESP courses seem to be proving very successful. The consumers are highly motivated, the instructors know very clearly what is required and such courses seem to avoid becoming EFNPP courses (English For No Particular Purpose: Coffey 1978), like so many school courses.

I realize, as do L.A. Hill and the Tongan Senior Education Officer (Curriculum), that any such decision will be very unpopular, to say the least, with parents, government officials, and members of parliament. As Hill puts it,

> In many countries parents insist on their children all learning a foreign language, because they believe that it will help them to get a good job; so if it is taught only to tertiary students, parents whose children do not reach that level will cause trouble to their members of parliament, the Minister of Education, etc.

(I like that 'etc.'.) Hill does not suggest a way to overcome this resistance; nor does the Tongan education official; nor do I.

However, by an interesting coincidence, or perhaps as yet another example of serendipity, a 1980 BBC TV documentary, and the book it was based on (Glasser 1977), describe a similar situation, happening almost in reverse in Europe. The book and the documentary describe a small southern Italian village, San Giorgio, where parents were very anxious to get higher education for their children. The young people realize that their parents, 'by sending them in for higher education . . . have already made a choice on their behalf to send them away [from San Giorgio] simply because there is no chance whatsoever for [them] to get a job as an engineer, a doctor, an accountant, a lawyer and so on, in a tiny place like this. So by the very fact of education they are being made into exiles from fairly early childhood'.

English teaching was not, of course, the reason for the exiling of the young in San Giorgio. But their parents' desire for higher education *was*. In other countries parents' insistence on their children learning English has a similar origin and might well have similar effects.

> In the early 1960s, the Italian government raised the school leaving age to 16 and made it easy for nearly everyone to proceed to the state universities. Today, of Italy's two million unemployed, half have a university or similar qualification. There are also two million job vacancies, but they are not the sort of jobs that [San Giorgio's] parents hoped for as a reward for their *sacrificio* – the sacrifice they made to get them a good education. (BBC TV script 1980).

According to Glasser, who has been involved in development in various countries for fifteen years, what we (developers? agents of change? English teachers?) have been doing

> is to impose upon people a series of very violent emotional changes as the price of achieving industrialization and technological change. And this realization is such an emotional shock to them that you get a violent explosion in that society which leads to misery, cruelty and all those other things which we now (1980) see in Iran and Kampuchea . . .

I do not feel that I have reached any conclusions. I think I have asked some questions that are not perhaps asked when countries embark on or modify English teaching programmes. I have suggested one or two alternative approaches to the problems of English teaching, alternative approaches which might reduce the frustration and inadequacy felt by planners, administrators, teachers, and 'consumers'.

The questions and approaches I have outlined are one of the results of my English teaching experiences in Europe, Asia, Africa, and the South Pacific: experiences that have left me with many doubts, a great deal of unease, and a growing realization that more of the same might not be the answer. Edward de Bono in *The Use of Lateral Thinking* (1967) has a very apt metaphor about the digging of holes and deepening and enlarging existing holes instead of deciding to dig new ones:

> It is not possible to dig a hole in a different place by digging the same hole deeper . . . If the hole is in the wrong place, then no amount of improvement is going to put it in the right place. No matter how obvious this may seem to every digger, it is still easier to go on digging in the same hole than to start all over again in a new place . . . The disinclination to abandon a half-dug hole is partly a reluctance to abandon the investment of effort that has gone into the hole without seeing some return. It is also easier to go on doing the same thing rather than wonder what else to do: there is strong practical commitment to it . . . Yet great new ideas and great scientific advances have often come about through people ignoring the hole that is in progress and starting a new one . . .

Perhaps ELT/ESL/EFL/TESOL 'experts' should consider climbing out of their current ELT holes and should start looking for sites for more useful, more productive holes, even though, as de Bono says, 'experts are not usually the first to leap out of the hole that accords them their expert status, to start digging elsewhere'.

Tasks

Task 1

Rogers believes we should not automatically assume that English has to be learned throughout educational systems in the developing world and he thinks it should be taught only to those who really require it. His argument is based on the five points listed in note form under column A in the table below. You may agree with his argument, but in this task try to imagine possible counterarguments to each of the points, producing any evidence from your own experience in support. List your counterarguments and evidence under column B. (Leave column C blank. You can fill this in after reading Abbott's article pp.14–18.)

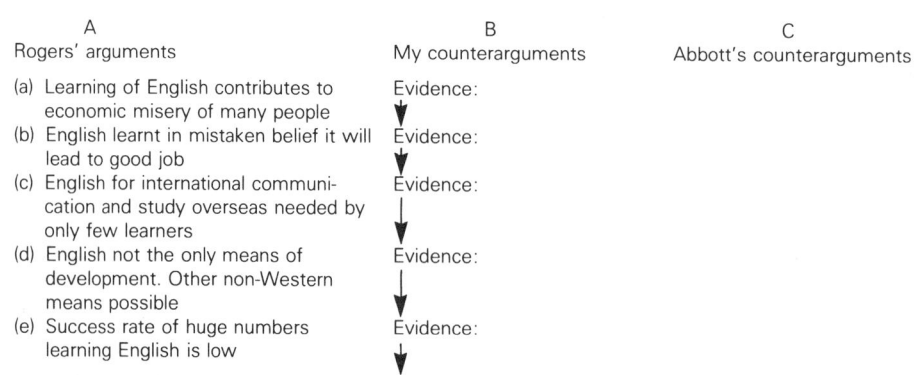

A Rogers' arguments	B My counterarguments	C Abbott's counterarguments
(a) Learning of English contributes to economic misery of many people	Evidence:	
(b) English learnt in mistaken belief it will lead to good job	Evidence:	
(c) English for international communication and study overseas needed by only few learners	Evidence:	
(d) English not the only means of development. Other non-Western means possible	Evidence:	
(e) Success rate of huge numbers learning English is low	Evidence:	

Task 2

Rogers says in the article that his argument: 'is not directed at the teaching of English to migrants or immigrants who come to live in an English-speaking country and who do not speak English.' (p. 5)

   (i) Why do you think he excludes this group from his argument?
   (ii) Does it make more sense for secondary school pupils from the English-speaking 'host community' to learn an im/migrant language rather than one of the languages (e.g. French, German) traditionally offered in secondary school systems in English-speaking countries?

(One answer to this question is put forward by Quinn in this volume.)

Task 3

Peters (quoted in Widdowson 1983: 17) has this to say about the difference between education and training:

> A person could be a trained ballet dancer or have mastered a...skill such as pottery making, without being educated. What might be lacking is something to do with knowledge and understanding: for being educated demands more than being highly skilled.

   (i) Do you think that someone who learns a language is merely mastering a skill or is being educated? Think of an example from your experience.
   (ii) Are the aims of ELT overseas to produce educated or skilled individuals? Or is it impossible to separate the two? Can you provide evidence from teaching situations you know to support your argument?
   (iii) Do your answers lead you to support Rogers' views on ELT or not?

Task 4

Business students in a university institute in Tunisia (where English is used mainly for international communication outside the country) learn English because, amongst other reasons, the university administrators often feel that the students will need it in their job when they leave college. However, a survey conducted among businesses (Thornton 1980) showed that employers were interested in job applicants having a good qualification in business studies and were not so concerned about their competence in English. How might the employers' attitudes affect student motivation to learn English and how might this in turn affect the content and design of English materials for these students?

Task 5

Rogers believes that we should look at the costs and benefits of language policy and its implementation. One decision that many multilingual developing countries have to take is whether to adopt English or a local language as the official language to be used in government and administration. Thorburn (1971) lists a number of possible consequences (we shall assume in this task they are *benefits*) arising from the adoption of either English or the indigenous language as the official language of a nation. They are:

   (a) More efficient and effective administration of the country.
   (b) Increased trade relations with other countries.
   (c) Access to world technology and culture.
   (d) Greater national unity.

(e) Equality of opportunity for all citizens.
(f) Development of national cultures.
(g) Increase in standard of living.

(i)   Which of these seven benefits (a–g) do you think are, in fact, influenced by the choice of either English or a local language as official language?

(ii) Select *one* of the benefits you isolated in (i) above. If you had to decide whether this benefit could be best achieved through the choice of English or a local language as official language, what facts and figures would you try to collect to help you reach a decision? You could try grouping the facts and figures under different headings as follows:

Political
Social
Economic
Cultural
Attitudinal
Linguistic

Task 6

Rogers introduces the concept of appropriate technology, suggesting that local solutions to problems may be more effective than those imported from the West. We can extend this notion of appropriate technology to include theories and practice in ELT. There are obvious dangers in applying ideas in contexts for which they were not designed. Maley (1985) suggests one solution (a kind of 'intermediate technology') to the problem of introducing more 'communicative' techniques into 'traditional' classrooms. He believes, taking examples from China, that it is possible to use an existing pedagogic framework but change what occurs within it so that more communicative activity takes place. See if you can do this with the following examples:

(i)   Maley says that students follow a traditional three-part study scheme of (a) preparing each lesson before the class, (b) going over it in class with the teacher, and (c) revising the lesson later – essentially going over the same content three times. Can you think of ways of keeping this three-part format but varying the content of each part to create a more communicative (and more interesting) approach?

(ii) Students memorize vocabulary, which consists of long lists of esoteric words and idioms, which they are unlikely ever to use. If you were to continue this practice of memorizing vocabulary, how would you ensure that it was useful?

(You can compare your solutions with Maley's by reading his article.)

Chapter 2

Should We Start Digging New Holes?

GERRY ABBOTT

Editor's introduction

Abbott, replying to Rogers, supports the need for a radical examination of the role of English in the developing world but takes issue with a number of Rogers' arguments. Is not Rogers, he asks, failing to distinguish between problems related just to ELT and those of a more general educational nature? If we consider English as one subject among others on a school curriculum, rather than as one subject in isolation, we can counter a number of Rogers' points. Thus, if the criterion for maintaining a subject on the curriculum is that students successfully learn it (and this begs the question what we mean by 'successfully'), and if they do not, we abolish it, then not only English but a whole range of other subjects will be removed from the curriculum. This would clearly be unacceptable, and we would do better to look for underlying causes of low school achievement across the curriculum, such as poorly-trained teachers, lack of resources and sporadic attendance. Of course it can be argued that learning a second language (in this case English) is essentially different from learning other school subjects in that it involves not only assimilation of linguistic content but also of the values and behaviour of another culture. (See Serpell and Emenyonu this volume.) This assumes that the reference group for English belongs to a different culture from those learning the language. This may indeed be so in EFL situations where Abbott's vision of language learning as a broadening cultural experience might be relevant, but it is not the case for those countries which now use English as an additional language intranationally. (See Judd this volume for a classification of situations and consequences in the classroom.)

Once it has been decided that English has a place on a curriculum, the question remains of when it should be introduced. Remember that Rogers felt it should be taught once a genuine need could be ascertained. Abbott feels this approach could lead to charges of elitism. Again, this seems to be singling out English unnecessarily. By the time students reach higher education, and in many countries upper secondary schools, they already form an elite, irrespective of whether they have studied English or not. An unfortunate situation would, of course, arise in a country where access to education was dependent on English and the government allowed English to be taught only to a restricted group.

Debates about the part English should play in an educational system cannot be conducted without considering the role of local languages. Expansion in the number of areas of national life in which English is used tends to mean a reduction in those in which local languages are used and vice versa. Both Abbott and Rogers agree that, at least at primary level and below, there is a strong case for using a local language, rather than English, as the medium – an issue raised in many of the articles in this book. Both writers, however, tend to gloss over the theoretical justification for such a policy and the practical problems of implementation. The common-sense view (but possibly this is an ethnocentric view derived from a monolingual culture) seems to suggest that becoming literate in a local language would be psychologically and cognitively better for a child, though in fact this has not yet been conclusively proved. Abbott thinks that, given commitment by a government, more mother tongue programmes could be initiated; the logistical problems, however, are still immense in many situations.

JOHN ROGERS' HEART-WARMING article 'The world for sick proper' (this volume) is the sort that demands a response. I found myself agreeing with the tenor of the argument, with the insistence on the need to ponder deeply upon the significance of English language teaching (ELT) for the individual, especially the young learner. And yet there are some 'buts' that have to be expressed in any debate upon the issues that Rogers raises. One purpose of this article is to contradict some of his tentative arguments; the other is to support his implied championship of mother-tongue education, whether in poor underdeveloped countries or rich and perhaps overdeveloped ones.

Rogers first asks whether English has helped the sort of children whose views he quotes, or whether in some way it has contributed to their misery. But it is his second question which has to be answered first: 'Is it ethical', he asks, 'to go on teaching English to so many children, and so encourage them to believe that it will entitle them to . . . a "better" life?' This question is couched in terms designed to elicit the answer 'No'. It also assumes that in giving the answer expected, we will be coming to some kind of policy-making decision. But of course we are the wrong people to ask. (I assume that Rogers is addressing teachers, teacher trainers, so-called 'experts' in ELT and so on.) A decision in Colombo that English is to be a national language is one that I can challenge, as an academic exercise; but it is not one that I can change. A decision that English is to be retained as the medium of schooling in Uganda is one that the Ugandan government must make, not the foreign ELT expert. The establishment of a role for English in *any* country is a part of that country's national education policy, and is quite rightly effected with little or no reference to outside expertise; expatriates who hold advisory positions soon become aware of how seldom their advice is sought, let alone heeded. On this subject, the first chapter ('The adviser and his dubious role') of Curle (1966) should be made compulsory reading for all would-be experts.

When governments decree that English is to be taught, it is possible that the language might, in various areas for various reasons and in various ways, be taught badly. In these cases, the ELT outsider's job is to try to help to improve the teaching, not to try to erase English from the curriculum against the wishes of the government. Rogers' question is 'Why go on teaching English if it is taught and learned badly?' The answer is, 'Because that is the law.' Besides, we do not abolish school subjects merely because most students fail to master them. Recent investigations have found that large numbers of first-year secondary schoolchildren in Britain have learned very little of the arithmetic taught in primary schools, but no-one dreams of suggesting that we should therefore delete arithmetic from the primary curriculum.

Another question, posed not only by Rogers but also by many of the teachers I have worked with in various parts of the world, is 'Why are attempts made to teach English to so many students who are never going to need it?' It is not the statistical accuracy but the assumed omniscience in this question that is dangerous. It is true that very few of the secondary students in a country like Ethiopia (and many others) will ever need to use English; but which ones are they? In the primary school, or in first-year classes in the secondary school, prediction is hazardous. Since a compulsory English course is part of a system of compulsory education designed by a government to give (or appear to give) equal opportunity to all, who can say which particular children should be prevented from learning English? And at what stage can such a judgement be passed?

As an outsider one can of course try, as I once did in Thailand, and Rogers (1969) did later in Ethiopia, to persuade the decision makers that English was not important enough to be on a particular curriculum. But in general, I believe that one has to be very careful to take into account the broad educational principle of equality of opportunity before offering such advice. Take, for instance, a territory where a knowledge of English is – whether we like it or not – considered an asset on the employment market, and where a large number of youngsters leave school after completing a compulsory period of primary education. Many of them leave school not because they want to but because there are too few secondary school places available. To delete English from the primary curriculum would be to make these young people even less employable. I know that many of them do not find reasonable employment anyway; but *some* of them do, and *sometimes* this is *partly* because they know *some* English.

Or take a very different case: the teaching of a foreign language in British secondary schools. I happen to believe that one very desirable educational opportunity is that of viewing aspects of life through the filter of a foreign language, and that we should therefore make this chance available to all our children. It has to be admitted that, for a variety of reasons (e.g. poor learner motivation and poor teacher performance in classes of wide ability range), the output of successful language learners is low. But that does not mean that the children have gained nothing of value from the course. The teaching of French to primary school children in Britain is a case in point: the children's later performance in French may not be significantly better than that of their secondary school peers who have not done any primary school French, but their attitudes may have changed for the better (see Burstall 1975) and this may be no mean achievement. Nevertheless, low foreign language achievement in schools has spurred the modern language teaching profession, first in the USA and now in Europe, to attempt 'individualization'.

Another recent move is towards 'compact courses', which provide intensive study over a brief period, instead of the usual handful of lessons per week over a period of several years. Now, there is no doubt a lot to be said in favour of such a policy, but the tendency will almost certainly be to start such courses later than the current ones; and of course, if compact courses were held after the age of sixteen, then all those who leave school at that age would be prevented from participating in them. FIPLV (the Fédération Internationale des Professeurs de Langues Vivantes) assures us (1982) that the aim 'is neither to reduce the time available, nor to lower standards, nor to narrow the focus'. We are also probably safe in assuming that no drastic delay such as I have just described is envisaged. But there are governments that might well be tempted to carry out a little social engineering by, for example, ensuring that access to English is reserved for the children of a social or even racial elite, children who (by reason of wealth, influence, sponsorship or whatever) reach the later stages of the school system. Without having to use a delaying mechanism, the Residential Schools of mainland Malaysia carry out this sort of racial preferment, in that they continue to prepare selected Malays for Cambridge English examinations with a view to subsequent higher eduction in other countries using the medium of English, while the non-selective schools catering for all races prepare students for exams not accepted as valid for university entrance in those countries.

Let us return to Rogers' argument. Most of his observations are on aspects of English-medium education, rather than the learning of English as a foreign language;

and I think it is fair to say that he tends to blame English where he should be blaming education; indeed, Rogers half admits this. No doubt it is a pity that Western education systems, along with their values and aims, were implanted or imported into countries (not all of them parts of former Western empires, remember) which could well devise more suitable ones for themselves. No doubt people such as Rogers and myself are disenchanted by the fruits of 'progress' that our own education systems have borne. And, no doubt, we are saddened when we see our own educational and social mistakes being re-enacted, sometimes as if to a script by some Third World Kafka. But could we outsiders really do any better in the circumstances? It is vital to avoid the paternalism that sometimes accompanies true concern: our own disenchantment with the product of our labours must not lead us to forbid the components to others who want them, or to interfere with the assembly of them. There is, after all, a good chance that others will make a better job of assembling them than we did. Again, if a nation's system of schooling is used 'to facilitate the integration of the younger generation into the logic of the present system' (Freire 1972), we may deplore its function; but we must not attach any special blame to English simply because it happens to be the nationally-appointed medium of instruction. Education has the same function in Tanzania, where Kiswahili has replaced English as the medium, and in Thailand, where the vehicle of learning is and always has been Thai.

What Rogers calls 'the dubious ethics of raising so many false hopes' probably applies to every education system in the world; with over three million unemployed in Britain at the moment, it certainly applies to ours. As he says, it is higher education of the kind currently offered, as much as anything else, which helps to alienate the young from their parents, including me from mine. It is the systems that are at fault, and perhaps what the world needs most is governments willing to redesign their educational ladders so as to help their young citizens to climb up different rungs towards more appropriate objectives, so that as adults they will contribute more effectively to the national wellbeing. Or perhaps young Kweku was right: it is the *world* that is 'for sick proper'.

So far, I have concentrated on denying the guilt that Rogers attaches to the teaching of English as a second language in Asia and Africa. I want now to look at the alternative or parallel possibility: the teaching and use of the mother tongue (MT) in education.

I am convinced that wherever it is possible to start schooling and to achieve literacy in the MT it should be attempted. Fortunately, the catchment areas of the world's primary schools, even in multilingual nations, often lie within one language area, and the teachers are often 'locals' – or at least able to function socially in the local language. Nevertheless, there are often reasons why even children entering school for the first time are forced to operate in an alien language. The absence of syllabuses or materials, the migration of families across language boundaries, and shortages of suitable teachers are a few typical examples. At secondary level, there is less room for manoeuvre, because the catchment area of many a secondary school crosses several linguistic boundaries; and I know from my Ugandan experience under Idi Amin that English was trusted as a non-partisan vehicle of communication, whereas such tribal languages as Luganda and Lusoga, and even the non-tribal Kiswahili, were not.

If we do as many Third World societies do – that is, sensibly accept the spilt milk of history and face the brass tacks of the present – we will find that English has been appropriated and is by and large being used to serve the ends of the peoples who need it.

But the ends do not necessarily justify the means: the need to rely on English (or French or Urdu) for secondary and tertiary education does not justify the neglect of and even contempt for the pupil's own language that some societies are guilty of.

In many countries, the government could, if it only put its mind to it, decentralize education sufficiently for all or most of its primary schoolchildren to start their schooling and become literate in their MT. Those who wonder why it matters so much that a child should be instructed in the MT should pause and imagine what it would have been like trying to become literate and operate at school in (say) Russian before, and perhaps even without ever, becoming literate in their own language; the intellectual difficulties and the emotional trauma can be tremendous. They ought then to consider the findings of such researchers as Tóukomaa (1982), who regards MT instruction as 'the key to the entire development of the child'.

It is no excuse to complain that there is no standard script for a certain language; my experience of helping to create a 'typewritable' orthography for the Kayan/Kenyah languages of Borneo leads me to think that such problems are easier to overcome than some people would have us believe. Where there is no accepted orthography and next to nothing to read, even a makeshift spelling system will do for a start. Dialectal variations are unlikely to be any more problematic than they are in English. Nor is lack of teaching material a valid excuse: there is almost always a wealth of folk stories and traditional lore to use as a starting point. It seems to me self-evident that a willingness to read, and an ability to write with fluency will be achieved far more easily through the MT than through any foreign language, whether it is Standard British English being imposed on West Africans in Lagos and West Indians in London, or Parisian French being marketed in Mali, or Bahasa Malaysia being imposed on the gentle Bidayuh of Borneo.

I suspect that Rogers would wholeheartedly support me when I say that ELT practitioners are often superbly placed to lend their skills to the support of MT instruction. The principles and practices of TEFL have, after all, much in common with those of first-language teaching at primary level, and are even more similar to those needed for the teaching of a non-MT but local medium of education such as Kiswahili or Bahasa Malaysia. Without having to speak the local language, ELT staff can pass on their skills to anyone who speaks English. Again, when we find that we are dealing with illiterate secondary school children, our first thought should be how we can get them to read – not how we can get them to read English. Teaching them (or helping other teachers to teach them) to read their MT – or the local medium of instruction, if this is more appropriate – is almost certainly the best thing to do; and ELT staff should do this without feeling guilty because they are not doing the job they are paid to do. By getting children literate in a local language they facilitate the reading of English, and this *is* what they are paid to do, surely. Besides, in my own work overseas in Africa and Asia, I have proved to my own satisfaction that outsiders are far more likely to gain local co-operation in ELT matters if they show a willingness to help tackle the country's linguistic problem as a whole than if they confine themselves to 'pushing' English all the time.

It is this wider and very worthwhile extension of our profession which I would like to see pursued; the application of our language-teaching skills to the teaching of those indigenous (or, in the case of migrant populations, exotic) languages that are vital for the communication process that we call education. To continue Rogers' borrowed metaphor, perhaps what is needed is not the digging of new holes, but the widening of those we have already dug.

Tasks

Task 1

Turn back to Task 1 of the Rogers article (p. 10) and fill in column C of the table with the counterarguments made by Abbott.

(i) Now compare your own arguments (column B) with Rogers' (column A) and Abbott's (column C).

(ii) Drawing on your own experience and these arguments, what conclusion do you come to on the issues of when English language learning should be introduced in educational systems and to whom English should be taught?

Task 2

Kennedy (1985a) has distinguished a number of levels at which plans and decisions about language are made, as follows:

Planning levels
Government
Ministry
Regional authority
Institution
Department
Classroom

(i) Suppose teachers in your particular situation wanted to make changes to methodology (your solutions to Task 6 of the Rogers article p. 12 would be examples) and suppose that these changes required a change in the way you *tested* your students,

　(1) Would the teachers be free to design and implement a new test themselves? Or

　(2) Would the teachers be allowed to design and implement a new test once they had the agreement of other people at different levels in the table above? (If so, whose agreement at which level would be required?) Or

　(3) Would the design of the test and the decision to implement it be entirely the concern of other people at different levels? (Again, if so, which people at which levels?)

(ii) Bearing in mind your answer to (i) above, do you think the present system allows teachers in your situation to respond effectively, in the domain of methodology and testing, to the needs and wants of their students? Give reasons for your reply.

(iii) If you answer to (ii) above was 'no', what realistic and feasible changes would you propose that might improve the situation?

(iv) Who would be affected, and at which level of planning, by the changes you proposed in (iii) above?

Task 3

The following claims have been made by those writing on the relationships between language and development:

(a) There is a correlation between multilingualism and economic underdevelopment (Fishman 1968a).
(b) A common language creates a unified society (Kelman 1971).
(c) Modernization can only take place in a monolingual society (Neustupny 1974).
(d) It is impossible to give more than a maximum of three languages equal treatment in a multilingual nation (Kloss 1967).

(i) Do you agree with these statements? Give reasons for your answer. Can you think of any examples of present or past language situations to support your argument?
(ii) How could a politically and economically powerful group in a multilingual society use such claims to promote their own language?
(iii) Can you think of any actual cases in multilingual settings where such claims might be used, or have been used, to promote (a) English at the expense of local languages; (b) one indigenous language at the expense of another?

If you find this difficult, the case studies later in this book or those in Kennedy (ed.) (1984) may provide some examples for you to think about.

Task 4

Both Rogers and Abbott argue strongly for wider use of the mother tongue in education.

(i) How do you think they would reply to the following viewpoint (Paulston 1986)?

While moral decency dictates the language rights of minority groups, it does not necessarily follow the state is under any obligation to economically support such rights, nor does it follow that minority groups have a right to impose their language on the nation.

(ii) What is your own reaction?
(iii) Can you provide any examples, past or present, of a state supporting minority language rights, or of minority groups imposing their language on a nation?

If you wish to find examples to help you in this task, a number of the collections on language planning listed in the bibliography at the end of this book contain case studies.

Task 5

Pattanayak (1986) argues that we should look carefully at mother-tongue programmes to see whether the language that is being used in the school (taught mother tongue – TMT) is in fact the 'home' language (vernacular mother tongue – VMT) of the minority group concerned or the mother tongue of another group within the nation concerned. He gives the following examples:

Country	TMT	VMT
Singapore	Mandarin	Hokkien
Italy	Italian	Venetian
India	Hindi	Maithili

Why do you think it is important to distinguish the two mother tongues (TMT and VMT) when evaluating the successes or failures of mother-tongue education?

Task 6

Both Rogers and Abbott mention that governments, when proposing to introduce changes in the use of English and local languages in education, may find themselves in disagreement with some of the parties most immediately affected by these changes, e.g. students and their parents. (See also the Gibbons article in this collection.) Rogers adds he has no idea how any resistance (for example to a policy to reduce the role of English) can be overcome by policy makers. (See Horvath in this collection for some discussion of this issue.)

Do you think that changes in language policy can be imposed by governments or that successful language planning must follow, rather than influence, public attitudes? Can you give any examples to support your answer?

Part Two

THE RELATIONSHIP BETWEEN LANGUAGE
PLANNING AND LANGUAGE TEACHING

Chapter 3
The Role of Language Planning in Second Language Acquisition

JAMES W. TOLLEFSON

Editor's introduction

The previous articles have raised a number of issues in the teaching of English overseas and implicitly demonstrated the relationships between governmental socio-political concerns and educational and language policy. Tollefson continues this theme by presenting an explicit framework for describing the potential links between language planning (LP) and second language acquisition (SLA) – using the latter term to cover, for the moment, both acquisition and learning, and foreign or second language situations. We shall see, as we proceed through this collection, how the problems raised by each article can be located within the framework. Tollefson addresses the question with which we are primarily concerned here, namely, to what extent can SLA be planned, and what influence do planning procedures have on SLA. He first outlines one particular model of SLA, consisting of four variables, (a) input (whether acquisition takes place in natural or classroom environments; the nature of teacher-pupil interaction); (b) the learner (age, personality, attitude and motivation); (c) learning strategies; and (d) the linguistic content of what is to be learned. Now materials writers and teachers are used to manipulating some or all of these variables and most syllabus designers would regard them as influential. The interest of Tollefson's approach is that he adds 'above' the SLA model a sequence of planning procedures which he believes may, to a greater or lesser extent, influence SLA. His framework starts from an analysis of the language situation, which forms the context for the planning procedures. These procedures operate at different levels, from government to ministries, curriculum boards, educational institutions and finally classrooms, with each level formulating policy which is in turn implemented by the level below. The framework is hierarchical, top-down, presenting a blueprint approach to planning and would no doubt need to be modified and extended once applied, to include for instance a feedback mechanism and a more process-based approach to planning. It should not be regarded as prescriptive and Tollefson is not saying that planning either does or should happen in this way. However, such an approach may be useful for the comparison of different situations and for diagnosis of problems and evaluation at the implementation stage. It could be an effective device to make the people involved at the different levels in the system aware that they were links in a chain of reaction. The ones higher in the system should be able to follow through a policy and assess its degree of success at any stage in the procedure, and the ones lower in the system, for example language advisers and syllabus designers, should be able to distinguish between those SLA variables that were part of the system and fixed (probably a considerable number in a highly centralized system) and those that could be negotiated or modified. Such analysis can only lead to more realistic, and hence in the long term more effective, implementation at each level and might help to avoid inappropriate and overambitious formulation of policy at all levels and the inevitable frustration in implementation. Appropriate materials and methodology which work in a particular context might be one result, rather than innovations that have a short and disappointing uptake.

MERRILL SWAIN (1979) expressed a view that is widespread among researchers in second language acquisition when she said that the 'why' of second or foreign language learning is a matter of fate, a result of the accidents of one's job, parents' language, school curriculum, and so on. In this view, factors such as motivation, nature of input, personality characteristics, learning processes, and quality and method of instruction are *unplanned* variables affecting rate and eventual attainment in second language acquisition or learning. This view is a common one and more or less accurately reflects language learning processes in the United States. Outside the United States, however, the facts are often quite different. Multilingualism is often the rule rather than the exception, and the acquisition or learning of second or foreign languages is often *planned* rather than accidental.[1] In constructing SLA models that reflect primarily the North American situation, researchers have not examined sufficiently the degree to which language acquisition is the direct result of planning by official and unofficial agencies. This article, therefore will outline the role of language planning in a model of SLA. Specifically, the impact of the language planning process on certain SLA variables will be explored.

Language planning

Language planning refers to all conscious, deliberate efforts to affect the structure and function of language varieties. Included are the creation of orthographies, standardization and modernization efforts, and planned functional allocation of varieties (Ferguson 1968).

Language policy may be considered a particular area of language planning. Language policy refers to conscious *governmental* efforts to affect the structure and function of language varieties (Fishman 1972c). The policy approach to language problems assumes that official action by government authorities can affect language structure and language use. Language policy involves choices by officials of particular courses of action based upon resources available, expert advice, and the circumstances of the particular language situation. These courses of action are aimed at achieving language related societal goals normally established by government authorities.

Language policy consists of two related processes: formulation of plans and implementation of plans. Formulation involves decisions of formally constituted bodies regarding the structure of codes and their functional allocation in a language community. The formulation of policy is stated in constitutions, legal statutes, official statements, and other actions of governmental authorities. Implementation involves all efforts to carry out the policies. It includes the writing of grammars and dictionaries, design of school curricula and government funding of publishing houses, cultural institutions and media.

A model of SLA

Swain's model of SLA, based on an earlier schema developed by Schumann (1976), includes four sets of variables: input, learner, learning, and learned variables. Planning variables are not included. *Input* variables affecting SLA are divided into natural interaction, involving native speakers, and instructional interaction, involving teacher-student and student-student interaction in both formal language classrooms and classes based on a functional or communicative approach. *Learner* variables include attitude and motivation; ego permeability and other personality factors such as sensitivity to criticism and tolerance of ambiguity; cognitive style; aptitude; age; and past language experience. *Learning* variables include unconscious acquisition processes and conscious learning strategies (Krashen 1976, 1978). *Learned* variables include the grammatical and pragmatic structural systems which learners must acquire. Studies of learned variables have focused on morpheme acquisition, complementation, politeness, and other elements of pragmatics (Larsen-Freeman 1976).

These sets of variables interact in a number of ways. Learner variables are affected in different ways by different learning contexts (input variables). Evidence suggests, for instance, that different personality types respond differently to varying approaches to curriculum. Proficiency level (a learned variable) affects the nature of input, as the structure and degree of foreigner talk input is, in part, determined by language proficiency. The stage of proficiency also interacts with learner variables, as one's success at communication activates different personality characteristics. What one knows in a second language affects the types of errors one makes (learning variables), and the nature of input affects the type of learning process one undergoes.

Swain's model, like other SLA models by Krashen (1976, 1978), Lamendella (1977), and Schumann (1978), does not include a planning component. Nevertheless, many of the variables in all categories may be directly affected by planning efforts. That is, such variables as the nature of input, approach to curriculum, attitudes, motivation and age of learners, content of curriculum (and what is learned), and the nature of the learning process may be determined, to a large extent, by a conscious, deliberate language planning process.

Language planning and second language acquisition

Language planning takes different forms in different settings. The focus of language planning efforts may be primarily linguistic, involving, for example, the development of a modernized vocabulary of technical and scientific terms. In such cases, the impact on SLA processes is limited: textbooks and curricula may have to incorporate the new terminology, and students may be expected to learn it. In other situations, language planning may be aimed at a major shift in the languages learned. An entire range of motivational variables may be affected, the composition of teaching staff may change, textbooks may have to be (re) written, and the distribution of language-related power and resources in the society may be altered.

The language planning process constitutes a set of intermediate variables which in turn affect input, learner, learning and learned variables. The language planning process is never simple but involves a hierarchy of decisions and planning levels which eventually affect SLA. The nature of the impact of language planning on SLA may be represented by the sequence of influences depicted in Figure 3.1.

Figure 3.1 suggests that decision-making occurs in a particular sequence, but often the direction of influence is complex. In decentralized language planning processes, for example, local micro-policy goals may largely dominate federal macro-policy goals. Often the language situation itself may be altered by planning decisions, such as when large scale SLA processes change language proficiency and use among subgroups of the national population. Despite such complexities, Figure 3.1 represents

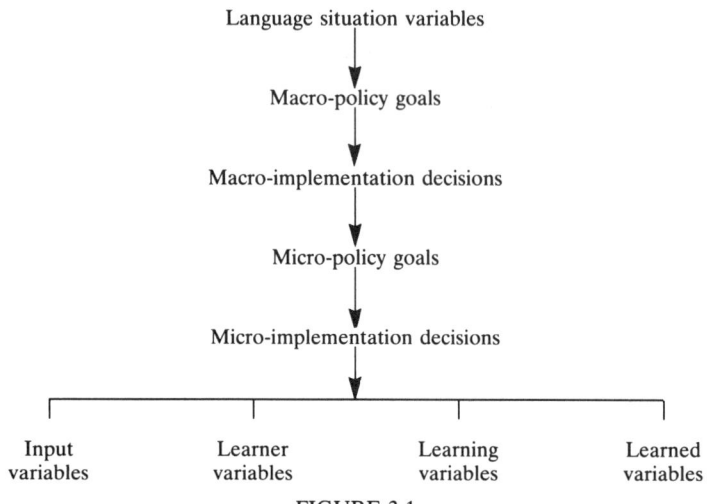

FIGURE 3.1
*Representation of the role of language planning in second language
acquisition.*

the general direction of influences on SLA of various stages in the language planning
process.

The language situation

The term language situation (Fishman 1972c) refers to a set of factors that include *who*
(ages, socio-economic classes, ethnic and regional groups, etc.) *speaks* (with what level
of proficiency) *what language varieties* (social and regional dialects, registers,
autonomous languages) *to whom* (ages, socio-economic classes, ethnic and regional
groups, etc.), *for what purposes* (e.g. business and trade, religion, education,
government activity). A detailed description of these factors constitutes a statement of
the setting within which planning decisions are made and SLA takes place. In a
relatively unplanned situation, these factors directly affect SLA. When language
planning is involved, planning decisions are often designed to change the language
situation, perhaps by bringing about changes in SLA. Among the many factors in the
language situation that affect SLA, three examples may be useful: language contact, the
role of language in socio-political structure, and types of language varieties in the
community.

Language contact[2] may be of two types: face-to-face and indirect. Face-to-face
contact between members of communities speaking different language varieties may
dramatically affect SLA. Lewis (1971), discussing the impact of Soviet migration
policies on SLA, demonstrates that changes in patterns of face-to-face interaction may
correlate with changes in patterns of language acquisition. Of course language contact
does not necessarily result in any particular pattern of language acquisition, since
intervening variables (e.g. language attitudes) may exist, as in Belgium (Lorwin 1972).
Indirect language contact involves radio, television, the press, and other means by
which speech communities have contact with other language groups. Often this indirect
contact is of little importance in SLA, but in border regions characterized by relatively

open political boundaries, indirect contact may be an important influence on SLA (Tollefson 1980).

The role of language in socio-political organization includes a complex set of factors: correlations between language and socio-economic class, between language and political power, and between language and decision making. In societies in which language is a major predictive factor in the distribution of power, SLA may be directly affected. McGroarty (1980) shows that language proficiency is related to the exercise of political rights and power in Canada, Australia, and the United States. Gumperz (1972) discusses the relationship between complexity of socio-political organization and the communication matrix of communities in North India. In general, socio-political complexity correlates with complexity of the communication system which individuals must acquire.

The types of languages in a community may vary substantially. Linguistically heterogeneous communities, with language problems quite different from relatively homogeneous communities, may contain languages in different stages of development (Fishman 1968a). Unwritten languages, which are seldom learned in school, affect SLA processes differently from written languages. Languages without technical vocabulary may be acquired for different reasons from those for which world scientific languages are acquired. Languages with great literary traditions are generally taught in schools more often, and differently, than recently codified varieties. Languages without a standardized variety, or with competing standards, present different settings for SLA processes. Language planning efforts are often designed to change the nature of language varieties (e.g. from one lacking technical vocabulary to one with full intertranslatability with world scientific languages). When these linguistic changes occur, changes in SLA are likely to follow.

Macro-policy goals and macro-implementation decisions

The formulation of a plan may be considered from different perspectives. A plan formulated at the federal level may require co-operation of local authorities. From the perspective of federal authorities, the implementation problem consists of formulating policy goals that will influence local authorities to implement the plan effectively. This is the macro-implementation perspective. For local authorities, the micro-implementation problem involves formulation of local policies and procedures, and adaptation of the local organization to the plan (Berman 1978, Tollefson 1981).

The term *macro-policy goals* refers to the aims of plans formulated by authorities with responsibility for the national community (i.e. operating within the macro-implementation perspective). Macro-policy goals generally are of three types: (1) language maintenance or language shift, (2) structural changes in a variety, (3) changes in the functional distribution among varieties. Hofman and Fisherman (1971) examine the impact of language policy in Israel on the rapid shift to Hebrew among immigrants. They also note that Israeli policy favours the maintenance of English, French, and Arabic, which are likely to benefit in the long run from government policy. Language policy in Yugoslavia strongly supports the maintenance of Albanian in the province of Kosovo, and this has resulted in efforts being made to encourage acquisition and use of Albanian among residents of the region.

Language policy may be aimed at achieving structural changes in the varieties of the community. Alisjahbana (1971) discusses problems in standardization of Bahasa Indonesia that resulted fron the impact of Dutch and English on affixes and word formation. These problems were overcome in the normative grammar for Bahasa Indonesia that has served as the basic language text since 1948. The development of that grammar, an important example of language planning, has had direct impact on which language variety is acquired in Indonesian schools.

Changes in the distribution of functions may be a major goal of macro-policy. Wurm (1968) proposes that Papua New Guinea Pidgin may one day, due to a combination of planning and the natural drift of social forces, expand its range of functions from that of a lingua franca to include official uses as well, thereby becoming the national language of Papua New Guinea. Such an expansion in function is occurring with Swahili in Tanzania, an expansion clearly due to government macro-policy goals and implementation efforts (Whiteley 1971). The clearest result of those efforts has been a great increase in the use of Swahili and in general proficiency levels. Thus in Tanzania, and elsewhere, for example in Israel, Yugoslavia, and the USSR, macro-policy goals have been aimed at a change in the distribution of functions. These goals have had direct impact on the acquisition of languages in those nations.

Macro-implementation decisions may commit funds to different projects in different countries. These projects may include, at the national level: teacher-training programmes, publication of textbooks and other materials, establishment of curriculum standards and requirements, and scholarships and exchange programmes. In addition, macro-implementation decisions may be made in the areas of official language use and statutory rights and responsibilities (e.g. requiring bilingualism in government job descriptions). In Yugoslavia, for example, federal, regional, and local constitutions and statutes spell out in great detail the role of language in official communication, education, and political rights. Such macro-implementation decisions may have a major impact on who learns which languages for which purposes.

Micro-policy goals and micro-implementation decisions

In general, macro-implementation decisions require more detailed formulation of policies for local communities and individuals. These more specific policies, termed *micro-policy goals*, involve the definition of bilingualism, the nature of evaluation instruments and curriculum, and so on. Once local and individual goals (based more or less on macro-implementation decisions) have been established, specific implementation actions must be taken by school administrators, language teachers, and others with direct contact with students and other individuals who are targets of macro-policy goals. These specific actions, termed *micro-implementation decisions*, include methodology and testing and have long been recognized as having impact on SLA.

Language planning and specific SLA variables

The effect on SLA of the language situation and language policy formulated and implemented at macro- and micro-levels will vary from setting to setting. The aim of researchers studying a particular SLA setting should be to delineate the extent to which input, learner, learning and learned variables have been affected by planning. My aim here is to outline which variables are often affected by planning.

Input variables

These are often subject to planning. The decision to teach, or not teach, a particular language may be a major planning decision. In Spain under Franco, severe restrictions on the teaching of Catalan and other minority languages were in effect. Elsewhere, languages taught in school are subject to detailed macro-level planning decisions affecting publication and availability of texts, availability and distribution of scholarships, and whether to teach a language as a subject or to establish it as a medium of instruction. In the United States, decisions in these areas generally are made by local or state school officials and may not be part of a co-ordinated plan. In Turkey, however, national plans have often included detailed statements in all these areas (Gallagher 1971), as is also the case in the Philippines, the Soviet Union, China, and many other countries. In general, to the extent that language is subject to planning in a particular setting, instructional variables tend to be strongly affected. Language acquisition processes in the classroom thus are commonly incorporated in language planning processes.

Learner variables

These too are subject to planning. Motivation can be manipulated; for example, governments can decide to reward language proficiency. Governments have a number of other means to control SLA motivation: language criteria in job descriptions, language learning scholarships and opportunities for overseas study. Equally important is creation of attitudinal and ideological motivation. In Tanzania, government policy has led to the association of acquisition of Swahili with Tanzanian nationalism; in Slovenia, acquisition of Italian by Slovenes is associated with a broader policy aimed at protection of Slovenian and other minority languages vis-à-vis Serbo-Croatian; in Turkey, literacy in the Latin alphabet was associated with both historical and nationalist ideology; and in Israel, acquisition of Hebrew is associated with both political and religious identity. In such cases, the planned attempt to form and to manage nationalist, religious, ethnic and other identities has direct effect on SLA, as language becomes an important symbol of these identities.

Other learner variables may be subject to planning when national educational plans are established. Age of students, previous language study and aptitude (e.g. as a criterion for admission) may be incorporated in national language teaching plans. A decision to begin required language study at a particular grade level, for instance, may have important implications: if certain ethnic groups tend to drop out of school prior to the period of required language study, then this curriculum decision will have direct impact on the composition of language classes.

In general, cognitive style and individual personality characteristics are not directly subject to language planning decisions, but rather may be indirectly affected by decisions in other areas.

Learning variables

These are manipulated indirectly by planning to the extent that various curriculum and other educational planning decisions affect the acquisition process. Highly structured programmes based on conscious learning of rules of grammar are likely to encourage students' use of conscious strategies and techniques. A curriculum requiring formal statements of memorized rules is unlikely to encourage unconscious acquisition. Acquisition is more likely to result from planning decisions that facilitate the following: overseas study; informal contact with native speakers; high quality instruction by teachers with native fluency; availability of a wide range of reading materials, films, etc.; current texts written by native speakers with formal linguistics training; and use of motivating media such as popular songs and current cinema. Even in settings in which the only major contact with native speakers is a foreign instructor, the existence of these factors can lead to acquisition of near-native fluency (Tollefson 1980).

Learned variables

These are mainly affected by micro-implementation decisions, although in highly centralized planning systems macro-implementation decisions may dominate (Tollefson 1981). While research on the order and rate of acquisition of various grammatical and pragmatic structures has been undertaken (e.g. Larsen-Freeman 1976), a great deal of work remains to sort out the effects of curriculum structure (cf. Perkins and Larsen-Freeman 1975). Curricula designed to proceed through a fixed order of structures typically include evaluation instruments measuring knowledge of those structures. Such curricula, which define successful learning in structural terms, may be established by decisions at either the macro- or micro-implementation level. In either case, to the extent that these curricula are successful, what is learned may be said to be the result of the planning process. Thus, although it is often unclear whether what is acquired is the result of curriculum planning, it is certain that planning has some effect in some instances. Future research should clarify this area.

Conclusion

This article is a preliminary effort to outline SLA variables that may be affected by the language planning process. Statements of cause and effect must be made with caution. In different settings, quite different conditions may hold. In one setting, interaction with native speakers may be encouraged through exchange programmes, scholarships and other means. The result may be acquisition of the contact language. In another setting, the language may first be acquired through intensive language instruction, which then may result in increased contact with native speakers (e.g. tourists, business people). In one setting, government policy may facilitate positive attitudes towards a language, leading to acquisition. In another setting, positive attitudes may be the result of widespread successful teaching of the language (cf. Deuchar 1976) or of other factors (e.g. availability of popular music).

Given the twofold complexity of language planning processes and SLA processes, the task of the researcher is to outline potential areas for planning, possible effects of decisions made in particular settings under specific conditions, and the interaction of planned and unplanned variables. In the attempt to formulate an adequate model of SLA, it will be essential that researchers maintain an international perspective toward language acquisition. The general indifference towards language learning evident in the United States leads to seemingly accidental acquisition, often in the face of great odds. But outside the United States, language learning is often a component in modernization and development programmes and in ethnic, religious, economic, and political struggles where language is a symbol and a means to achieve mobility, social and economic advancement, and political power. In such situations, planning may have a critical impact on language acquisition — as either an obstructive or a facilitative factor.

Notes

1. Krashen's distinction between acquisition and learning is an important one, as is the distinction between second and foreign languages. In this paper, I will use SLA to refer to second and foreign language acquisition and learning, and will distinguish the terms only when it is important within the overall framework of an SLA model.
2. Weinreich (1953) uses the term 'language contact' to refer to use of two or more languages by one individual. I use the term here to refer to a social rather than individual phenomenon. That is, language contact refers to communication between speech communities speaking different native languages.

Tasks

Task 1

Munby (1978) lists the following variables concerned with language course design:

(a) **Socio-political**
Attitude of government; status of English (optional/compulsory, medium/subject); expectations of institution/society; decisions on timing (e.g. when to start).

(b) **Logistical**
Number of trained teachers; accommodation; amount/suitability of equipment; extant materials; money.

(c) **Administrative**
Quantity, intensity, and mode of instruction; time-table.

(d) **Psycho-pedagogic**
Learner's motivation and expectations; traditional styles of learning.

(e) **Methodological**
Recommended language learning strategies and language teaching techniques; order of items and organization into teaching units; selection, adaptation, and production of suitable materials.

(i) From your experience in your own situation, work out (1) what influences decisions and/or (2) who takes decisions about each of these factors.

(ii) Now try to fit the factors and the people and influences associated with them into Tollefson's diagram on p.26.

Task 2

Munby believes that the course designer, when designing a course, should first find out the language needs of students learning English in order to draw up a language syllabus, and should then consider the five sets of variables listed above, modifying the syllabus and materials if necessary. Roe, on the other hand, talks of the 'total curriculum setting' (Roe 1977) and believes that all variables have to be considered together and at the same time to produce the syllabus and materials.

In the light of what you discovered when you did exercises (i) and (ii) in Task 1 which approach (Munby's or Roe's) do you favour and why?

You might find Holliday (1984) or Kennedy (1985b) useful follow-up reading.

Task 3

Teachers play an important role in the LP process since it is they who implement the policy in the classroom. Barnes (1976) has distinguished between two sorts of teachers, transmission teachers and interpretation teachers. Transmission teachers believe that their job is to impart knowledge of a subject to students lacking that knowledge and to evaluate and correct learners' performance. Interpretation teachers believe that their job is to encourage students to relate the knowledge they already possess to new knowledge and to develop thinking about the subject in co-operation with others. Many teachers switch between categories, of course, according to their objectives.

Using Barnes' descriptions, complete the table below to show the sort of communication you might expect in the classroom from each type of teacher.

	Interpretation teacher	Transmission teacher
Teacher talking to whole class		
Student to student talk		
Student initiates talk with teacher		
Teacher initiates talk		
Teacher informs		
Student asks questions		

Task 4

(i) Do you think planners can influence whether teachers use interpretation or transmission approaches? (In tackling this question, you will need to specify who these planners might be and where in Tollefson's levels of planning they might be working).

(ii) If you think planners can influence teachers, how would they go about doing it? For example, can changes in approach be effected through teacher training or a new course book?

Young and Lee (1984) have some interesting views on this issue.

Task 5

Tollefson believes that the learning environment, (e.g. whether the language is being acquired naturally outside the classroom or learned in a classroom) is an important factor in language planning.

(i) Look at the two extracts below.
    Extract (a) is from a language classroom (Ellis 1984).

Extract (b) is from a conversation between two friends (Crystal and Davy 1973).

(a) T = teacher, P = pupil.

T What did I dream?
   Can you remember?
P1 You turned into a toothbrush.
T Can I have a full sentence, Hugo?
P1 That you turned into a toothbrush.
T OK
   You...?
P2 You turned into a toothbrush.
T You...?
P2 You turned into a toothbrush
P3 You dreamed.
T You dreamt.
P3 You dreamt.
T OK. I dreamt that I turned into a toothbrush.

(b)

A You got a cold?
B No, just a bit sniffy cos I'm I am cold and I'll be alright once I've warmed up. Do I look as though I've got a cold?
A No I thought you sounded as if you were
B Mmm
A Pull your chair up close if you want. Is it
B Yes I'll be alright in a minute it's just that I'm
A What have you got?
B stupid I had about five thousand books to take back...

Can you list some of the differences between extract (a) and (b)? You might like to consider such things as:

Who initiates the talk
Who replies
Who evaluates
What freedom is given to teacher and pupil in (a) and to A and B in (b) to produce uncontrolled, unplanned speech
Whether the focus of each extract is on the form of the message or the content
Whether the answers to the questions are known or not?
What range of grammatical structures and vocabulary is produced in each extract

(ii) By now you should have a number of differences listed. These differences show that 'classroom' talk and 'natural' talk may not be closely related.
   (1) If you wanted to try to bring 'classroom' talk nearer 'natural' talk, what changes would you have to make to methods and materials?
   (2) Where in Tollefson's model would you need to make the decisions that would lead to such changes?

Ellis (1984) talks about methods and second language acquisition. It would be well worthwhile dipping into this book if you wanted to pursue this subject.

Task 6

Johns (1981) and Kennedy (1985c), both conducting surveys of ESP teachers at university level, found that the teachers mentioned a number of major, long-standing problems. They were:

(a) Low priority in timetabling. English was taught at unpopular times (e.g. early morning, lunchtime or late in the day) compared to the students' main subjects (such as engineering, law etc.).

(b) Difficulties meeting and working with main-subject teachers. (Blame was laid on both sides for this.) (ESP staff need to meet subject staff in order to gain further information on student needs.)

(c) English staff were classified administratively as 'teachers'; main subject staff were 'lecturers'. English staff felt they had a lower status than subject staff.

(d) Difficulty meeting other ESP staff, both in their own institution and in others, to exchange views.

(i) You may not have personal experience of this situation yourself, but can you work out some of the possible causes of these problems? Try to place the causes at the appropriate level in Tollefson's diagram on P.26.

(ii) If these problems were to be solved, what changes to the system would be needed, where would they have to be made and who would have to make them?

A number of these problems are essentially 'language management' problems. For a view of the relationships between language planning, management and language teaching, see Kennedy (1986a).

Chapter 4

Language Policy, Curriculum Development and TESOL Instruction: A Search for Compatability

ELLIOTT L. JUDD

Editor's introduction

Judd develops one aspect of the framework Tollefson introduced in Chapter 3, that of the language situation, or language context, within which LP may operate. It is, obviously, useful to have some system of distinguishing different situations, and although a number of terms already exist, Judd proposes some standardization. He suggests four categories, each representing a different set of functions for the use of English in a country and related to the questions of who uses English with whom, where, and for what purpose. The categories, which form a continuum of language use, are: English as a Second Language (ESL), where English is used in a variety of situations and registers for communication between native and non-native speakers, (typically 'immigrant' situations, see Quinn, this volume); English as an Additional Language (EAL), where English performs the function of a 'linking language' between different mother-tongue groups and is often used in government and education (see Serpell on Zambia, this volume); and English as a Language of Wider Communication (ELWC), where English performs no internal functions (these are taken by local languages), but is used as a medium of communication with other countries, notably in the spheres of business, science and technology (see Olshtain, this volume). Judd's fourth category, English as a Foreign Language (EFL), is slightly problematic. The other three categories are defined according to the use of English in a community, whereas English in an EFL situation has no role in communication; it is simply a subject on the curriculum. Either English has a function, in which case it can be assigned to one of Judd's first three categories, or it is not used and has a zero function. In the latter case, the outcome in the classroom may very well be that described by Judd under his EFL category, but this is confusing educational outcomes, which we mention below, with societal language use.

In the second part of his article, Judd attempts to relate the categories of language use to the design of ELT curricula and materials. There is no doubt that the language situation in any given country influences motivation and purposes for learning English, and materials writers and teachers should be aware of this as Judd illustrates, but we should be careful not to over-simplify. An analysis of the language situation will reveal certain facts about language use which could justifiably be interpreted as ends for language learning, the ultimate objectives or needs of language learners. But where needs are deferred, as they are for the vast majority of secondary-level language learners, or are only relevant for a few, (as in an ELWC situation), we may not be able to relate means and ends that closely, and indeed may use educational, rather than utilitarian, arguments for ELT provision. (This returns us to the Rogers and Abbott debate.) There is also the problem of the overgeneralization evident in the use of national, global categories which may conceal important differences in language use between sexes, ages, social classes, and urban/rural groups, which ideally should be considered in the classroom, though centralization of curricula and examinations may make this difficult. Judd's contribution, despite the reservations mentioned above, is valuable; he points out that in order to develop more effective language programmes we must first make an analysis of the language situation. Obviously, this is not the only thing we have to do, but, as we shall see when we have progressed through this collection, it is a necessary part of the language planning process.

THIS AUTHOR AND several other writers have previously argued that language policy has a direct impact on TESOL instruction and therefore should be considered as a crucial factor in planning ESOL programmes (Judd 1978, Richards 1979, Tucker 1977, Kachru 1976, Noss 1971, Bowen 1971). Each of these writers takes a slightly different perspective; yet underlying all of the articles is the basic premise that the socio-political environment in which English language instruction occurs has a direct impact on the shape of ESOL instruction. Failure to consider these socio-political factors can lead to dire consequences for all those involved.

At present English has been shown to be the major world language (Conrad and Fishman 1977). It is the native language of many throughout the world but for an even greater number English is learned as a second language. Those of us currently concerned with TESOL find ourselves flooded with terminology and acronyms to describe the theory and process of teaching English to non-native English speakers. The two most widely used terms are TESL, the Teaching of English as a Second Language, and TEFL, the Teaching of English as a Foreign Language. More recent terms are TEIL, the Teaching of English as an International Language ; TEAL, the Teaching of English as an Auxiliary Language (both used by Richards 1979); TEIAL, the teaching of English as an International-Auxiliary Language (Smith 1976); and TELWC, the Teaching of English as a Language of Wider Communication (adapted from Fishman 1977a).

As both a researcher and a teacher trainer, I see this plethora of terms as both a blessing and a curse. On the positive side, they show that the process of teaching English to non-native speakers is multidimensional and complex. On the negative side, my students, colleagues and I have spent a lot of time ostensibly discussing the heart of the matter only to realize that we had been using either different terms to mean the same thing or the same term to mean different things.

Therefore, one major aim of this article is to offer a redefinition of terms based on the examination of the socio-political context in which English functions. Once this is accomplished the terminology will be discussed in terms of its practical impact on ESOL curriculum design and instruction.

A classification of English language use

Basic framework

When I was a graduate student the classical terms used were TESL and TEFL. The basic differences between these had to do with the language environment in which the non-native speakers were learning English. In a TESL situation, the dominant environment is English and the non-native speakers are learning the language of the majority of the population. For example, a non-English speaker coming to the United

States or Great Britain would be studying ESL, or English as a Second Language. On the other hand, a non-native English speaker who studies English in an environment where the dominant population speaks a language other than English is studying EFL, or English as a Foreign Language, as in the case of a Costa Rican student learning English in Costa Rica or a Japanese student studying English in Japan.

Several questions arise from this simple dichotomy: exactly what is a dominant or nondominant English-speaking environment? For example, if a non-English speaker goes to Montreal, is s/he in an EFL or an ESL situation? One could answer that it must be ESL since Canada is a dominant English-speaking country. However, since the province of Quebec is dominant French-speaking and French is one of the official languages of the country, then studying English there must be EFL. Of course, one could counter this point by noting that in certain neighbourhoods in Montreal English dominates, thus rendering it ESL. But other neighbourhoods are French-dominant and thus we are back to EFL.

The two terms may also be considered ambiguous in certain multilingual countries where English is officially recognized as one of the principal languages. For example, in Nigeria or India are we teaching ESL or EFL? Certainly, English is an official language in both places and dominates in certain socio-linguistic contexts, especially among the educated. Yet despite this official recognition, English may only be used by a small minority of the total population and in very limited situations, and for most people English is a foreign language (see Prator 1968 and Kachru's 1976 response). The same ESL/EFL debate has occurred with respect to the Commonwealth of Puerto Rico.

A final point of controversy revolves around the term 'foreign' in EFL. Is a foreign language used in an English conversation between:

(a) two non-native English speakers who each speak different primary languages, or
(b) two non-native English speakers who speak the same primary language, or
(c) one native and one non-native speaker of English?

Perhaps it includes all of the above situations. The question becomes even more complex when *foreign language* is used by some to mean English conversations between non-native English speakers from different countries and by others to mean English conversations between non-native speakers in the same country.

Because of these difficulties with ESL and EFL, people have resorted to some or all of the other terms mentioned earlier in the paper. Rather than criticizing these terms or proposing completely new ones, which further add to the confusion, I propose a redefinition of some of the existing terms. The classifications to be presented have in fact already proved useful in both socio-linguistics and TESOL courses that I have taught.

English as a second language

An ESL situation can be redefined as a situation in which non-native English speakers spend the vast majority of their time communicating in English. More precisely, the speakers will be using English to express in basic language, all of their ideas and feelings, with the possible exception of those that arise in intimate conversations with close friends and family. In an ESL context the four skills – listening, speaking, reading and writing – will all be used, and the English language will be employed in a variety of registers ranging from the very informal to the highly formal. Of course, the exact proportion for each of the language skills and registers will vary from person to person and situation to situation, but in an ESL situation nothing can definitely be ruled out. It should also be remembered that the non-native speaker will be communicating primarily with native speakers of English. Here again though, depending on the specific case, there is the possibility that there will be communication with other non-native English speakers in English.

Examples of an ESL situation can be seen in the United States, Great Britain, English-speaking Canada, Australia and New Zealand. One might also include certain nations like Jamaica, Barbados or Trinidad if dialect questions are ignored.

English as an additional language

An EAL situation can be defined as one in which speakers learn English after they learn another primary language and use it for the purpose of communicating with others who have different primary languages. Such situations are found in countries that are multilingual and recognize English as the language for intracountry communication. EAL corresponds to Richards' description of English for Intergroup Functions (1979), or Smith's English as an Auxiliary Language (1976).

The key difference between EAL and ESL concerns socio-linguistic contexts. Since students already speak a language that fulfills a variety of communicative needs beyond the intimate levels, English is used in more limited ways than in an ESL situation. EAL tends to be used only in rather formal registers and in certain areas such as national governmental affairs, intracountry commerce and in the mass media. In addition, the proportion of the population in an EAL context who actually use English is much smaller than in an ESL situation and those who use it tend to be of a high social, political and economic level. As in an ESL context, in an EAL situation all four language skills will be employed, although percentages will vary from country to country. The other important socio-linguistic characteristic of many EAL situations is that a localized version of English has probably emerged (see Kachru 1976).

Many of the countries that fall into the EAL category are former British or American territories such as Nigeria, Fiji, Liberia, Botswana and Ghana, to name a few. Other countries in the EAL category are countries where English is one of several co-official languages such as in French-speaking Canada, Afrikaans-speaking South Africa, India and Puerto Rico.

English as a language of wider communication

ELWC is used in a country where English serves no intranational purpose and is needed only for international communication (Richards 1979, Conrad and Fishman 1977, Smith 1976, Bowen 1971). Since English has become the major lingua franca of the world, many people need to use English for scientific, technical and commercial purposes.

An ELWC situation is characterized by the fact that the register range in English is often limited and formal and the lexical and topical repertoire is narrow. Furthermore, the skills to be mastered are also limited. In many ELWC contexts the skill used the most is reading; face-to-face contact with people who use English in any form is rare. Writing is used little because the need to encode information in English is much rarer than the need to decode. In an ELWC situation some will need to use oral skills: those people, for instance, who must deal with visiting English-speaking colleagues or those who might occasionally travel to an English-speaking country for business or lecturing. Yet even in these cases, the percentage of time spent yearly in oral language use is quite small. In most ELWC environments one or more native languages serve intracountry daily communicative needs and, as in an EAL situation, only a small highly educated elite need and use English. Examples of countries that clearly fall into this category are Japan, Taiwan, Indonesia, Tanzania, and Germany. There are many more.

It should be noted in passing that many countries that are in the EAL situation are moving or have already moved to an ELWC situation, as indigenous languages become more standardized and gain more prestige (Conrad and Fishman 1977, Rubin and Shuy 1973, Rubin and Jernudd 1971, Bowen 1971, and Fishman, Ferguson and Das Gupta 1968).

English as a foreign language

The last major category is EFL. An EFL situation is one in which English is studied as one of many foreign languages and serves little communicative function for students once they finish the actual course. Communicative use is limited and may focus on literature and high culture. Translation may also be stressed. The use of English for any purpose outside the classroom is minimal and of short duration. At most it might serve 'in temporary contacts with foreign-language speakers in everyday situations, whether as visitors to the foreign country or with visitors to their own country, and to establish and maintain social contacts' (van Ek 1976: 24–5). For many even such temporary usage might never occur. Thus, in an EFL situation very few people, other than those in the teaching profession, use English on a regular, long-term basis. In short, English has no special use or status over any other foreign language.

Some general comments on the catgories

The four categories taken together make up a continuum of English language use. In terms of both the percentage of time spent using English and the number of registers employed when speaking English, they can be ranked from high to low as follows: ESL, EAL, ELWC and EFL. Not every country or every educational situation can be neatly labelled by any one of the categories. Some countries (for example Malaysia) may be in the process of switching between categories and certain groups of students may need two categories of English: ESL when they study at an American university, and later EAL or ELWC when they return home. Yet, despite these weaknesses, the four categories offer the ESOL professional some useful perspectives in developing instructional materials and teaching strategies.

Applications to ESOL instruction

The four categories have a practical value in the development of ESOL programmes which correspond to the realities of English use. Instructional programmes that are compatible with the socio-political situations in which they are located are more likely to succeed, while those that are in conflict with the English language policy of a given country run a greater chance of failure (Judd 1978).

In an ESL situation, programmes need to stress all four language skills. Students must also be exposed to a variety of registers in English and must develop an ability to interact with a variety of native speakers in a variety of different circumstances. Curricula that stress pattern drills and rote memorization of vocabulary, dialogues, and grammatical paradigms will fail to prepare the students to deal with the realities of the ESL situation. Since considerable English use is required of a student in an ESL context, emphasis must be placed on linguistic creativity and innovation and both academic and non academic topics have to be introduced. In addition, teachers should be native speakers and have a complete understanding of the varieties of roles that English plays in an ESL context.

In an EAL situation, the curricula and methods of ESOL instruction change. Again, all four skills need to be emphasized, but materials can focus on the more formal registers of English and less attention need be paid to the informal ones. Since English is used on fewer occasions than in an ESL situation, those studying in an EAL context can be introduced to a narrower range of topics and the lexical items chosen can reflect only the situational demands which students will encounter. It is still important to stress the need for linguistic creativity, since those in an EAL situation will be expected to respond to a variety of linguistic situations. The need for native English-speaking teachers is not imperative in an EAL situation; teachers who are fluent English users are more important. Fluency here is defined as the ability to engage in all communicative functions in which the students themselves will need to function.

In an ELWC context, the curriculum can place less emphasis on listening, speaking and writing and focus on reading. Within the reading component, formal registers associated with the language of journals, reports, and business correspondence should be studied. It is within the ELWC context that English for Special Purposes (ESP) or English for Science and Technology (EST) find their greatest application because of the narrowness of topics and the limited use of English language registers. A notional-functional approach, such as the one suggested by Findley and Nathan (1980) or Wilkins (1976), might provide a good method of organizing and presenting the English language. If ELWC students need to write, speak, or listen to English it will probably be only for short spells and the English involved will be very limited in focus and register. Materials that assume too wide a focus or emphasize equally all four skills run the risk of not preparing the students for real situations and can cause resentment. ELWC teachers need not have the oral proficiency of native speakers but they should have full fluency in the written medium. Tapes, or other materials which provide native language speech models, should suffice for the limited amount of oral work that may be necessary. It is important that ELWC instructors possess some technical knowledge of the subject areas to which the students are being exposed.

In an EFL situation the fluency and registers of English are limited. Therefore, fluency among teachers is less of a prerequisite than in the other three contexts and there is no need to recruit native English speakers. In an EFL programme controlled materials and a classical audio-lingual, or even a grammar-translation, approach may be employed since students will probably have little future need for English. As mentioned earlier, some students may have short-term contacts with English speakers. If such contacts tended to recur, then the notional-functional approach with its 'minimal competencies' (see van Ek 1976 or Findley and Nathan 1980) may prove quite useful. Such a presentation of language should appeal to students' interest, whether or not they will have any direct contact with English speakers. Whatever teaching method is employed and whatever manner is used to organize materials, topics should be chosen for immediate student interest; there is no need to focus on long-range, long-term goals.

Conclusion

This article has emphasized the importance of understanding the exact role of English in the overall language policy context in any given country. Such knowledge can aid those who are interested in both language policy and the teaching of English. It is easier to reach sound curricular and instructional decisions when one has analysed the role of English in different countries around the world. Furthermore, those involved in both the teaching and the learning process are more likely to be successful when the instructional approach relates to the various uses to which English is put. When English language instruction meets the needs of the students, motivation will be higher. The long-range impact will also be greater because speakers will develop a knowledge of real English for real communication. In conclusion, it is crucial that we realize that the role of English varies around the world. No single ESOL curriculum or instructional strategy will suit all circumstances. As G. Richard Tucker says, 'Educational or national policy serves to define the parameters within which language problems can be developed' (1977:16), and only through an understanding of the English language policy of a given country can we help devise the proper curricular and teaching approach for its particular educational environment.

Tasks

Task 1

(i) Using as an example either your own country or, if different, the one in which you work, try to classify the role of English in that country, using Judd's terms – ESL, EAL, ELWC, EFL.

(ii) Turn to one of the chapters in Part 3 of this book and classify the situation you find described there.

(iii) Try comparing a number of different countries you know, using Judd's terms.

For another view of the relationships between the role of English and ELT see Kennedy (1986b).

Task 2

The table below (adapted from Moag 1982b) shows some features of the different situations described by Judd. From your own experience, fill in the table using a scale 1–3, 1 to indicate 'high', 3 to indicate 'low'.

Note any categories you have problems with and ask yourself why the problems occur.

Feature	Category			
	ESL	EAL	ELWC	EFL

(a) Language policy
   (i) Degree of official recognition given to English
     (low to high)
(b) Language use in English
   (i) Percentage of population using English (low
     to high)
   (ii) Influence of English-using group in society
     (minor to major influence)
   (iii) Range of activities conducted in English
     (limited to full)
   (iv) Use of English in formal situations (yes/no)
   (v) Use of English in informal situations (yes/no)
   (vi) No. of learners relative to no. of users (large
     to small)

See also Fasold (1984, chapter 3) for a discussion of the use of formulae to ascertain the roles and functions of languages in any given society.

Task 3

Look back at the results of Task 2.

   (i) Which features do you think would have an impact on how and what teachers taught in the classroom?
   (ii) Are there any other features that have an important influence in the classroom and that you think should be added to the table in Task 2?

(The 1982 article by Moag includes additional features if you need help with this question.)

Task 4

In some countries, English is used primarily for external communication, Judd's ELWC category. In these countries, English at secondary level and above may either be a subject on the curriculum, with the medium of communication being a local language; OR schools and universities may be entirely English-medium with no local languages being used (officially, at least).

   (i) Do these differences in the choice of language as medium of instruction cause problems with the ELWC category?
   (ii) Would the differences lead to different student needs and wants?

A good collection of articles on the relationships between language and other subjects in the curriculum is Tickoo (ed. 1986).

Task 5

Shaw (1981) conducted a survey amongst university students in three countries, Singapore, India, and Thailand, to find out their attitudes towards and motivation to learn English. The students were asked to rank four groups of people (a-d) in order of importance for the student's need for English. The results are below (1 = most important, 4 = least important).

'It is important for me to speak English so that I can talk to':

	Singaporeans	Indians	Thais
(a) Fellow countrymen in specific social or business situations	1	1	3
(b) Fellow countrymen who do not know my first language	2	2	4
(c) Native English speakers	3	3	1
(d) Non-native speakers from other countries'	4	4	2

(i) What can you infer from these results about the use of English and local languages in the three countries concerned?

(ii) How would you classify the countries in Judd's terms?

(iii) Would these results indicate that there were likely to be differences or similarities between the English courses offered to these university students in the three countries?

Another interesting investigation of language attitudes (towards French and Arabic in Morocco) is contained in Bentahila (1983).

Task 6

Moag (1982a) in an interesting article on the 'life cycles of English' suggests that non-native varieties of English (see Abbott p 138 this volume for an illustration), better known as 'New Englishes', often change their roles and functions over time as the society in which they are used alters economically and politically. He lists a number of stages of development which, in fact, reflect the history of English in colonial and post-colonial times.

Stage 1. Introduction of English by native speakers of English to a non-native community. Very restricted contact between native speakers and non-native speakers.

Stage 2. English begins to be used more widely, in education, for example, and by a local indigenous elite. Both the uses and functions of English expand.

Stage 3. Use of English expands still further in the society and new varieties of English emerge and are widely used.

Stage 4. The new varieties become institutionalized as they begin to be used e.g. in education, in the press, and by writers. An 'internal' model of English begins to be used and accepted.

Stage 5. The uses and functions of English are restricted, English once again begins to be used only by a local elite.

(i) Can you think of any English-using countries that have been through some or all of these stages? If you find this difficult, the case studies in Part 3 of this book will help you.

(ii) The emergence of new varieties of English sometimes presents problems to English teachers when assessing their pupils' language. A common feature of many varieties of New Englishes, particularly colloquial varieties, is for example the dropping of the '-s' marker on verb forms (e.g. she go to school; he drink coffee). Many writers (see Platt, Weber and Ho, 1984, Chapter 10 for example) would advise the teacher not to assume automatically that such forms were 'wrong', but to view them as 'inappropriate' for a particular situation. If you agree with this view of 'inappropriate' rather than 'incorrect' language, when would you accept forms like 'She go to School' in a student's spoken and written work and when would you regard them as inappropriate?

Chapter 5

The Fact-finding Phase in the Policy-making Process: The Case of a Language of Wider Communication

ELITE OLSHTAIN

Editor's introduction

Olshtain develops the theme of the link between language planning (LP) and language teaching and extends it in a number of important respects. She emphasizes that language planning, like any other planning, takes place in a particular cultural and political environment which will inevitably influence all levels of planning from government to the classroom. Outsiders concerned with language use and its language learning implications cannot afford to under-estimate these effects. LP is not undertaken for its own sake and generally has a non-linguistic objective; it might be seen as an aid towards modernization or the establishing of a nation's identity. It is therefore a means to an end, as is its implementation in the classroom, and the decision takers and policy makers are likely to view it in the light of their own political and cultural beliefs. Indeed, they may feel that an analysis of the language situation, which Olshtain regards as a necessary step before policy decisions are taken, is irrelevant. Those involved in the sorts of language surveys advocated in the article should be aware of the possibility, some might say likelihood, that their findings will be ignored when policy decisions are taken.

The author is quite specific as to the content of a survey to investigate language needs and use. It should, according to Olshtain, include an investigation of the role of all languages in the society concerned, not just of English, and should collect data from a number of different areas, so that societal needs, group and individual attitudes to the languages concerned, and the political and economic issues related to language may be isolated. The complexity and ramifi-cations of decisions related to LP are indicated by the number of areas for investigation that Olshtain lists under societal needs – education, the labour market, pressures for modernization, uses in administration, and social status of the languages concerned. She points out that there may often be conflict between general societal needs and individual wants. Thus, a survey might reveal an occupational requirement for reading skills, but individuals involved in actual language programmes might very well want a broader approach, perhaps feeling that the concentration on one skill would be detrimental to their learning or a tacit admission of their language learning inadequacies. There is an appropriate emphasis on attitudes in the article. Few language policies will succeed if the attitudes of those affected by them are not taken into account in some way (see also the next article by Horvath). Moreover, since motivation to learn is closely linked to attitudes, it is self-evident how important this variable is in the gauging of learning outcomes. Olshtain indicates the powerful nature of instrumental motivation, for example the need to learn English for career promotion, while not denying that the need for group affiliation may also be significant in a society where learners desire to be associated with an English-using elite.

Introduction

LANGUAGE-POLICY AND LANGUAGE planning, as a field of study, have gained consider-able importance in the last decade or so. Not only have sociolinguists focused their attention on this area, but a definite multidisciplinary approach has been brought to bear upon the process of making and implementing language policy. We are witnessing an intensification of interest in this field which is at least partially due to the phenomenon of a 'shrinking world' but is primarily related to two important trends in today's world: rapid modernization and national consolidation of new nations. Either or both are taking place in various parts of the world, increasing the need for careful language planning.

Various scholars have come to grapple with the definition of terms like 'language planning' and 'language policy'. In the present paper we shall concern ourselves mainly with a language policy-making process leading, ideally, to the development of a language-teaching program. The following definition of 'language policy' will therefore underly the approach presented here:

> Language policy-making involves decisions concerning the teaching and use of language, and their careful formulation by an authority which has the power to do so, for the governance of others. The language policy-making process leads to the implementation of these high-level decisions, which in turn leads to the making of further decisions at lower levels. Decision-making is therefore a permeating aspect of the process of developing a teaching program on a national scale [C. H. Prator – personal communication].

The language policy-making process is viewed today by sociolinguists as a pragmatic and eclectic field of interest, where cultural, psychological, attitudinal, economic, linguistic and other factors must all be considered. The definition suggested above is broad enough to allow for the inclusion of such factors.

The term LWC (Language of Wider Communication) was coined and first introduced by Ferguson in 1962 in 'Language factors in national development' (in the collection of essays by Ferguson 1971b). Ferguson suggests (pp. 52–3) that languages be arranged on a scale in terms of their use in written form:

W0   language is not used for normal written purposes
W1   language is used for normal written purposes
W2   original research in physical sciences is regularly published in the language
W3   translations and résumés of scientific work in other languages are regularly published.

On the basis of these definitions of the different levels of language development, it seems that W3-type languages are best candidates for the role of an LWC since they can help a community whose primary language is W0, W1, or W2 gain access to scientific and technological writing and provide a tool for communication with the rest of the world. This type of LWC is often referred to as an 'international language.' An LWC can, however, be used for internal communication within one political or national unit which is multilingual in nature. Amharic functions this way in Ethiopia; Tagalog in the Philippines, or English in India. In such cases the role of the LWC is most significant in terms of unification.

The LWC, from the point of view of the present paper, can be best defined as a world language used to enable communities whose primary languages are not widely used outside their own area to communicate with members of other speech communities, either for the promotion of foreign trade or in order to gain access to scientific, technical and literary materials that do not exist in their own language. Sometimes such an LWC fulfills major functions within the community itself, e.g. when it has an official or semiofficial status. Even then, however, its major role is to help further the overall process of modernization.

There is little doubt today that English has gained the strongest and most widespread position as an LWC throughout the world. This is not surprising since the use of an LWC is closely related to the process of modernization. This spread of English usage, described and quantified in Fishman, Cooper, Conrad (1977), has increased enormously in the last decade or two. It is spoken natively by most of the population in the United States, Australia, the United Kingdom, New Zealand, Barbados, Jamaica and Trinidad. It is the only official language in a number of countries where it is not the native language of the majority of the people – Nigeria, Uganda, Zambia, Botswana, Fiji, Gambia, Ghana, Liberia and Mauritius. Most of these countries have maintained English (the language of the former colonial power) as their present LWC. In other cases English is one of two or more official languages of the country, spoken natively by the majority of at least part of the population – Ireland, Canada, Cameroon, South America, Puerto Rico, etc. (Fishman et al. 1977: 7–10).

In a large number of countries English is neither the national nor one of the official languages, but it is given special status either because of historical factors (i.e. the country was an English mandate or colony), or because of social and economic pressures to communicate with other speech communities as, for example, in Israel, Kenya, Burma, Ethiopia, Malaysia, Pakistan, Egypt and others. In some of these countries English may be the medium of instruction in the school system, or at least for a part of the course of study, while in others it may only have the status of a major foreign language, which is a compulsory and highly regarded subject on the curriculum.

In many other countries English is taught as one of the foreign languages available to students within the school system, but in practical terms it is recognized as the most important foreign language: Japan, Italy, Brazil, Mexico and others. Even here the role of English in the process of modernization, science, and technology is significant. It is for this variety of situations, which share many significant factors, that a model of policy formulation and implementation is needed. The present paper will attempt to describe the first phase of the policy-making process – the fact-finding phase.

The fact-finding phase

The fact-finding stage is the period of time devoted to the careful consideration of the actual language situation in a community and to an evaluation of the needs and aspirations of the members of that community that could be fulfilled by developing a suitable language policy resulting in an appropriate language programme. During this first stage the investigators – linguists, sociolinguists, sociologists and educationalists – are at work collecting data, which are needed by the authority or organization empowered to make policy in order to start functioning effectively.

It is often hard to convince a political authority of the necessity of such a fact-finding survey. Leaders tend to think that they know the situation well enough and to urge the policy-making body to come up with fast remedies. In such cases, the first task that the policy makers have to undertake, is to demand an in-depth fact-finding stage, prior to the taking of any decisions.

The fact-finding stage is, practically speaking, devoted to the identification and definition of language needs or language problems. Such problems must be defined within the social, cultural and political framework in order to allow the policy makers to establish relevant goals, strategies and predicted outcomes. Neustupny (1968) specified language problems as being of two kinds: those that can be called 'conscious' and those of which the speech community is not fully aware. It is very important that the data collection techniques allow for the incorporation of both types of language problems or needs.

In the present paper we shall concern ourselves with an LWC and therefore the notion of 'language problems' can be more narrowly defined as the overall situation of the LWC vis-à-vis the other languages within the community, with special emphasis on the function which the LWC fulfills. More specifically, we are interested in the needs of the members of the pertinent community to use the LWC and the lack of ability on their part to do so, since policy decisions should aim to remedy such a situation and minimize the gap between 'actual needs' and the ability to fulfill them.

The fact-finding investigation must begin with the overall language situation within the community. The need for such an in-depth study of the entire language situation has been clearly stated by Prator (1975:146):

> One of the basic concepts of the Survey, then, was the recognition that the language situation of a country should be studied in its totality and that any success in defining the role of one language in a given setting should help define that of all the languages used in the same setting.

Studying the various functions that one particular language fulfills in a social setting provides us with information about the whole 'matrix of communication', as Gumperz (1972) calls it:

> The totality of communication roles within a society may be called its 'communication matrix'.

It is possible to build up a picture of the various languages and the functions and roles which each of them fulfills within the particular community. An in-depth study of the language situation is, therefore, very significant for policy-making.

Ideally, such an in-depth study of the entire language situation in any country can best be carried out when there is an overt and widely felt need for such a survey. Such a need can be felt when local authorities find it hard to make decisions concerning the effective allocation of financial and human resources because they lack information on the actual language situation. It may also be felt when the public is aware that the programme of instruction available within and outside the school system is failing to meet its expectations and requirements. Overt needs often create a social, psychological or political motivation to change, and when such motivation exists, it is the right moment to administer questionnaires to the public.

Two examples of surveys conducted for the purpose of evaluating the language situation of English as an LWC are the Cohen and Aronson (1964) survey carried out in Israel and the one by Harrison, Prator, Tucker (1975) carried out in Jordan.

The Cohen and Aronson report was the result of a number of developments that took place in Israel: planning and initiation by the Director-General of the Ministry of Education and Culture, beginning in 1953 (when the Director-General died in 1954 the project was abandoned until 1958); in 1958 a Research Department was established in the School of Education at the Hebrew University, which undertook to conduct a country-wide survey of the teaching of English in Israeli schools; an advisory panel was set up to guide the research team and experts were brought into the country from England. The survey was finally published in 1964 and proved useful in initiating a long process of implementation.

In Jordan in 1972, the Ministry of Education and the University of Jordan invited a team of specialists to examine the English language teaching situation. They prepared a report (Campbell et al. 1972) in which, among other things, an English language policy survey was proposed. In response to this report, the Ministry of Education requested Ford Foundation assistance in order to carry out a survey of English language instruction in Jordan. Survey activities began in June, 1972. In January, 1973, one hundred copies of the prepublication version of the report were sent to the Ministry which eventually created a National English-Language Planning Committee to coordinate implementation.

In both cases the initiative for the survey came from the Ministry of Education. We can assume, however, that this initiative was taken because there was widespread public feeling that the situation regarding English was not up to expectations. As a result, there existed a favourable situation for conducting a survey.

There is a significant difference between the two surveys: while the Israeli survey was done mostly within the school system, evaluating teachers, programmes, textbooks, syllabus requirements, etc., the Jordanian survey included (in addition to the evaluation of the English situation in education) a field study of the societal needs in Jordan at the time, and questionnaires in Arabic were administered to a sample population. This, therefore, comes very close to an in-depth study of the entire language situation. In a country like Jordan, the language situation is relatively simple: one common first language for most of the population and one major foreign language – English as the LWC.

Summarizing this introduction to the fact-finding stage in the policy-making process, we can conclude that three different sets of factors need to be investigated in depth before decisions are made:

(1) Societal needs.
(2) Group and individual attitudes.
(3) Political, national and economic considerations.

The collection of data pertinent to these factors can be carried out by means of two basic techniques: collection of facts that are overtly stated in governmental and other institutionalized documents, and the administration of personal questionnaires, which reach for the less overt feelings and thoughts prevailing at any particular time among the members of a community.

Societal needs

Societal needs, with regard to the LWC must be defined on the basis of the objective and practical ways in which the members of the community need to use that LWC.

Thus, the educated strata may need the LWC for advancement in their professional positions; blue-collar workers may need the LWC in order to use manuals and instructions that accompany technical equipment; and those who serve tourism may need to communicate mainly in the spoken language. Language policy-making must be based on a detailed mapping of all areas in which the need for the LWC is felt.

Societal needs can be investigated and evaluated qualitatively and quantitatively, yet a conflict might exist between individual attitudes and the overall societal needs. In a country that was colonized, the attitude of the members of the community might be anti-LWC because it represents the earlier colonizing power, although their real, instrumental need for the language might be great. In another instance, there might be a different individual perception or group perception in terms of the type of LWC they need and the realistic function of the language. Thus, in a country where tourism is an important industry certain groups (e.g. cab drivers, tour guides, porters) may only need the spoken language to communicate with the tourists, but the group serving tourism as a whole might feel that they need to become proficient in reading and writing as well in order to feel 'equal' with the higher social classes. In such cases there is a conflict between actual societal needs and the perception of individual needs on the part of certain individuals or groups within that society.

In order to establish the societal roles of the LWC, several areas have to be investigated:

(1) The role of the LWC in education.
(2) The role of the LWC in the labour market.
(3) The role of the LWC in the process of modernization:
    (a) accessibility to technological information
    (b) operating modern technology
    (c) training professionals outside the country
    (d) participation in international conventions
    (e) hosting experts from other countries.
(4) The role of the LWC in administration.
(5) The social status of the LWC.
(6) The degree of 'spread' throughout the social system.

Each of these areas deserves special attention and may have to be treated differently according to its specific characteristics.

The role of language in education must be investigated from three points of view:

(1) The degree to which the individual learner needs to use the language as a medium of instruction in order to further his/her education.
(2) The degree to which the LWC functions as the language of study, although it is not the medium of instruction within the school system.
(3) The overall effectiveness of instruction of the LWC within the school system.

In the last two decades there has been a growing belief that literacy should be taught first in the mother tongue of the student; this approach received its greatest impetus from the historic UNESCO conference which produced the monograph, *The Use of Vernacular Languages in Education* (1953). As a result of this monograph, even in those countries where English is the medium of instruction, it is not used as such in the early grades.

In Nigeria, where English usually becomes the medium of instruction after two or three years of the vernacular, it is now felt that throughout primary school English should be a minor subject only, and the vernacular should be the medium of instruction, as stated by Taiwo (1979); in fact, a special project was designed for that purpose – the Vernacular Primary Project (VPP).

Similarly, in Ethiopia, where Amharic is considered the official language of the country, English is the medium of instruction from grade seven and up (British Council Information, 1976). There is, however, a very strong drive in Ethiopia to make Amharic eventually the medium of instruction throughout the school system, but the preparation of teaching materials, teacher training, etc., might require considerable time, and so far English is still the medium of instruction.

A very different picture presents itself in countries like Portugal or Italy, where English has never been the medium of instruction in the regular school system, and where it is, in fact, only one of several foreign languages offered. In Portugal, English is not even the foreign language most widely chosen by students and follows French, which is the number one foreign language. English is, however, rapidly growing in importance (British Council, 1978).

It becomes obvious that without information on the existing role of English in the educational system of a country – at one extreme it could be the medium of instruction, at the other just one of several languages taught in school – no policy decisions can be made. In fact, policy makers need to have information on the situation of English in countries other than their own in order to gain a more universal perspective of the decision-making process.

The second dimension of English within the educational system is its function as a 'language of study'. For our purposes we shall define a 'language of study' as the medium without which one cannot pursue a certain subject in depth – whether the subject is academic or professional. Thus, the medium of instruction in a particular country might be the local language exclusively, even at university level, yet if the reading of references must be done primarily in English, then English must be considered a 'language of study'. A term often used for this type of LWC is English for Academic Purposes (EAP), or English for Science and Technology (EST). Munby (1978:3) expresses this very clearly:

> There are a number of reasons for the rapidly growing need for ESP programmes. One of the most significant is the spread of higher and further education with the concomitant need to gain access to the required knowledge that is available, either exclusively or most readily, in English.

The countries in the Middle East have relatively few institutions of higher education where English is the medium of instruction; but English as a language is important for all universities whether the medium of instruction is English or the local national language. Malaysia is now moving rapidly in the same direction with Malay having replaced English in secondary schools and in universities.

Finally, before any new policy-decisions are made, we need to evaluate the effectiveness of the operating instructional programme within the school system. Usually, policy has to be made in order to change an existing system, perhaps to make it more responsive to actual societal needs.

In Thailand, for instance, where English is not a medium of instruction but is a study language and needs for EAP are growing, there is a strong feeling that high-school graduates are not sufficiently proficient in English. Many adults are highly motivated to continue their studies in English when they realize how important it is in terms of job requirements. Adult evening schools often supply these needs (British Council Information, 1977). There is a discrepancy between the achievements of the English instruction programme and actual societal needs. This should call for a revision of policy making based on data produced in a fact-finding stage that will paint the complete picture of the present societal needs in Thailand. A special evaluation and comprehensive investigation into the teaching of English in the country will be necessary of the type that was employed in the two surveys mentioned earlier – the Cohen and Aronson (1964) survey in Israel and the one by Harrison, Prator and Tucker (1975) in Jordan.

When we consider the role of English as the LWC in education, we must distinguish between actual roles, which can be investigated, and potential or desired roles which might be incorporated in future policy making. In order to assess the role of English in education, two main paths of investigation must be followed:

(1) Official documents stating aims, curriculum, school situation, etc., need to be consulted. The Ministry of Education in a country can usually make such documents available to the investigators. In some countries there are special research institutes which carry out various surveys within the school system that might be of great value to the investigators dealing with the LWC situation.

(2) Conduct an in-depth survey in a proper sample of schools in the country in the following areas:
   (a) language achievement based on specially prepared tests to compare actual attainment to stated objectives
   (b) evaluation of the curriculum
   (c) analysis of textbooks
   (d) analysis of teaching methods
   (e) analysis of teacher training
   (f) measure the opinions and perception of teachers, students and parents by means of questionnaires.

Only by combining the results from both types of investigation can we come up with a complete picture of the 'actual' role of English in education and on the basis of these findings prepare recommendations for the desired role. Such investigations may take several years or several months, depending on the particular situation, size of the country, linguistic complexity, co-operation of local authorities, availability of suitable personnel and availability of funds.

The role of the LWC in the labour market

This is the second area which needs to be assessed under the heading societal needs. It is important to work with the full spectrum of social groups and with representatives of a wide variety of geographical areas in order to get a fair representation of the society with which we are working.

When collecting information on the labour market, we may have to concern ourselves with various official assessments available from governmental or other labour agencies, which can provide us with the picture of the overt needs. At the same time, however, we need to interview, and collect information from, individuals in the field representing the employers, the working employees and the future employees who are still job seekers. This may help us complete the picture and yield some information on less overt needs.

The role of English in the modernization process

In order to evaluate this we need to assess a number of factors affecting the process itself. All of these factors will relate to the accessibility of technological information and know-how. How can such technological information become accessible to a community whose primary language is not an LWC? Several questions need to be considered:

(1) To what extent are technological and scientific journals available in the local language(s)?
(2) To what extent are the instruction manuals and catalogues that accompany modern machinery made available in the local language(s)?
(3) To what extent do professionals receive training abroad?

In a rapidly developing society, the three factors mentioned above are the most important in terms of developing human resources of high calibre to help implement technological progress. If, however, such materials are not available in the local language(s), the first thing members of the community will need to do is acquire an LWC in order to further their knowledge in the technological and scientific fields. If the LWC is not readily available to large sections of the population, then neither will developed technology be available to them, unless special efforts are made on a national scale to translate important reading matter into the local language(s) and to produce local scientific and professional journals. The function of an LWC in this area should be considered when the aims of the school ELWC programme are being laid down.

The use of English in administration and legislation

This is probably most relevant in countries which have a colonial history, whether they still consider English an official language or not. In Fishman, Cooper and Conrad (1977), Chapter One provides a detailed and enlightening picture of English as a 'world language', with information on cases where English also enjoys the status of an 'official' language.

Group and individual attitudes

Sometimes individual and group attitudes towards a language are a true reflection of societal needs, while at other times there is a conflict between societal needs, which are based on economic and social circumstances, and individual needs, which have psychological roots. In a context of current or prior colonization, societal needs for the language of communication may be great, but individual attitudes may be strongly opposed to that language, which is viewed as the language of the oppressing power.

Therefore, individual attitudes and attitudes of particular groups in the society need to be assessed independently of societal needs.

Individual attitudes towards a language represent the covert feelings and thoughts about the language itself, the people who speak it natively and their culture. Positive attitudes will reflect high regard for, and appreciation of both the language and the culture it represents. Negative attitudes may be caused by various factors based on practical experience or historical rivalry. Negative attitudes, whatever their roots, create a certain psychological distance between the learner and the subject matter, and can, therefore, influence the learning-teaching process. Moreover, both positive and negative attitudes may exist side by side – the famous 'love-hate' relationship, where there is appreciation and respect on the one hand, and emotional hatred on the other. In North Africa such attitudes exist towards French.

Much research has concerned itself with the effect of positive or negative attitudes on success in second language acquisition. Gardner and Lambert (1972) view attitudes as one of the basic components of motivation. A learner can be instrumentally motivated to learn a language when there is an overt utilitarian value to knowing that language, or a learner may be integratively motivated if there is a strong desire to know more about the members of the group of people who speak the language.

In the present discussion instrumental motivation is closely linked to societal needs. When societal needs require the practical use of the LWC, then instrumental motivation can be expected to follow. In other words, the individuals within the society will sooner or later recognize the utilitarian value of knowing the LWC and, therefore, be instrumentally motivated to learn it.

Integrative motivation, on the other hand, can only come as a result of a positive attitude toward the LWC, the people and the culture it represents. Such motivation is strongest when the learner or user of the LWC wishes to identify with the native speaker of the LWC. To this notion of integrative motivation we should add the dimension of the social status of the LWC within the community. If there is a general feeling that the LWC is a social symbol, integrative motivation might be more related to the attitude of various social groups towards the more educated (English speaking) social group within their own society, than to their attitudes towards Americans or Englishmen. The notion of upward social mobility is, of course, related to this interclass attitude.

A questionnaire is, at present, the most feasible and manageable tool for attitude assessment. The preparation of such questionnaires requires that the investigator make an evaluative and judgmental hypothesis as to the kind of response that a certain attitude will elicit. We predict, in other words, the behavior resulting from a presupposed attitude and we express it in the form of a question to which the subject will respond. A great deal, therefore, depends upon the wording of the questions.

A lot has been written about the wording of questionnaires and the various traps that an investigator must try to avoid. Perhaps the most important danger inherent in a questionnaire is the fact that, when we are asking about attitudes directly and overtly, we might, at the same time, influence the attitudes of that individual. So much of what we are concerned with in terms of that 'predisposition' has to do with an individual's covert and only partially conscious thoughts and feelings. Yet, until a better tool is developed the questionnaire and the interview remain the most effective means for collecting information on attitudes.

Political, national and economic considerations

Political, national and economic considerations are often closely interlaced and can, therefore, be viewed as an integrated factor. At the initial fact-finding stage, however, we need to devote some attention to each of these factors separately. Viewed at the highest level, *political considerations* have to do with the particular regime in power, and how it views the question of language in general and the LWC in particular.

National considerations are particularly relevant to nations which are still in the process of nationalism, defined by Fishman (1968b) as a sequence of states moving from the ethnic group to the nationality. During this process, and for a period of time following the process, language comes to be viewed differently by the members of the group.

Economic considerations relate to the desire of the particular community or nationality to become an integral part of the world wide community in terms of technological, economic and scientific activities. They are of two different sorts: economic developments, which provide incentives for members of the society to learn English; and economic limitations – usually shortages of funds – that have to be taken into account when policy is made. These two different types of economic considerations might be in conflict most of the time and the making of certain choices will depend on national priorities.

Conclusion

During the fact-finding phase of the policy making process, the data gatherers are concerned with the identification of both overt and hidden language problems. A complex picture of the linguistic situation is built up from factual data on: societal needs, group and individual attitudes, and political, national and economic consider-ations relating to the use of the LWC. Researchers or experts then prepare a document which incorporates their findings and policy making recommendations. This document constitutes the first step in the process of language policy making.

Tasks

Task 1

Look at Olshtain's definition of an LWC on p. 46. It is not the same as Judd's definition.

  (i) What are the differences?
  (ii) Which definition do you think is more useful and why?

Task 2

Olshtain makes the point that language planning should consider the roles and functions of all languages in a given society, not just English. Turn back to Task 6 on the Judd article p. 43. Look at the five possible stages of the 'life-cycles' of English. Each stage dealt only with English. Read through each stage and try to work out how the roles and functions of the local languages would be affected by the changing role of English at each stage. For example, would local languages be used by more or fewer people at each stage; would they be used by different people, in different situations, for different social functions?

Task 3

Olshtain highlights the importance of English as an International Language (EIL) often used as a means of communication between non-native English speakers who do not share a common language. It is important to realize, however, that learners of EIL may have different reasons for learning English and therefore different needs and wants.

(i) Look at the following learner profiles (from Underhill 1981).

Learner profile 1
Kamel is a Kuwaiti naval cadet. He is going to follow a naval training course in Germany. This course will be taught in English; Kamel, therefore, needs EIL to communicate with German instructors and other naval personnel. Because the situation in which English will be needed is known in some detail, it is possible to identify which language skills, activities, and vocabulary areas should be taught.

Learner profile 2
Laszlo is a Hungarian doctor working in Libya. English is the main language used to communicate with his patients, most of whom are Arabs or East Europeans. He has to talk to the patients to find out what is wrong with them, and then be able to explain the treatment he recommends. He has to read medical journals in English. English is also the main language for social activities outside his own national group. In the course of these social activities he will sometimes be communicating with native English speakers.

Learner profile 3
Fumiko is a Japanese guide at an exhibition centre in Japan. She constantly requires English when guiding visitors, many of whom are not native English speakers, around the exhibition. As well as entertaining them socially, she must give technical translations and explanations. For this purpose she requires an advanced and accurate knowledge of English; some of her visitors will be diplomats and executives.

Learner profile 4
Georges is a French nuclear safety expert who has to visit many different countries to explain and check on safety standards in nuclear power stations. He must therefore be able to communicate in English with senior managers in any part of the world on a subject where accuracy is very important. He must be able to read highly complex technical documents.

Learner profile 5
Mitsuko is a Japanese housewife who frequently visits other Far Eastern countries on holiday and also goes with her husband on business trips. She needs to communicate with business associates and other people she meets on holiday; communication rather than accuracy is important.

(ii) From the information in the profiles, try to find out:

Why the learners need English.
Who they will be using English with.
What topics they will need to know about.

Fill in the table below with the information.

Learner	Why	Who	What
1			
2			
3			
4			
5			

(iii) Consider how a course designed for each learner might be similar/different. You might like to think about the question using guideline categories such as the following (but feel free to add your own): topics; skills; grammar/lexis/phonology; functions; emphasis on accuracy or fluency.

Task 4

Job advertisements can be a useful indication of language needs. Boys (1981) conducted a small survey of job advertisements for office, technical and professional staff in Chile. She found that out of 956 jobs advertised, 21% required English, and 0.8% required other foreign languages (French, German, Portugese). In a follow-up survey of 422 advertisements requiring English, she analysed the types of job most frequently advertised. The results are given in table 5.1

TABLE 5.1
Jobs most frequently advertised

Jobs	Number of advertisements	Percentage of total
Bilingual secretaries	94	22
Engineers (14 specializations)	89	21
Accountants (book-keepers and accountants)	44	10
Salespeople	43	10
Business administrators	27	6
Marketing executives	19	5
Technicians (5 specializations)	16	4
Receptionists	11	3
Others (19 jobs)	79	19
TOTAL	422	100

(i) Who in the language-planning process would find this information of use? (Olshtain mentions a number of interested parties in her article. Tollefson's article will also be useful, p. 23–31.)

(ii) What decisions related to language and language education might they make as a result of receiving the information?

Task 5

Olshtain distinguishes between integrative and instrumental motivation. Pride (1979b, p. 53–4) adds another type of motivation which he calls 'expressive' motivation.

This relates to the need, felt by vast numbers of learners of English, to use the language in order to express something of their own way of life and experience, both to those who speak the language natively and to those who do not – these latter audiences including both members of their own society and those of other societies.

This point is developed by Serpell in this volume (see p. 102).

On pages 45–6 of her article, Olshtain lists a number of countries which use English as an LWC.

(i) Try to identify those countries where you might expect to find a high level of expressive' motivation among learners wanting to communicate with members of their own society.

(ii) In what ways might ELT materials designed for the learners you identified in (i) be different from/similar to materials designed for groups showing integrative or instrumental motivation?

Task 6

Table 5.2 is taken from Lieberson (1982: 57). It shows the percentage of goods exported by a random sample of countries to a number of nations classified according to their official

TABLE 5.2
Export markets, classified by language, for a sample of nations

Official language of the importing nation	Exporting nation									
	Bolivia (1975)	Costa Rica (1974)	French Guiana (1975)	India (1975)	Lebanon (1973)	Nether- lands (1975)	Poland (1974)	South Vietnam (1973)	Uganda (1975)	Zambia (1973)
English	19	31	46	21	10	12	8	46	47	24
German	8	13	–	3	–	32	16	2	6	10
Dutch	6	9	4	–	–	14	–	–	2	–
Japanese	8	–	–	10	–	–	–	24	8	–
Italian	4	3	–	2	2	6	4	1	3	12
Spanish	9	26	–	–	–	1	–	1	–	–
French	3	3	41	3	–	25	3	16	4	8
Russian	5	–	–	12	–	–	29	–	–	–
Other	–	3[a]	8[b]	12[c]	52[d]	4[e]	13[f]	65[g]	5[h]	10[i]

Source: United Nations, 1976, Table 3 for each exporting nation.
– Signifies no representation in the leading markets for that nation.
[a] Finnish
[b] Portugese
[c] Persian (8 per cent); Bengali (2 per cent); Polish (2 per cent)
[d] Arabic
[e] Swedish (2 per cent); Danish (2 per cent)
[f] Czech (7 per cent); Hungarian (3 per cent); Bulgarian (3 per cent)
[g] Chinese (38 per cent); Malay (15 per cent); Tamil (12 per cent)
[h] Arabic (2 per cent); Serbo-Croat (3 per cent)
[i] Portugese (5 per cent); Swedish (1 per cent); Chinese (2 per cent); Serbo-Croatian (2 per cent)

language. For example, according to the table, in 1975 19% of Bolivia's exports were imported by nations whose official language is English, 8% by nations whose official language is German, and so on.

(i) Would this information be useful to those planning a language policy in the exporting countries? If so, in what way might it be useful?

(ii) What further information about trade would also be useful as input to language policy decisions?

Little has been written on the connections between language and national aspects of business/ economics. Ridler and Pons-Ridler (1984) and Vaillancourt (1983) are exceptions.

Chapter 6

Innovating in Schools

BARBARA HORVATH

Editor's introduction

Horvath's article arises from an issue in a particular context, that of the introduction of community language programmes in Australian schools, and thus relates closely to Quinn's article later in this collection. The theoretical aspects of the paper, however, are very relevant to our discussions so far, since they are concerned with innovation processes and strategies for change. Implementation of language policy invariably involves some degree of change operating within an educational system and it will fail, or be only partially successful, if the change implied by the policy for some reason does not take place. Innovation theory may be useful, therefore, both to draw up a plan that will successfully initiate change and to act as a means of evaluating the causes of a policy's failure or success. We have already seen how complex a task investigating aspects of the language situation is. Horvath now gives us some insight into the difficulty of implementing a plan and getting it accepted by those whom it will affect.

Drawing on the work of innovation theorists, Horvath suggests a number of areas which could be of relevance for our purposes – the structure of the plan itself through which change will be implemented, the participants involved at different levels, and the various strategies that can be adopted to aid acceptance of an innovation. The three strategies Horvath introduces are characterized by increasing involvement in the plan of those affected. Thus, power–coercive strategies enforce policy by decree through legal and economic sanctions. It is doubtful whether language planning that aims to change language use, i.e. change behaviour closely linked to a sense of personal identity, will succeed unless those affected are already in some way in agreement with the policy. Where they are not, other strategies probably need to be used that provide information about the change (rational–empirical) and preferably involve those affected (normative–re-educative). The latter approach inevitably means compromises and a more long-term incremental approach to change, which can be applied at lower levels of LP implementation. Thus, curriculum development that involves changes in materials and methodology is unlikely to succeed through legislation alone. More often than not, especially in centralized systems, or when innovations are 'imported' from outside the local context, this is the approach adopted, with little regard for involvement of the teacher or the student in the reform. Problems arise where there are few opportunities for feedback and little contact between, to use Horvath's terms, implementers (teachers), clients (students), and suppliers (materials writers).

Any attempt to characterize change, involving as it does complex relations between human behaviour and administrative systems, is bound to be oversimplified, but Horvath illuminates a neglected area in LP and provides a framework which might be usefully applied to policy implementation at all levels.

Community languages in schools: an innovation

WHEN WE TALK about incorporating community languages in schools, we are talking about innovating, about planning change in the education system in some way. Depending on the way we want to bring the community language into the school, of course, we may be talking about a major or minor innovation. For example, deciding to teach Polish in secondary school, or to allow Polish to be a matriculation subject, represents less of a change to the education system than does teaching Polish in the primary schools. In the first instance, the organizational structure for teaching foreign languages is already there; bringing in another language, a community language, requires little more than a specialist teacher to be added to the language staff. However, to bring community language teaching to the primary schools represents a relatively far-reaching change. Primary teachers have traditionally been generalist teachers and, therefore, to bring in specialists challenges this tradition. Language teaching methods appropriate to this age group are not nearly as well developed as they are for older learners and so we need not only teacher training but also support for basic research. If we are talking about bilingual education, particularly maintenance bilingual education, then we are talking about an even more extensive change to the education system.

Whatever the size of the innovation, it is important to have some understanding of the *process* of innovation. How do new ideas, programmes, products, or organizational structures (collectively called innovations or sometimes technologies) get introduced? What sort of processes, or stages, does the innovation go through before it becomes fully integrated into the system? And who are the people who carry the innovation process along? I want to discuss these three aspects of the innovation process: change strategies, stages in the process of innovation, and participants in the innovation process. Change strategies have to do with how a technology comes to the attention of a potential group of people who have a problem to which the innovation represents a possible solution. The stages in the process of innovation provide a framework for understanding what happens from the time the innovation is seen as a possible solution to the time it is incorporated fully into the system. By studying the participants in the process of innovation we can see who makes it happen, what roles are played by various participants at various stages in the process.

Given a framework provided by innovation researchers, we are better able to understand the problem at hand, the incorporation of community languages in our schools. By looking at the Australian education system from this point of view, we might get a better undertanding of how to proceed with planned changes to that system.

A typology of change strategies

Chin and Benne present a typology of change strategies for planned change which will allow us to identify in our situation the kinds of strategy that are being used or that will be most useful for achieving the adoption of the innovation.

The three types of strategy recognized by Chin and Benne (1970) are:

(1) Rational–empirical
(2) Normative–re-educative
(3) Power–coercive

Rational–empirical strategies

These strategies assume (i) people are rational and (ii) that they will follow their rational self-interest once it has been revealed to them. In line with these strategies,

> A change is proposed by some person or group which knows of a situation that is desirable, effective, and in line with the self-interest of the person, group, organization, or community which will be affected by the change. Because the person (or group) is assumed to be rational and moved by self-interest, it is assumed that he (or they) will adopt the proposed change if it can be rationally justified and if it can be shown by the proposer(s) that he (or they) will gain by the change. [Chin and Benne, p.34]

The strategy basically involves a system of research, to develop the knowledge needed to address some problem, and then education to inform the potential users of the knowledge so that they may act in accord with the research. This combination of research and education works best where the population is ready to accept the new innovation e.g. computers or new maths and science teaching methods, but is not effective where this is not the case (e.g. the fluoridation of water). It is especially not effective as a single strategy according to Chin and Benne, where the new technology is seen as a threat to traditional attitudes and values.

Of the many forms of this kind of strategy, one is particularly relevant to the kind of planned change we are dealing with. This has to do with linking this rsearch-plus-education approach to innovation diffusion approaches. The research-plus-education approach often entails setting up a model programme which is well researched and which appears to be feasible to install in practice settings. However this strategy alone is subject to failure if it is assumed that all you need to do is show that the technology achieves a desirable result and that people will adopt the technology once they know the results. By adding the diffusion approach, the question of how the technology will get a fair trial and how it will be installed in the ongoing system will be addressed.

Normative–re-educative strategies

These strategies pay closer attention to the values and attitudes of the potential group of users of the innovation. It is assumed that patterns of behaviour are supported by socio-cultural norms and by the commitment of individuals to these norms.

> Change in a pattern of practice or action, according to this view, will occur only as the persons involved are brought to change their normative orientations to old patterns and develop commitments to new ones. And changes in normative orientations involve changes in attitudes, values, skills, and significant relationships, not just changes in knowledge, information, or intellectual rationales for action and practice. [Chin and Benne, p.34]

Supporters of these strategies take the position that people must take part in their own re-education if re-education is going to occur at all, and so action-research is encouraged. There is an emphasis on a collaborative relationship between the researcher and the client, where the client is involved in working out the solution to the problem. Often the re-education process involves working in groups where attitudes and values, which may be nonconscious elements that are getting in the way of solving the problem, are brought to consciousness and publicly examined.

These strategies emphasize 'experienced-based learning as an ingredient of all enduring changes in human systems' (Chin and Benne, p.49) and further recognize that people have to learn to learn from their experiences, hence the need to develop research into small group dynamics, attitude change strategies, etc.

The normative–re-educative strategy differs from the rational–empirical in that the latter describes a situation in which simply knowing some information is sufficient to cause someone to act. The former strategy adds a further step which intervenes between knowing and acting, i.e. changing the attitudes and values that impede acting in one's own self-interest.

Another different feature about this strategy is that, unlike the rational–empirical strategy, it is not necessarily the case that innovations need to be imported from without. Creative adaptation to changing conditions, by contrast, can as easily come from within the group.

Power–coercive strategies

These strategies emphasize political and economic sanctions in the exercise of power, but strategies can also build upon moral power or play on sentiments of guilt and shame. The power–coercive strategy generally goes unnoticed when it is used by those in legitimate control of the system, but becomes particularly worthy of note when it is used by those who have no such legitimacy.

> In general, power–coercive strategies of changing seek to mass political and economic power behind the change goals which the strategists of change have decided are desirable. Those who oppose these goals, if they adopt the same strategy seek to mass political and economic power in opposition. The strategy thus tends to divide the society when there is anything like a division of opinion and of power in that society. [Chin and Benne, p.53]

In cases where these strategies are used by people who are seen as legitimate wielders of power, changes are brought about through bureaucratic order, governmental legislation or judicial decree. Others who use these strategies need to achieve power outside of the legitimate channels of authority, which may be accomplished by organizing discontent in some way; nonviolent demonstrations, for instance, would be one way of dramatizing some situation in need of public attention. Less dramatic realizations of this strategy involve delegations to those in authority, petitions, public meetings, pressure groups, letters to the editors of newspapers, etc.

Although there are many problems with this kind of strategy, two in particular diminish its effectiveness. Those working for change may wrongly assume the change has taken place once a law is passed (e.g. the Women's Liberation Movement vis-à-vis right-to-vote legislation.) Getting the law passed is only one step in instituting change.

The second problem has to do with the nature of power elites and gets us back on the normative–re-educative strategy. Simply decreeing alone that an innovation (e.g. multicultural education) will become part of the curriculum, will not achieve the goals of those who want to change the school system in this direction. Those who have the power to institute the changes, including administrators, principals and teachers, are also those who, in fact, were in charge of the system that required changing but who did nothing about it until pressured to do so. Unless they are re-educated (i.e. their values and attitudes are changed, it is quite likely that the change will be ineffective. Chin and Benne express some doubt about re-educating power elites and suggest the need to 'build counterpower to offset and reduce the power of the presently deciding group where this power interferes with the achievement of desirable educational goals' (pp. 56–7). Thus, an effective use of this approach would yield some power to those not normally seen as having it legitimately.

The process of innovation

The process of innovation can be viewed as a series of stages or decision phases (the description here comes from Lambright and Flynn (1980) and is based on the model proposed by Rogers et al. (1977). The following four stages are proposed:

(1) Pre-adoption
(2) Adoption
(3) Implementation
(4) Incorporation.

Pre-adoption

This stage begins with the recognition of the problem and lasts until some innovation is seen officially as a possible solution to the problem. The official recognition may take many forms, including having the innovation discussed at meetings of bureaucrats who are empowered to introduce changes into the system.

Adoption

The adoption stage is a process during which a number of smaller decisions are made so that there is a gradual matching of a need with a technology. It may involve a search for solutions other than the innovation initially considered; consultants are often hired to give advice on various possible solutions. Gradually, both the problems and the solutions become better defined and linked over time. Formal adoption of the innovation occurs when resources are allocated to the innovation.

Implementation

The innovation that has been adopted is given a trial run during this stage. It can be changed or rejected during this phase. It is possible to extend the innovation with further testing and training of personnel. There is a gradual meshing of the innovation within the system. The innovation may well be rejected at this point, but it will be seen to have been rejected on increased knowledge. By contrast, by the end of this phase it may be viewed as a 'necessity' rather than an 'extra'.

Incorporation

When an innovation is regarded as a necessity, it becomes part of the routine operation of the system. It is no longer on trial and rejection is no longer contemplated.

Participants

Five different kinds of participant can be recognized. There are the *adopters*, those who officially and formally have the authority to make decisions and allocate resources to the new technology. There are the *implementers*, middle managers and employers who carry out the policy set by the adopters. The *clients* are those who receive the services. The *suppliers*, are those who supply the technology to the system. The first three of these participants must want the innovation and, of course, the supplier must be willing and able to supply the technology. The coalescing of this group does not occur automatically; this is where the fifth participant, the *entrepreneur* comes in. The entrepreneur forms links among the local participants and may be someone who is also participating as an adopter, implementer, client, or supplier.

Some of these participant groups can be further divided. Adopters for instance, are often subclassified into early adopters, late adopters and laggards. Obviously, when an innovation is first being introduced, the entrepreneur would be eager to identify early adopters, rather than laggards, to promote the innovation.

Success or failure of innovations

Although there is much to be said about whether or not an innovation succeeds or fails, I only want to focus upon two notions that are of particular relevance here.

Success has been found to be related to characteristics of the innovation itself.

> If a technology does not work, it will not be adopted. If a technology that has been adopted operates below expectations, it may well be abandoned. Separability helps, especially in larger scale innovations. [Lambright and Flynn, p.25]

Lambright and Flynn studied a number of cases of innovative programmes and found that when a complex programme came as a whole package it was more likely to be rejected outright than when it was offered as a combination of programmes that could be separated. In the latter case, some of the programmes could be rejected, others modified, still others accepted as they were, without jeopardizing the overall programme.

> Technologies that are separable tend also to be incremental. They are easily understood, or at least not perceived as threatening. Thus, they are clearly advantaged. Large-scale, costly, and seemingly irreversible technologies have greater problems in being adopted and used than those that are small, cheap, and seen as easily abandoned if they fail to work. [pp.259, 261]

The other important factor leading towards success, especially when considering a local organization's adoption of an innovation, is the extent of intra- and extra-organizational support that is given. Without support, the local organization has a reduced capacity to innovate.

Resistance to change

Although this subject has not been explicit in the models of change discussed so far, implicitly the *resister* has been lurking in the background all along. Identifying the resisters and their reasons for resisting will be important to the agents of change.

Educational change in Australia

The title of this section is overly ambitious. I merely want to place some observations that I have made about how educational change proceeds in Australia within the framework developed so far. My observations have been limited and this section therefore necessarily is only a cursory look at change. Furthermore, I will constrain my view of change by dealing only with one educational problem: the mismatch between the language the child has learned before coming to school and the language used by the school as a medium of interaction.

This is no place to trace the history of the reactions of the education system to the presence of migrant children in the system; a quick review will suffice for our purposes here. Initially, no changes were made at all; then ESL (English as a Second Language) classes, usually withdrawal classes, were begun; next, some intensive English language centres were started; then people began to worry about 'the complete child' and multicultural education was proposed; finally the child's first language received some attention. We are now at the point of deciding how to treat the child's first language at school – should it be a subject to be taught or a medium of instruction?

Using the framework developed so far, we can first of all clarify what our 'innovation' is, at what stage in the innovation process we now find ourselves, who are the participants in the process of innovation, and what strategies are being used to institute change. Given this understanding of our own situation and the understanding that comes from the research into change processes, we ought to be able to arrive at a language plan for incorporating community languages in the schools which will have some hope of success.

Let us start by clarifying the innovation. Recalling that Lambright and Flynn found that separable innovations were usually incremental and seen as less threatening, I would suggest that the innovation be regarded as a package of alternatives rather than as a take-it-or-leave-it programme. The variety of situations (numbers of languages in a given school; degree of maintenance of the language in the community; availability of trained teachers; community support for programmes, etc.) alone would dictate that no single programme would have a chance of being successful. So, multicultural education, community languages taught as school subjects, community languages as media of instruction, and perhaps even support for ethnic schools would all be regarded as part of the innovation package.

However, it is essential to compare these different programmes within the innovation package, to clarify what goals can be achieved by each programme and to point out which of the programmes is most likely to achieve the educational goals of providing a sound education for children. In other words, all of the programmes can be seen as positive steps but some are much better than others in that they are more likely to satisfy the goals that have been set.

At what stage in the process of innovation are we? If we consider the innovation package as a whole, I would suggest that we are through the pre-adoption stage; the 'problem' has been recognized officially (e.g. the Galbally report (1978), various policy statements from state departments of education, research reports). The adoption stage, recall, is one in which serious consideration is given to various solutions and there is a gradual clarification of both the 'problem' and the solutions. During the next stage, implementation, the innovation is given trial runs. I would suggest that we have only begun the adoption stage, given the whole innovation package. Even though there are some examples of community language programmes and bilingual education programmes, they are too few, too recent, and their futures are too uncertain for them to be regarded as trial runs of an adopted innovation. The fact that we are in the adoption phase has important implications for the planning of change. This is the time, for instance, to encourage debate about the alternatives, to clarify the 'problem' and to bring the solutions in line with the problem and to do feasibility studies on the implementations of the various solutions.

We have identified five participants in the change process. In the scheme set out by Rogers et al., (1977), the adopter is the policy maker; in our system one would expect this to be someone at the head office in charge of programmes affecting migrants; however, my observation is that, whilst policies do appear to come down through the bureaucratic hierarchy, those policies are often quite general statements open to various interpretations. I would suggest that the role of the adopter is played most directly for purposes of designing a language plan, by the local school principal. It is the principal who has the power of instituting change in his/her school within quite broad guidelines set by the department and other agencies, such as the Schools Commission. The implementers are the teachers and the aides, the clients are the children and their parents. Whether or not the clientele is to be limited to only children of non-English speaking backgrounds is still uncertain. The suppliers are those who design the curriculum and produce materials. And who plays the role of the entrepreneur, the one who brings these other participants together? It seems to me that this role is played by such organizations as the Schools Commission and, in some cases, by the Minister of Education, especially when the power–coercive strategy has been most effective.

If we turn now to the change strategies outlined by Chin and Benne, we can examine what strategies have been used so far. I would put this report clearly within the rational–empirical strategy; various conferences, in-service programmes, etc., represent the normative–re-educative. However, I am convinced that much of the reason these other two strategies have been used at all, is that people outside of the legitimate power structure have brought pressure to bear on the system. In effect then, I would argue that the most effective strategy so far has been the power–coercive. Interestingly enough, in talking to department of education people more often than not it was the pressure of migrant support groups that was cited as a reason for instituting change. Hardly ever was a rational argument given on the basis of 'sound educational philosophy'. It was obvious that this pressure was resented and even seen as an impediment to change, but it also was not apparent that any change would have been contemplated without such pressure being applied.

There does seem to be a real problem with using the rational–empirical strategy as a single strategy to institute change in this case. The majority of people in decision-making positions are monolingual Anglo-Australians and the promotion of a multilingual, multicultural education system is simply not in their self-interest. In fact for many participants (except for the clients) their self-interest is threatened. When they do act out of self-interest (self-preservation?), it is only after the power–coercive strategy has been effective.

Implications for the community language plan

If the interpretation of the process of incorporating community languages into the education system given above is correct, then there are implications that must be drawn for devising a plan to continue the adoption of this innovation.

The innovation

The innovation should be seen as a package of programmes. The programmes should allow for alternatives which can be shown to be appropriate to particular subdivisions within the clientele (e.g. children who enter school speaking little or no English; children of migrant background who have only understanding competence in a community language; Anglo-Australian children; etc.) Where some programmes in the package can be seen as incremental steps, the plan should have a schedule which will ensure that those steps are taken.

The state of change

At this point, various alternatives should be supported and evaluated; I believe that model programmes where school staff and researchers work collaboratively are best, because thay can achieve both the further development of the programme (e.g. bilingual education; teaching a community language as a school subject; etc.) and deal with the changing of values and attitudes of the school staff in the least threatening way.

The client

Although I have said that the clients are the children (and their parents), there are persuasive arguments that require that we set priorities on which clients should participate initially in the programmes.

The adopter

If I am correct and the principal of the school is to be seen as the adopter, then the planning must be done at the level of the local school.

The strategy

If I am correct that those with legitimate power do not identify with those who want change, then it is justified, it seems to me, to involve the community, those who are pressing for change, in the decision-making process. Chin and Benne call this 'a strategy of building countervailing power to offset the existing concentration of power in people not identified with the interests (of the people seeking change)'. (p.56) Both rational–empirical and the normative–re-educative strategies will have to be used to achieve the adoption of this complex innovation.

Tasks

Task 1

Any person attempting change must take into account those factors that are 'fixed' and those that are open to change. Look back at the list of five variables related to course design in Tollefson Task 1 p.31. Suppose a Ministry of Education in a developing country had hired an ELT adviser from, say, Britain or the USA to work for three years with English language teachers in either a secondary-school English department ('General English') or a University English Language Service Centre (ESP) to develop new materials.

    (i) Which factors in the list given in Tollefson Task 1 should the adviser take as 'fixed' and which as open to change?

    (ii) How would your answer to (i) above affect the materials and the methodology the adviser might want to introduce?

Holliday and Cooke (1982) provide an interesting account of operating with 'fixed' and 'negotiable' factors in ESP programmes.

Task 2

Horvath suggests three different strategies for change:

    Power–coercive
    Rational–empirical
    Normative–re-educative.

Looking again at the situation of the adviser in Task 1, which strategy or strategies do you think s/he might apply and how?

    After doing this task, you might like to look at Kennedy (1987) who gives an example of putting change strategies into practice in the area of teacher education.

Task 3

Reports of failures to change situations are rare; this is unfortunate as we can learn as much from failures as from successes. One exception is Britten and O'Dwyer (1987) who describe an attempt to encourage teachers to evaluate their own teaching instead of being evaluated by others. They designed and distributed 'self-assessment questionnaires' to British teachers working in Moroccan secondary schools, to be used voluntarily and without external supervision of any kind. Few teachers used the questionnaires. In conclusion the authors state:

    (a) Some form of constraint is needed to ensure the appropriate use of (the questionnaires).

    (b) It would be desirable for users to belong to a group, for example a teacher development group among colleagues.

    (c) The failure...shows that...teachers' attitudes towards teacher self assessment can ...be very reserved.

    (i) Do you think the introduction of a 'constraint' suggested in (a) above is a good idea or not? Give your reasons. If you believe it is a good idea, what form should it take?

    (ii) What would be the advantage of the 'teacher group' suggested in (b) above?

    (iii) Can you suggest any additional reasons for the teachers' failure to use the questionnaire?

    (iv) How could you use these reasons to develop a strategy to try to encourage the teachers to use self-assessment?

Task 4

Horvath makes the point that for an innovation to be accepted, it must be seen by potential adopters to work. She also points out the advantages of small-scale and cheap innovations. This brings us back to the notion of appropriate technology which we looked at in the Rogers article Task 6. Appropriate technology is normally a term used in discussing development projects but Markee (1986b) believes we can apply it to discussions about ELT. The argument is that different methods, materials and teaching resources will be appropriate in different cultural contexts.

Look at the two imagined situations described below (taken from Abbott and Wingard 1981).

Example 1
A dozen young men and women in their late teens and twenties are sitting at desks placed in a semicircle. We can see (and hear by their accents) that they come from various countries ... Miss Taylor – her students call her Liz – is explaining something ... Now they are listening to a cassette recording and writing on their handouts ... The class ends. The students put on their warm coats and, chatting to each other in English, go out into the High Street. Above the door it says 'Oxbridge School of English'.

Example 2
The room is full of cheerful young boys, row upon row, sitting four to a bench. There are a dozen benches, all bolted to the floor. These eleven year-olds are listening respectfully to their teacher, whom we cannot understand because he is explaining something in their mother tongue. One or two children per bench have a grubby textbook, and they all have a grubby exercise book ... The class ends. The boys stand up while the teacher leaves, then rush shouting out of the stuffy room into a hot, sandy compound. In all the noise, not a word of English is heard.

(i) List the differences revealed by the two extracts and any other differences you might expect.

	Example 1	Example 2
Methods		
Materials		
Resources		
Other		

(ii) Would you say the content of each list is 'appropriate' to the situation or would you want to make any changes? If so, what would they be?
     Could the teacher make the changes you propose or would they be the responsibility of other poeple? If the latter, what position would such people hold in the educational hierarchy?

Task 5

The following quotations (from Kennedy 1988) refer to problems of initiating change in areas other than ELT (agriculture and medicine for example).

(1) Financing fixed-term projects is not as effective as long-term programmes working through existing institutions and organisations.
(2) Top-down programmes are not successful because they never really involve the farmers. Allied to this is the realization that for farmers to participate there must be benefits that they can appreciate.

(3) The case against the disease was relatively easy to solve; the real problems lie elsewhere...transient politicians and civil servants, changing policies, very low wages and above all a brain drain.

(i) Do you think the same sorts of problems occur in the context of ELT projects? Can you give any examples from your own experience?

(ii) If you were running a materials project similar to that outlined in Task 1 of this chapter, how would these quotations help you in drawing up a plan for the project?

There has been suprisingly little written on ELT project design and implementation, and still less on project evaluation. Some useful ideas, however, can be found in ELT documents 116 (1983); Alderson (ed 1985); and British Council Evaluation of Educational Projects seminar papers (1986).

Task 6

It is important, when initiating any form of change, to get those who will be affected by the change as closely involved with the project as possible. It is essential to know, therefore, the reasons why some wish to take part in changes and others do not. One theory is that individuals calculate what they will gain and what they will lose by being involved in and supporting any change. If gains outweigh losses, the individuals are likely to respond positively to change.

(i) Suppose a head of department wanted teachers to take part in an ELT materials project and wanted them not only to teach the new materials but, wherever possible, to take a part in their design and writing. Look at the following list of possible gains (you may wish to add to it) and put them in order of importance to teachers.

Job security
Further professional qualifications
Approval of superiors
Improved service to the students
Increase in teachers' knowledge
Increase in teachers' skills in classroom
Intellectual satisfaction
Increased contact with colleagues
Financial rewards
Professional advancement

(ii) Which ones would a head of department have the power or influence to offer as inducements to teachers?

(iii) What losses would teachers be likely to put against the gains offered under (ii)?

(iv) On the basis of your answers to (i), (ii), and (iii), what is the likelihood that the head of department will succeed in getting teachers to collaborate in the materials project?

The whole area of innovation is fascinating, though little has been written with respect to ELT. A good introductory book for those interested in the general area of educational innovation is Nicholls (1983).

Part Three

ISSUES IN LANGUAGE PLANNING AND LANGUAGE TEACHING

Chapter 7

A Rationale for the Choice of English as the Official Language for Independent Namibia

Editor's introduction

In this third section of the book we shall be looking at particular instances of language planning and policy in different parts of the world and seeing how they relate to our earlier discussions. The first case is that of Namibia, which, as South-West Africa, was a German colony and then a League of Nations mandated territory under South African rule. The mandate officially came to an end on the demise of the League, a fact which was not, however, recognized by South Africa, which continues to govern it as before, despite a ruling against South Africa by the International Court of Justice in 1971. The opposition to this situation is led by SWAPO, the exiled South West African People's Organization, and the United Nations Institute for Namibia, which was the source of the document from which this extract was taken. There could be no clearer illustration of the close link between the history of a country, its politics and its languages. The political reasons for language policy decisions, so often kept concealed, are in this case evident, since the choice of an official language for Namibia is very much a statement of adherence to a particular political system and language choice is seen as one major instrument for social and political change. In this sense, the choice of English as the official language for an independent Namibia — rather than Afrikaans and English (the present system) — is predictable, given the nature of the social and political system with which Afrikaans is associated. English has, in addition, already been adopted as the official language of SWAPO so the reasons given in this document for the adoption of English are, to some extent, a rationalization of a decision which had already been taken. Nonetheless, the criteria that the chosen language will need to meet are interesting and remind us that, in many cases of language policy, the decision which language to use for what purposes is not a simple one, but one which can only be taken after weighing up a number of different demands from various sectors of society. The eight criteria range from socio-psychological constructs, like acceptability, to practical considerations, such as feasibility.

In some cases, the complex nature of the decisions to be made is not recognized, perhaps for ideological reasons, and this may lead to conflict if groups within the society in question feel they have been unfairly treated. The authors of the document show an awareness of this complexity. Thus, although there are strong reasons for promoting the local languages in Namibia, the decision to choose one of them as the official language could have lead to divisiveness, which would be problematic for an independent Namibia. This does not mean that the local languages cannot play an important role, especially in education, a fact that is recognized in the document. Of the other possible options (Afrikaans, German, French and English), Afrikaans and German are rejected mainly on grounds of acceptability, and English is preferred to French partly for the reason that it is the more important world language of the two. Notice that the choice of English as official language represents policy which cannot be implemented until Namibia gains its independence. What happens then, in terms of implementation, will depend, to a large extent, on the attitudes of the Namibians to their different local languages, the use they put them to in reality, and the availability of resources required to make English the official language in practice as well as in theory.

PRIOR TO PRESENTING a rationale for the choice of an official language for Namibia, a brief perspective of the prevailing situation in Namibia is offered as a background to the ensuing discussion. The rationale will then be developed by suggesting a set of criteria that an official language must meet. Various languages will then be considered in view of these criteria.

Under the oppressive rule of South Africa, Namibia's history is characterized by the attendant evils of apartheid, namely racial and ethnic separation, job discrimination, economic exploitation, political suppression, educational retardation, and linguistic isolation and fragmentation. The forces of divide and rule, cornerstones of the colonial system, have by design contributed to maintaining and enforcing the ethnic and linguistic separation that persists in Namibia today. In post-independent Namibia a major priority for the new government will, therefore, be to minimize any divisive tendencies and practices in the country on the one hand, and on the other hand, to reinforce all such factors that may contribute to national unity i.e. to create conditions conducive to national unity, whether in the realm of politics, economics, religion, culture, race or language.

It will be remembered that the South African regime has to date capitalized on and exploited the existence of various languages in Namibia. It has deliberately magnified minor differences and even manufactured others. It has used language differences to create ethnic divisiveness. It has attempted to drive the people to focus on linguo-tribal affiliations and differences instead of on national unity. The practice of creating such divisiveness is clearly an ideological position in line with the age-old practice of divide and rule.

An official language: the criteria for choice

In view of the factors related to this perspective and the needs of an independent nation, the chosen official language for Namibia will need to meet a number of criteria. The most significant of these criteria are listed below. There are many orders of listing possible; the one offered here attempts to lead broadly from a national to an international perspective of requirements for an official language:

Criterion 1: unity

The language chosen should contribute toward the new nation's primary task; that is, achieving unity and national reconstruction in the wake of a deliberate policy of ethnolinguistic fragmentation pursued by the illegal occupying regime. Inasmuch as any official language has the capacity to contribute substantially toward such unification, it would be expected to be able to neutralize any competitive or disruptive socio-linguistic forces likely to emerge if one language were chosen from amongst others.

Criterion 2: acceptability

The chosen language should be one which in the specific case of Namibia has positive rather than negative associations for the people. This would mean avoiding languages that may be associated with the oppression and injustices which have characterized Namibian history, and which are still being perpetrated.

Criterion 3: familiarity

The language chosen should be one with which Namibians, both inside and outside the country, have some familiarity and, preferably, one with which there has been some short- and long-term experience in the educational system.

Criterion 4: feasibility

The question of the cost and effort involved in promoting a language to official status has to be included amongst the criteria. Added to this is the question of whether the necessary resources are available in the chosen language for short-and long-term implementation plans. Are there learning programmes and accompanying books and materials readily available? If not, can country and group-specific programmes and materials be prepared in time? Are there sufficient expatriate professionals fluent in the chosen language available for recruitment to help with teaching, teacher training, crash courses, curriculum design, educational administration, and other areas crucial in any emergency language development situation? Would there be adequate training facilities available in educational or other institutions in countries where the language chosen for Namibia is used?

Criterion 5: science and technology

Namibians, after independence, will want to harness the resources of modern science and technology to the development of their country. This means applying such resources to Namibia's mineral wealth, crop and livestock production, and fishing, as well as to the specific challenges of desertification and aridity, to mention only a few. Thus, the chosen language should be language of wide communication in virtually all fields of science and technology as well as a library language rich in published materials to facilitate training and research programmes inside and outside the country.

Criterion 6: Pan-Africanism

The chosen language should facilitate the growth of bonds between Namibian and other progressive communities in Africa. It would be advantageous if the chosen language were one common to many of Namibia's immediate neighbours, as well as being widely spoken throughout Africa.

Criterion 7: wider communication

Namibia is likely to re-orient from a South African outlook, as at present, to an international one after independence. Such an outlook is already developing as members of the Liberation Movement pursue pre-independence personnel training and other strategies in close liaison with many countries and organizations throughout the world. Use of an international language of wider communication, in direct contrast with the insularity and limitations of other languages, is therefore implied. This language would be used by Namibians as they develop sea and air communications, and as they develop international trading and negotiating at administrative, diplomatic and commercial levels.

Criterion 8: United Nations

The history of Namibia's struggle for independence is intimately linked with the United Nations Organization. There is every reason to suggest, therefore, that Namibia's main official language, if other than an indigenous language, should be one of the principal languages of the United Nations with which Namibian negotiators are already familiar.

These criteria do not include mention of any objective standards of quality which a chosen language would have to meet. It has been pointed out that the choice of an international language, or lingua franca, is 'never based on linguistic or aesthetic criteria, but always on political, economic and demographic ones'. (Quirk et al. 1972:3)

Having set up these criteria, the next step is to consider how those languages which might be deemed eligible for Namibia's official language match them. Indigenous Namibian languages, Afrikaans, German, French, and English are examined for their suitability as the official language for independent Namibia.

Indigenous languages

It has been stated that 'every language is equally well adapted to the uses to which the community puts it'. (Halliday et al. 1970). If this were so, Namibia could choose as the official language one of the local languages spoken by substantial numbers of people in the country. However, against this has to be set the fact that no local language is spoken by a large majority of Namibians throughout the country. And because of this, choosing one of the local languages as the official language could arouse unnecessary intra-linguistic competition and strife. It is conceivable that other Namibians whose languages are not strong enough candidates on a numerical basis for national status might oppose the claims of this language. They might then prefer to assign such a status to a foreign language which may at least have the merit of being extra-ethnic.

Furthermore, the choice of a local language might be seen as being based on tribal preference or bias. Thus, it would seem that for political reasons, after independence, choosing a local language might have some disadvantages. Then, on the ground of the first criterion (unity) the choice of a local language would seem to be unsatisfactory. As Fishman points out:

> Instead of trying to cope with hundreds of local languages as instruments of government, education, industrialization, etc., most African states have decided to assign all of them equally to their respective home, family and neighbourhood domains and utilise a single, major European language (usually English or French) for all formal, statusful and specialized domains. This approach tends to minimize internal linguistic divisiveness since it does not place any indigenous language at an undue advantage as the language of nationhood. [Fishman 1970: 284]

Finally, while the second and third criteria (acceptability and familiarity) could identify a local language as a satisfactory choice, the fourth, fifth, sixth, seventh and eighth (feasibility, science and technology, Pan-Africanism, wider communication and United Nations) criteria would seem to preclude this being so.

Afrikaans

Next, it might be argued that Afrikaans should be a natural choice for Namibia's official language. Afrikaans appears to satisfy the third and fourth criteria (familiarity and feasibility) but fails on the first and second criteria (unity and acceptability) both of outstanding importance, as well as on the fifth, sixth, seventh and eighth criteria (science and technology, Pan-Africanism, wider communication, United Nations). On these grounds, Afrikaans fails to qualify.

German

German, a language in use in Namibia as a semi-official language, could also be considered. Like Afrikaans, however, it is a language which has been used to rule Namibia and has direct association with oppression and injustices in the country. Like Afrikaans, therefore, it fails to satisfy the first and second criteria (unity and acceptability). Even though it can be argued that German could stand up to the demands of criteria three, four, five and seven (familiarity, feasibility, science and technology, and wider communication), it fails on criteria six and eight (Pan-Africanism, and United Nations) and it can in any case be taken that no language which fails to satisfy the second criterion (acceptability) has any real chance of being selected as the official language by a Namibian government responsive to the sensitivities of the masses.

French

The French language is another possible choice. It has been offered as an optional subject to students at the United Nations Institute for Namibia since 1976, and is, of course, an international language widely spoken throughout Africa. French could satisfy the requirements of many of the criteria, notably the first, second, fourth, fifth, seventh and eighth (unity, acceptability, feasibility, science and technology, wider communication, and United Nations) but only partly those of the sixth (Pan-Africanism) and not those of the third (feasibility) at all.

English

Turning finally to English, it becomes apparent that, whereas the other languages previously suggested fail on one or more of the criteria, English qualifies with all of them. Because of its special role as the language already chosen and used by the Liberation Movement it would seem well suited for the demands of the first criterion (unity). On the demands of the second criterion (acceptability), though it might be argued that as a language of former colonialism in many parts of the world, English would be unsuitable, for Namibians there has been no direct negative association with the language. For criteria six and eight (Pan-Africanism, United Nations) English is well qualified. It is a language spoken widely by all of Namibia's neighbours except one. It is spoken, or understood, throughout Africa, and it is one of the two principal languages of the United Nations. Finally, for criteria three, four, five and seven (familiarity, feasibility, science and technology, wider communication) English is pre-eminently suitable. It is already one of Namibia's official languages, and though it is not taught in Namibia for actual use it features as a subject throughout the educational system. In addition well established techniques of implementing the use of English exist both for foreign students in Britain and other English-speaking countries and in countries where English is learnt as a foreign or second language (EFL-ESL) through organizations such as the British Council and UNESCO, as well as many university departments. Furthermore, there are many professionals available with long experience in teaching and developing English programmes throughout the world, and in using or adapting the wealth of English learning materials developed in past years. In all branches of science and technology, including medicine, English is paramount as an international medium for offering direct access to workers and specialists in these areas. The latest published sources concerning scientific and technological development are printed in English, worldwide, and make English probably the leading international library language for reference and research. Lastly, the spread of English throughout the world in recent years for utilitarian purposes places it in an outstanding position as a language of wider communication. For all these specific reasons, the choice of English as the main official language seems to be well-supported.

Broader considerations may now be offered. A study of recent choices in Africa indicates that many recently independent countries in Anglophone Africa have, on independence, adopted English as the official language of their independent states. It is stated that much of Africa south of the Sahara is in the process of becoming English speaking. Ali Mazrui (1975) suggests that English is already becoming the 'first' language in the sense of its functional primacy in the lives of many Africans. Significant sectors of the population of many states conduct most of their public thinking in English which communicates the affairs of business, law, government, politics and education; in some cases, English dominates their private lives as well. He cites the growing numbers of educated African families that use English as the language of the home, pointing out that functional primacy of English in the parents leads to chronological primacy in the children. If his assertion is accurate, it would appear that English is steadily gaining ground on the African continent particularly among the educated Africans.

The foregoing discussion thus supports the Liberation Movement's choice of English as the official language of liberation and for independent Namibia. This choice of English for Namibia made by SWAPO represents a position which has been re-affirmed on a number of public occasions by senior spokesmen of the Liberation Movement. As the only organization fighting for Namibia's independence, SWAPO's policy statements have tremendous influence and force on Namibian people both inside and outside Namibia. Thus, the fact that SWAPO has chosen English to be the official language at independence has invested it with the character of a language of liberation. Because of this, at the United Nations Institute for Namibia, as well as at other educational institutions and liberation support centres, training is conducted in English throughout. As a result, Namibians now are highly motivated to learn English and there can be little doubt that after independence such motivation will continue and be strengthened by the encouragement of a full government policy.

However, while the advantages and benefits of investing in a language of wider communication, such as English, are undeniable, local languages have vital roles to play in society. Modern language planning policies seek increasingly to establish these roles within their overall objectives, in order to help promote and safeguard national identity. Ideally, in fact, an indigenous Namibian language is needed for local intercommunication when the country becomes independent. There is no language that need be inherently inadequate for this purpose. Any language has the conceptual, structural and lexical potential to develop as new challenges are posed. But no such development has been allowed with any indigenous language in Namibia. The Bantu education system has relegated the use of Namibian indigenous languages, like their speakers, to subordinate positions, without giving any of them an opportunity to flex their muscles intranationally against the dominance of Afrikaans. Thus Namibian leaders have been motivated to agree to choose a highly developed international language like English as the official language for a future independent Namibia.

A major consideration has, however, to be borne in mind at all stages of the national language planning and implementation process. This is that the choice of a Western language, like English, may lead to a Eurocentric orientation. Experience indicates that when Eurocentricity becomes dominant questions of existing or potential multi-lingualism may end up being shelved because the use and development of national/local languages are deemed, in terms of priorities, to be of secondary importance. To quote Kashoki (1979): 'Africans have been psychologically conditioned to believe that only European languages are structured to aid development'. Similarly, Perren notes (1969: 205): 'Language is a manifestation of social cohesion, and education must be based on a society's own interpretation of its future needs... the language in education is far too important to national development to be *directed* by visiting experts'. (Italics added.)

It seems, therefore, prudent to be aware of the extent to which the formulation of English language teaching and training programmes anticipates a system patterned along Western lines and accepts initiation in thought and action by non-Namibians who may be motivated by the values of highly industrialized societies of questionable relevance to those desired for Namibia. There is no doubt that a clear view is needed of the perceived roles of indigenous and imposed languages and their relationship as the nation aspires for integration.

Tasks

Task 1

There are seven major local languages in Namibia. Afrikaans is the lingua franca. Afrikaans and English are the two official languages. Afrikaans is the language used by the administration and the medium of practically all secondary and most primary education. As we have seen, English will be the sole official language in an independent Namibia.

We talked in Judd Task 6 (p.43) about the 'life cycle' of different languages and how their roles and functions change over time as political and socio-economic conditions change. What changes do you think will occur in the uses of the local languages, and of Afrikaans and English after independence and beyond?

Further reading on Namibia can be found in Language in Education in Africa (1986).

Task 2

The article points out some of the dangers of choosing English as the future official language in Namibia. Such a policy could lead to a number of criticisms.

(a) The important role given to English could prevent a distinctly Namibian identity emerging.
(b) English would become the language of an elite.
(c) Local languages would be devalued.
(d) English would bring with it an English rather than a Namibian cultural impact.
(e) The importance of English would increase dependence on the West and Western solutions would be adopted to solve Namibia's problems.

(i) How would you answer these criticisms of the policy?
(ii) What could be done to try to allay these criticisms?

One very definite view on these questions can be found in Phillipson et al. (1986).

Task 3

The document from which the extract in this volume is taken considers alternatives for the use of languages in education over a proposed nine-year basic education period. The proposals are:

(a) Local language as medium for six years, English as medium for three years, and both languages as subjects throughout.
(b) Local language as medium for four years, English as medium for five years, and both languages as subjects throughout.
(c) Mixed medium – English and local language – both also as subjects throughout.
(d) English as medium throughout and English and local language as subjects throughout.

(i) Which option do you think is preferable? Give your reasons.
(ii) What further information might you need to know before coming to a decision?

Task 4

Look at Fig. 7.1, the map of language and population distribution.

(i) List the languages spoken in order of number of speakers.
(ii) How might the information from the map help in the drawing up of a language policy?
(iii) What further information would be useful? (The Olshtain and Tollefson articles might help you here.)

Whiteley (1973) is an article on the sort of information that can be included in language surveys and the care that needs to be taken in its interpretation.

Task 5

Look at the following extract from the document from which this chapter is taken. 'The [present, South African] administration is actively promoting the development of local languages...and developing a variety of materials...in them'.

(i) Knowing what you do about the situation in Namibia (see introduction to the chapter), why do you think the authorities are conducting this policy of local language promotion?.
(ii) In what ways might this present policy make the further development of local languages difficult when Namibia achieves its independence?

Task 6

One of the implications of the wider use of English in independent Namibia is that large numbers

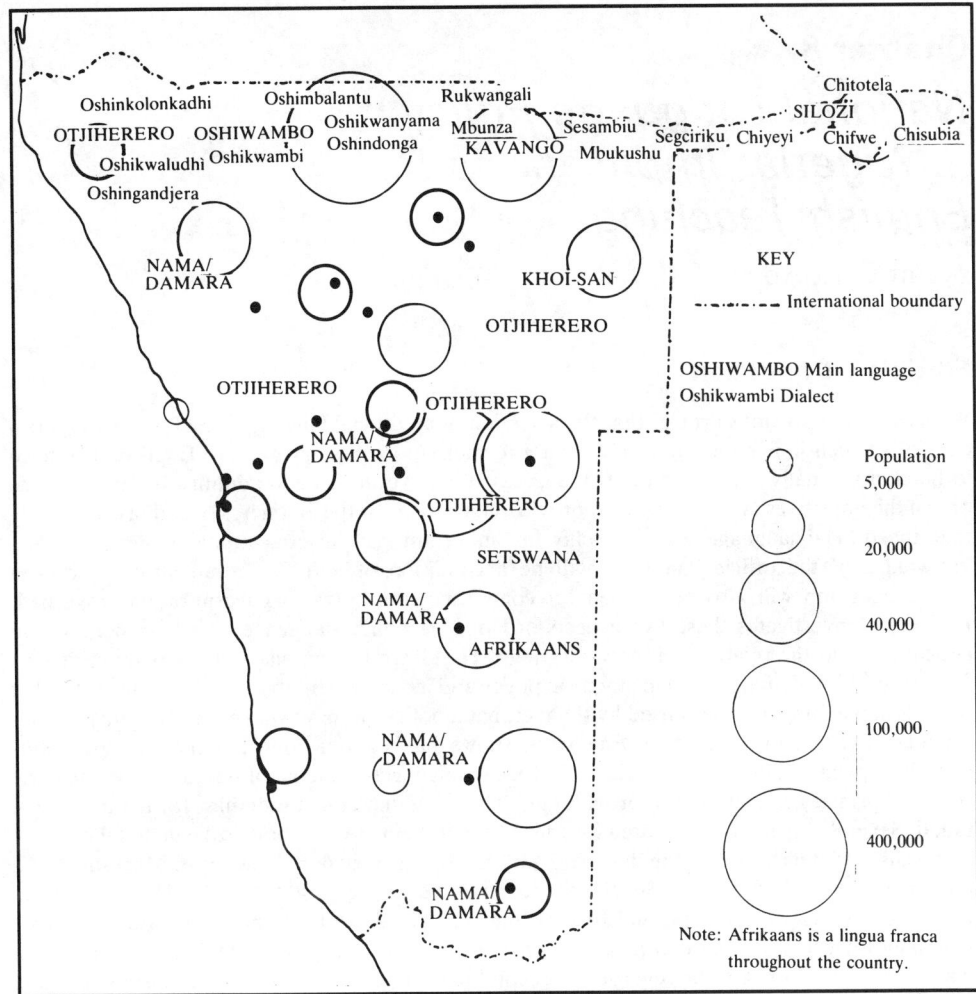

FIGURE 7.1
Namibia – language and population distribution.

(one estimate suggests thousands) of teachers of English will be required. One way of meeting this need would be to employ English-speaking expatriate teachers.

(i) What would be the advantages and disadvantages of this proposal?

(ii) If such a scheme for the employment of expatriate teachers were ever to be initiated by any future independent Namibian government, what suggestions would you make to maximize the advantages and minimize the disadvantages you listed in (i)?

Chapter 8

National Language Policy in Nigeria: Implications for English Teaching

ERNEST N. EMENYONU

Editor's introduction

We saw, in the previous article, that the selection of an official language may involve making a choice between indigenous languages and a former colonial language, like English. The term 'official' is normally applied to the language used in government and administration, but since one of the objectives of education is to provide manpower for these spheres of activity, it is likely that the official language will also play an important part in educational policy, and that knowledge of the official language will be a condition of entry to administrative posts in government and will also be needed for communication between governors and governed. Emenyonu investigates these two aspects of language policy (language in government and in education) and the relationship between them. He illustrates the distinction, made earlier by Tollefson (this volume), between language policy and its implementation, and demonstrates that failures in planning may be caused by the fact that a policy has never been implemented but has remained as a statement of intent. Emenyonu shows that Nigerian educational policy documents contain explicit statements about the use of local languages as media of instruction in the early stages of primary education, but provides evidence that implementation has, for the most part, failed. Several reasons are suggested for this; some of them are very practical, such as the lack of materials and teachers for the local languages. But Emenyonu believes that unsuccessful implementation at this practical level is the result of the perceived status of English and the local languages in Nigerian society, and that as long as English remains the high-status language, command of which is regarded as a passport to academic and professional success, the local languages will continue to be regarded as second best, at least for educational purposes. These attitudes, Emenyonu believes, have led to an inappropriate language policy in the schools which, in turn, has led to educational under-achievement, (recalling the earlier argument in this volume by Rogers). This problem would be partly solved, Emenyonu suggests, if the position and features of English in Nigeria were re-assessed and its role as an Additional Language were recognized (see Judd this volume). The result would be that the status of English would be reduced – English would come to be regarded as another 'local' language at the disposal of Nigerians, rather than as an imposed language – and the status of local languages would be raised.

The author believes this would encourage the introduction of more appropriate curricula and materials. Furthermore, if the aim of classroom teaching were to produce competence in EAL, greater attention could be paid to fostering communication skills and less time devoted to instilling mere knowledge of the language code. This, in turn, would mean accepting local varieties of English as pedagogical models rather than the present official, external, standard form. We shall see this question recurring in the articles that follow.

NIGERIA, AFRICA'S MOST populous country, is as diverse in human resources as it is in languages. Its population is about 80 million and it is often asserted that one out of every six Africans is a Nigerian. Similarly, with a total of about 400 different languages (see Hansford, Bendor-Samuel and Stanford, 1976), it is a living reality that Nigeria accounts for about twenty-five per cent of sub-Saharan African's spoken languages. Despite this multiplicity of indigenous languages, Nigeria's official language today is a foreign language: English, a colonial legacy. The language question in contemporary Nigeria's social and educational life is closely interwoven with the political determination of the status of English vis-à-vis Nigeria's indigenous languages. Very often, the issue transcends educational and linguistic considerations and borders on controversies over nationalism and charges of neo-colonialism and language imperialism. (See Essien 1981). Three of Nigeria's indigenous languages are designated as 'major languages' and appear to be serious contenders in the struggle to succeed English as the official language in the country. Recently, Nigeria has chosen nine of its indigenous languages for educational purposes namely: Hausa, Ibo, Yoruba, Edo, Efik, Fulfulde, Ijo, Kanuri and Tiv.

In the 28 years of Nigeria's existence as an independent nation, her leaders have trodden cautiously on the issue of a definitive pronouncement on the choice of an indigenous language as the official language. Despite such clear calls on Nigerian linguists to 'develop a common language out of the many spoken in the country',[1] English has remained the official language of government, business and administration, the safe neutral non-commital lingua franca, though its adoption for that purpose is deeply resented by many Nigerians. It seems safer to live with English, its colonial associations notwithstanding, than to delve into the explosive issue of making a choice from one of the ethnic languages in the country. Because of this, Nigeria remained almost twenty years after its independence in 1960, without an unequivocal and explicit language policy. It was not until 1977 that the then Federal Military Government made the first bold bid to formulate a language policy for the country through the publication of a document entitled *Federal Republic of Nigeria National Policy on Education*. It was to be further entrenched in *The Constitution of the Federal Republic of Nigeria 1979* which stipulates under sections 51 and 91 as follows:

> The business of the National Assembly shall be conducted in English, and in Hausa, Ibo and Yoruba when adequate arrangements have been made therefore. [Section 51]

and that

> The business of a House of Assembly shall be conducted in English, but the House may in addition to English conduct the business of the House in one or more other languages spoken in the State as the House may by resolution approve. [Section 91].

The language policy at best highlighted the importance of Nigeria's indigenous languages and their place in the educational system but instead of advocating the replacement of English as the official language, it prescribes an ambiguous and uneasy co-existence. This paper examines the ramifications of this language policy and its implications for the teaching of English in Nigeria.

Nigeria's national language policy

The national language policy is stated in five sections (1, 2, 3, 7 and 10) of the *National Policy on Education*, as follows:

(a) *Section 1. Philosophy of Nigerian education*
Paragraph 8: The importance of language
In addition to appreciating the importance of language in the educational process, and as a means of preserving the people's culture, the Government considers it to be in the interest of national unity that each child should be encouraged to learn one of the three major languages other than his own mother tongue. In this connection, the Government considers the three major languages in Nigeria to be Hausa, Ibo and Yoruba. [p. 5]

(b) *Section 2. Pre-primary education*
Paragraph 11: To achieve the above objectives, Government will:
(3) ensure that the medium of instruction will be principally the mother-tongue or the language of the immediate community; and to this end will (a) develop the orthography for many more Nigerian languages, and (b) produce textbooks in Nigerian languages. Some of these developments are already being pursued in the university departments of linguistics and under the auspices of some state Ministries of Education. The Federal Government has also set up a language centre as part of the educational services complex under the Federal Ministry of Education. This language centre will be expanded so as to have a wider scope. [p.6]

(c) *Section 3. Primary education*
Paragraph 15(4):
Government will see to it that the medium of instruction in the primary school is initially the mother-tongue or the language of the immediate community and, at a later stage, English [p.8].

(d) *Section 7. Adult and non-formal education*
Paragraph 52:
The objectives of adult and continuing education should be:
(a) to provide functional literary education for adults who have never had the advantage of any formal education;
(b) to provide functional and remedial education for those young people who prematurely dropped out of the formal school system; (p.21)
(5) ...The recognition of approved training courses outside the formal system of education will be a continuous process, implemented by the National Commission, together with the Federal and State Ministries of Education.
(6) A new, nationwide emphasis will be placed on the study of Nigerian arts and culture. The National Commission will work out the overall strategy for the inclusion of Nigerian arts, culture and languages in adult education programmes. (p.22)

(e) *Section 10. Educational services*
Paragraph 84(6):
Language Centres are being set up at Federal and State levels for enhancing the study of Languages especially Nigerian Languages [p.29]

In summary, the Nigerian National Language Policy stipulates the use of the local language as the medium of instruction for the first three years of primary schooling, and English as the medium of instruction in the last three years. During the period when the local language is the medium of instruction, English would be taught simply as a school subject. This means that the Nigerian child begins formal learning of two languages from the early age of six. The Policy further requires 'each child to learn one of the three major languages other than his own mother tongue'. In practice, therefore, the Nigerian child is expected to have learnt three languages in the course of his school career. Two of these (including English) are foreign to him. By implication, therefore, the Policy encourages, and seeks to enhance, enlightened multi-lingualism in Nigerian society.

Implementation of the Language Policy

More than five years after its promulgation, the Language Policy has yet to make its impact felt in Nigeria's educational system and in social and cultural environments. The greatest impediment to the implementation of the policy is the Government's failure to take systematic action and lack of any programme for enforcing the policy. There have been workshops on some indigenous languages and on the production of textbooks on such languages, but the most fundamental things have been disregarded.

There is no known federal machinery for monitoring the implementation, or otherwise, of the policy throughout the Federation. The bulk of the policy deals with language education at the primary level. Yet education is a subject on the concurrent legislative list. This means that each state can legislate on its system of primary edducation, including on the language policy. Adebisi (1977: 29) has pointed out an instance in which a state government openly declared that 'there is absolutely nothing in the country's educational system which prevents a school from using any language for instruction'. Some state governments are sponsoring work on curriculum reviews and the production of textbooks and readers in their individual local languages. No state government has, as a matter of policy, introduced into its local primary schools the teaching of another Nigerian language which is not indigenous to it. Nor has the federal government enforced the stipulation of 'each child learning one of the three major languages other than his own mother tongue' in the government owned and controlled secondary schools.

Two major projects have been undertaken by two state governments in the development and use of indigenous Nigerian languages for primary education. The former Western State Government encouraged and supported the University of Ife experiment known as 'The six-year primary project'. The Institute of Education at the University of Ife started the project, 'a bilingual primary education system that involved the use of Yoruba language as the medium of teaching mathematics, science, Yoruba, social and cultural studies and the special teaching of English as a second language throughout'. (Afolayan 1977:28) The project has since been completed and evaluated. Despite the high commendations by the project assessors and evaluators there has been no pronounced follow-up action by the government. (For a detailed report, see Afolayan 1976.)

The second major experiment in the use of indigenous languages in Nigerian education was sponsored by the Rivers State Government. Known as 'The Rivers readers project', it was essentially 'an attempt to respond to a unique situation by co-ordinating the efforts of a large number of people through a flexible and relatively informal organization'. Its aim was 'to produce readers and supporting materials in all the languages and major dialects of the state so that children can begin to learn to read in their own language before going on to English.'(Williamson 1976: 135–153) Although the project has attained a measure of success it has not achieved its primary objective. Williamson (1976: 151) reports that 'The Project has aroused a good deal of interest in the various language areas of State, and at the local level enjoys considerable support. We have not yet, however, achieved the aim of the Project, which is to have every child learning to read first in his or her own language.'

English language in Nigeria

English has been called different things by different people at different times in Nigeria, a foreign language, a second language and a lingua franca. Yet each of these terms is inadequate when the practical role of English is considered in Nigeria. D.W. Grieve (1964) refers to English as a second language and yet states that it 'has a status higher than that of a second language'. Chinua Achebe (1975) maintains that, although English is a foreign language in many respects, it is the 'one central language enjoying nationwide currency'. In government circles, English is referred to as the official language of communication, administration and instruction but Ebo Ubahakwe (1973) reveals that it is used by 'no more than 5% of the Nigerian population'. This imprecise, and often ambivalent, definition of English creates problems for the English-language teacher. It leads to ambiguous attitudes, in the teachers as well as the learners, towards the language. It also leads to confusion in pedagogical approaches to English as a subject and invariably results in half measures being taken to solve the problems of English language learning and teaching in Nigeria, no matter how profound the analysis of such problems may be. Ubahakwe (1973) has aptly argued that 'the varied and conflicting functions which the English language currently performs in Nigeria are at the root of our teaching and learning problems in the language'.

The Federal Government of Nigeria is committed to a programme to eradicate mass illiteracy in the country. Many scholars have argued persuasively that this goal can be more easily achieved if the mother-tongue medium instead of the multilingual policy is adopted in language education. (See Bamgbose 1977, Banjo 1977.) For some Nigerians the only worthy goal for encouraging serious studies in the teaching and learning of indigenous languages, is to hasten the dethronement of English in Nigeria and replace it with a Nigerian language. Yet it would appear that even such linguistic nationalism may not provide the answer to the difficult problem of mutual intelligibility across ethnic groups in Nigeria or the need for a language of the masses.

The present national language policy advocates 'equal time' for English and the indigenous languages on the curriculum. While English is studied as a foreign language in the first three years of primary education, it automatically becomes the medium of instruction in the last three years. The general observation here is that learners who go through this system end up knowing neither enough of the English language nor enough of the local language to be able to communicate freely in it, especially in writing.

At the secondary level, the standard of performance of the average Nigerian student in English leaves much to be desired. Many people have blamed this, as well as the general decline in educational standards, on the fact that English is being taught too early in the school system. There have been no empirically decisive studies to justify a definitive pronouncement on the matter. It is necessary to encourage, along with the Ife six-year primary project, a parallel experiment in which English is used as the medium of instruction throughout the six-year primary career.

Implications for English teachers of the national language policy

Judd (this volume, p.36) says that 'Language policy has a direct impact on TESOL instruction and should therefore be considered as a crucial factor in planning ESOL programmes.' He further argues that 'the sociopolitical environment in which English

Language instruction occurs has a direct impact on the shape of ESOL instruction. Failure to consider these sociopolitical factors can lead to dire consequences for all those involved'. Quoting from Tucker (1977:16), Judd concludes, 'Educational or national policy serves to define the parameters within which language problems can be developed and only through an understanding of the English language policy of a given country can we help devise the proper curricular and teaching approach for the particular educational environment.'

It is not enough to ask that a language be taught in schools. Its status must be defined, its roles spelt out in order to facilitate decisions on the curriculum, methodology, the preparation of teachers, the nature and provision of texts and other resources that are pertinent to a teaching-learning situation. At the moment, although English and the indigenous Nigerian languages are simultaneously taught in the schools, it is the mastery of the English language that is most emphasized as relevant to further intellectual pursuits and success in careers. Yet politically, the dominant position of English over the indigenous languages is resented. While pleading the cause of an indigenous language as a choice for the national language in Nigeria, Liman Ciroma condemned the premier position occupied by English, maintaining that 'as long as the country succumbed to the psychological superiority of a foreign language, our mastery of which is suspect, so long will our thought processes continue to be blocked, distorted and falsified and our output mediocre'.

What is important is to define clearly the needs of English language learners in Nigeria at any given time and then develop policies and strategies that would meet those needs.

Given its present roles in the educational system and the specific needs of Nigerian learners of English, one will agree with Elliott L. Judd that English in Nigeria is neither a foreign language nor a second language. It would more appropriately be an additional language. Judd says that,

> an EAL situation can be defined as one in which speakers learn English after they learn another primary language and use it for the purpose of communicating with others who have different primary languages. Such situations are found in countries that are multilingual and recognize English as the language for intracountry communication...The other important socio-linguistic characteristic of many EAL situations is that a localized version of English has probably emerged [this vol. p.38].

This aptly describes the position, role and features of English in the Nigerian situation. If English became an *additional language*, it would have a proper place, not only in the National Language Policy, but in the educational system as a whole. There would no longer be the unwholesome competition with the indigenous languages, which the latter must always lose. The system would then provide a forceful motivation for the study of Nigerian languages at all levels of the educational system. Instead of the present system, where a pass at the credit level must be obtained as a pre-entry qualification into the universities and most other institutions of higher learning, the policy could be modified so that at the end of the secondary school, every student would be required to pass English and one Nigerian language in order to qualify for the award of the West African School Certificate. This would ensure the continued and vigorous study of Nigerian languages beyond the primary school while making it possible also for English studies to be undertaken and pursued for their interest and without terror.

The immediate implication of this for the teacher of English would be the realization that various young Nigerian children would be learning English under some basic assumptions that related to their needs and experiences. For instance, in the primary English syllabus, emphasis would be placed on oral practice activities, which would enable the children rapidly to learn to hold conversations in English 'about things they would ordinarily talk about in their own language with people of their age group' Finocchiaro (1964:37). The over-riding goal here, or elsewhere in the educational system, would not be to aspire to any ideal standard of English, but instead to equip Nigerian learners with an adequate English vocabulary with which they could communicate with their counterparts from other parts of the country on subjects which are appropriate for their age and experience. It would, therefore, not be necessary to go in search of native speakers of English who could be ideal models. English teachers would no longer be aspiring to produce young English speakers who are only Nigerians by an accident of birth, but rather young Nigerians who have enough English to be able to convey their Nigerian experiences, when they have to, to one another. It would no longer be considered absurd when a Nigerian spoke English with a Nigerian accent, and/or mannerisms, as those would be understood by the Nigerian audience. Nor would it be awkward to talk, in its proper context, about Nigerian English.

Conclusion

This paper has examined the ramifications of Nigeria's linguistic problems within the context of the country's national language policy. This policy advocates the development of indigenous Nigerian languages for the purpose of a mother-tongue medium policy of education. Despite this encouragement and support for indigenous languages, the English language is, for all practical purposes, preserved as the official language of government and business and in particular is cultivated as an elitist language for high intellectual pursuits and sophisticated careers. The paper recommends a redefinition of the place, role and function of English in both the Nigerian educational system and Nigerian society.

English should be considered and taught in Nigeria as an additional language which would have the effect of not denigrating the indigenous languages. Forceful motivations should be provided for the study of the indigenous languages and due recognition given to them in the educational system as well as in the public service. No aspiring student who showed exceptional performance in other subjects should be denied the opportunity of higher education in Nigeria merely because he did not show exceptional performance in the English language. The Federal Government should go beyond ordinary pronouncements of language policy and devise the necessary machinery for effective implementation. It should also pay adequate attention to the provision of teachers in required numbers for the success of the policy. In particular, there should be a carefully thought-out scheme for the professionalization of teaching to ensure that all those who teach are adequately trained and special incentives should be offered to specialist language teachers, particularly teachers of Nigerian languages. There should be additional provision for the training of teachers of Nigerian languages at the teacher training colleges, colleges of education and faculties of education in the universities. Similarly, there should be provision for the training of specialist teachers of English.

There should be a restructuring of the English curriculum at all levels of the Nigerian educational system so that the English-language curriculum will reflect the new role and status of English in Nigerian society.

Notes

1. *West Africa*, 20 August, 1979. The appeal was made by Liman Ciroma the then Secretary of the Federal Military Government of Nigeria.

Tasks

Task 1

Before you complete Task 2 make sure that you understand the present language policy in Nigeria as presented by Emenyonu.

(i) How many languages are spoken in Nigeria?
(ii) What is Nigeria's official language?
(iii) How many 'major languages' are there and what are they?
(iv) List the nine indigenous languages designated as suitable for educational purposes.
(v) What is the language policy at primary level? Which language is medium of instruction and which languages are school subjects?

Year	Medium	Subject
1		
2		
3		
4		
5		
6		

Task 2

Emenyonu gives a number of reasons which, in his opinion, explain the failure of Nigerian language policy. The reasons are listed below in the order in which they are mentioned in the article.

(a) It is politically safer to maintain the present roles and functions of English.
(b) The central government does not have a programme to implement the policy.
(c) There is no means by which the central government can monitor implementation of the policy in the different states and regions of Nigeria.
(d) State governments can legally set their own policy with regard to the languages used in education.
(e) English is regarded as the passport to academic and professional success.
(f) The true role of English – to be an additional, rather than a second or a foreign language – has not been recognized.
(g) A qualification in English, but not one in any local language, is necessary for entry to university.

(h) No thought has been given to the provision and specialist training of teachers, especially those who teach Nigerian languages.

(i) The English curriculum does not reflect the role of English as an additional language in Nigeria.

(You may like to add further reasons of your own – lack of financial resources for example.)

These statements refer to decisions that need to be taken at different levels in the language planning process. (See Tollefson p.26 if you need a reminder.)

(i) Try to place the different statements in a hierarchy of decision making.

(ii) What changes would need to be made to the present system for a successful implementation of the policy?

Task 3

Emenyonu says that the English primary syllabus would need to change once English were recognized as an additional language. He suggests that oral activities whose content reflected the interests of the learners would need to be designed. One way of implementing his suggestion would be to design a syllabus based not on linguistic structures, but on a series of tasks which necessitated the use of English.

(i) Draw up a list of topics that you think Nigerian primary school children would like talking and finding out about.

(ii) Now think of one task that you might design using one of the topics in (i) above.

You might like to consider the following questions (not in any order of priority) when designing the task.

(a) How will the task be set up? (will it be, for example, individual work, pair work, group work, work done with or without the teacher?)

(b) What will the task be about? What will the topic be?

(c) What will the purpose of the task be (e.g. to compare, describe, evaluate, etc.)?

(d) What will the outcome be (e.g. a text completed, a diagram filled in, etc.)?

(e) Will the students need to justify their end product?

(f) Will the task be evaluated in any way (e.g. by the participants, by others, by the teacher), or will it be self-evaluating (i.e. considered successful if satisfactorily completed)?

(g) Will there be one right answer or will the task be open-ended?

(h) Will the task involve competition or collaboration?

(i) Will information necessary for completion of the task be shared by all or will transfer of information between participants be necessary?

(j) What media will be involved (written/spoken text)?

Candlin and Murphy (eds 1987) is a useful collection of articles on task-based learning. Tongue and Gibbons (1982) describe an activities-based syllabus for Hong Kong primary schools.

Task 4

(i) If English were 'reclassified' as an additional language in Nigeria and school curricula were designed to fit in with this notion of the roles and functions of English in Nigeria, the content of teacher-training programmes would need to be revised. What additions or changes would you expect to see in terms of training in methods and materials?

(ii) Look at the outline below of a syllabus for the first year of a course at a teacher-training college for future lower-secondary-school teachers of EFL/ESL.

(1) English language (including study of grammar, reading and writing skills, phonetics) (7 hours/week).
(2) Literature (including Forster, Hemingway, Goldsmith, Shaw) (3 hours/week).
(3) Cultural studies (including topics such as English youth, education, racial problems, American political institutions and mass media) (2 hours/week).
(4) Historical studies (including Great Britain, early times till 17th century; America, early times till 20th century) (2 hours/week).

Would you think this syllabus appropriate for Nigeria? What changes would you make, if any? Give reasons for your answers.

One of the issues raised by (ii) above, was the place of literature on a teacher-training course for ELT teachers, an area admirably covered in Brumfit and Carter (eds 1986). Carter and Long (1988) is a textbook integrating language and literature studies for learners of English.

Task 5

'Below the overt recognition of the external standard there is a strong covert commitment to the local vernacular. The internal standard is simultaneously admired and disliked' (Bell 1982: 255). This quotation is about attitudes towards British and New Zealand English.

(i) Do you think the same thing could be said of the attitudes of Nigerians in Nigeria towards British English, Nigerian English and the local Nigerian languages?
(ii) Would such attitudes help to explain the difficulties of implementing language policy in Nigeria?
(iii) If the attitudes described by Bell exist in countries like Nigeria, do you think that a language plan should (1) attempt to change those attitudes or (2) work with them?
(iv) If you answered (1) to (iii) above, how would you go about changing attitudes? (The article by Horvath in this volume might help you.)

Task 6

Schmied (1985), referring to attitudes towards English in Tanzania, believes that attitudes in individuals and groups vary according to:

(a) Their level of education.
(b) Their tribal/racial group.
(c) Their location (rural/urban).

(i) How might these elements influence attitudes towards language?
(ii) What difficulties would differences in attitudes present to those drawing up a language plan?

Chapter 9

The Cultural Context of Language Learning: Problems Confronting English Teachers in Zambia

ROBERT SERPELL

Editor's introduction

Serpell, talking about Zambia – this paper is the text of a lecture – reinforces some of the issues raised in the last article. He believes that the high status given to English in Zambia has led to the benefits gained by competence in English being exaggerated and the promulgation of an inappropriate language policy (English-medium education throughout the system). He admits, however, that this view might well be contested by parents naturally eager to ensure a good job for their children. (We shall see later in the Gibbons article on Hong Kong how influential parental pressure can be in educational policy.) Serpell argues for the recognition of a Zambian variety of English with its own place in the curriculum alongside other varieties of English and the local languages. His suggestions mirror those put forward by Emenyonu, but he extends the latter's arguments in a number of important ways. He looks more closely at language use and first language acquisition among Zambian children, suggesting that not only the language but the pattern of interaction changes radically when the child enters school for the first time. Pupils' use of language is highly situational; that is to say, they can talk about topics related to life outside the classroom in their own languages, and they associate English closely with their lessons and their knowledge of the language is based on the contents of their English textbook. Serpell points to the gap between home and school, represented respectively by the local languages and English, which he believes is partly responsible for underachievement. He goes on to list a number of strategies that children adopt in order to survive in a language medium with which they are unfamiliar. These strategies may conceal from the teacher the children's lack of comprehension, which presumably builds up and gradually becomes more serious as the pupils progress through the school. This is a clear example of a problem which has arisen as a consequence of an English-medium policy. The solutions, however, are far from straightforward. A switch to local languages as media of instruction would not necessarily solve the problems. We should, perhaps, first examine the present policy to see whether the difficulties arise less from the policy itself than from the way it is put into effect. If the problems arise from the implementation, then, possibly certain action could be taken which would make it more successful. Serpell himself gives some idea of the nature of the investigations that would be required, focusing much of his discussion on pupil behaviour. A great deal of mother-tongue research has been based on quantitative evaluation, and successes or failures have been reported in terms of a group's test results. Such research is necessary, but there is also a need for more observation of what actually happens in classrooms, which will give us some idea of why students get the results they do. It may be that it is all that happens in the classroom that is at fault and not the policy itself.

THE TERMS OF reference for my talk today are momentous. The cultural context of learning is a growing field in cross-cultural psychology, whose dimensions are the subject of considerable controversy. Language learning is a heavily researched field, which also has its share of controversy. And, finally, here am I, a mere researcher and university lecturer, proposing to address an audience of English teachers in Zambia on the subject of the problems which confront them. My hope is that I can justify this exercise by offering you a glimpse of some theoretical concepts which seem to me to have a certain relevance to the Zambian scene. My attempt to draw, from the theoretical analysis, conclusions which bear upon the problems which you, as professionals, face in your work will no doubt shock some of you, leave others among you cold, but, perhaps, also will interest a few of you by adding one or two new dimensions to the problems which you confront every day. The central theme of my talk will be that the cultural context in which English is learned in Zambia is characterized by a deep ambivalence – a conflict of values which leads to contradictions in our educational policy, in our parental attitudes and in our students' motives.

Language usage

The heart of this cluster of value conflicts is the pattern of language usage in Zambia. The concept of 'language usage' is central to the discipline now known as 'sociolinguistics'. During the late 1960s and the 1970s, a number of themes emerged in the research literature on language which broke away from Noam Chomsky's influential reinterpretation of grammar. One of these themes was that grammar cannot be properly understood without reference to the meanings of utterances. Notable examples of this theme were Charles Fillmore's theory of case grammar, which focuses on semantic relations and M.A.K. Halliday's division of language functions into three dimensions: the ideational, the interpersonal and the textual, which are all semantically relevant. His account of language development is entitled *Learning how to mean*. Dell Hymes and many others use the term 'communicative competence' to mark the fact that competent use of language involves elements of what Chomsky tried to exclude from the domain of linguistic theory by dismissing it as performance rather than competence.

A second theme was that language use varies according to context and that such variation is systematic, not random. John Gumperz has been especially interested in the ways in which an individual who speaks more than one language draws on his or her multiple speech repertoire, switching from one code to another to mark more and less subtle features of the social situation. William Labov, on the other hand, has been a leading exponent of the view that a so-called monolingual community reflects in its different varieties of speech a whole range of social variables, including social status, age, sex and ethnic affiliation as well as features of the social context in which speech is occuring. One especially important outcome of the work of Labov and his colleagues has been the documentary evidence showing that non-standard varieties of English are systematically structured and not just a bundle of random errors. As a result, it has been possible, for instance, for certain pressure groups to introduce the notion that Black English, a variety of English shared by a section of black society in the USA, should be used as the official medium of instruction in certain primary schools.

The status of English in Zambia

After citing a few of the theoretical trends which have influenced my thinking about language and language learning, let me turn now to a sketch of the socio-linguistic status of the English language in Zambia. Most of what I have to say on this subject was said for me yesterday by Mr John Mwanakatwe,[1] who described in glowing terms (or, as his adversaries in the debate on English in Zambia might prefer to put it, in lurid detail) the high prestige which attaches to English in contemporary Zambia. I should just like to add to his account two small items: first, a philosophical word of caution and, second, a theoretical catchword from the field of socio-linguistics. First, the word of caution: to describe a social situation is not necessarily to condone the values which that situation seems to embody. I would agree with Mr Mwanakatwe that it is a sociological fact that English is held up as the language of prestige and as the passport to economic success in Zambian society. But, although I count myself a loyal Zambian, I would not go on to say that I am happy about this situation. For instance, I find it a sad comment on our society that one of the admission requirements of our national university is an advanced knowledge of English: It is a happier comment that the regulations for the degree of Master of Arts at the University of Zambia permit a candidate to submit a thesis written in a Zambian language.

The sociological catchword I would like to bring in (albeit cautiously) to Mr Mwanakatwe's description of English in Zambia is 'diglossic', a term used by sociolinguists to describe a society that has two languages. (An individual having two languages is said to be bilingual.) The term diglossia refers to the functional separation of two languages in a society and the man who coined it, Ferguson, used it in particular, to refer to the stratification of varieties of the same language. Ferguson demonstrated that the stratification of varieties of one language occurs in countries as unlike as Egypt, Haiti and Greece. The languages spoken in these countries have little in common, but all of them are found in two varieties: one for public, high-status, prestigious aspects of the culture and the other, as he called it, the 'language of hearth and home'. Now, Joshua Fishman picked up this idea of Charles Ferguson's and applied it not to monolingual societies where two varieties of one language are spoken, but to bilingual and multilingual societies and suggested that countries like Zambia, countries which have had a history of colonial occupation by a foreign cultural group, also have a sort of diglossia in which the former colonial language is the high, public, prestigious language and the indigenous languages take on the role of the 'languages of hearth and home', or, as Ferguson put it, 'the L code', the low code.

I said that I would want to apply this concept to Zambia with caution for a number of reasons. First of all, obviously the term diglossia refers to two languages or two varieties of the same language, whereas in Zambia there are several languages at play, one at the top and lots at the bottom. That is not a very serious reservation but, I think, the worrying part about this model is the notion that up/down is the only dimension you are talking about – that one language is up on top and the others are down at the bottom. It seems to me that if you think about what is implied by the expression 'language of hearth and home', any such language will be a very important language: the one that is very close to your heart, the one that is very dear to you, and in some ways, therefore, it will be a more important language to you than the one which you reserve for the public, more formal occasions. You are perhaps, more yourself when you are using the 'language of hearth and home' and you are playing a role, a public part, when you are using the so-called 'high language'. There is clearly a functional separation and I think that, as Mr Mwanakatwe illustrated for us, part of that functional separation has to do with prestige. But also I think that this is where we come back to the ambivalence I mentioned earlier. We have to realize that the language which does not have the prestige has a lot of other things going for it – it has the 'heart strings', if you like, pulling on its side!

In any discussion of the role of English in Zambia, and still more so in any discussion of the role of English in Zambian education we must bear in mind that we are in a situation of historical change. The first generation of those who actually started off their education in the English medium is now reaching the university. In other words, the 1965 decision, outlined by Mr Mwanakatwe, which was at first implemented rather gradually and really became very widespread policy by the late sixties, has now been in force long enough for people to have been right the way through the educational system, up to the university level, with English as the sole medium of instruction. But if you think of the educated population of Zambia as a whole, it is clear that the majority did not go through that system. They went through the old system of starting in a Zambian language and moving over to English between Grades four and seven of the primary system. So, there must be some changes going on in our society. There must be generational differences in perspective on the language of instruction in schools. I think it is very dangerous to speculate about what those trends are. I am not here blaming Mr Mwanakatwe for trying to be a prophet. He was asked to prophesy in his talk and it is always a challenge to try to do that, but I would want to be very cautious when predicting what the impact will be on the people who have been through this system. I do not think, for instance, we can assume blandly that the people who went through this system will have none of the ambivalence towards English that the previous generation had.

Linguistic flexibility in Zambian society

Before I examine the way in which most Zambians use English today, let me add one more feature to the sketch of the language situation in Zambia as it affects the English language. Here again, I would like to use a technical catchword which I will be referring to later on. This is the notion of 'code-switching'. 'Code' is used here as a general term to cover language, dialect or language variety. People who have various codes at their disposal tend to switch to and fro between them. And here the work of Gumperz is, I think, both illuminating and tantalizing.

John Gumperz started his work on code-switching by suggesting that you could predict which code a bilingual or trilingual person would use by looking at the situation s/he was in. So the first kind of code-switching that he documented he called 'situational code-switching'. An obvious illustration of this in the Zambian school context is the fact that most people, as they walk out of school, start speaking a Zambian language, having spoken English inside the school. But, of course, even inside school, if you listen hard, you will hear a lot of languages other than English being spoken. So a situation may be more than a physical domain, like the territory of a school. It may be very narrowly defined, for instance, the participants in a conversation. So, within the classroom, although conversations with the teacher may generally be held in English, children tend to chat with their friends in, say, Nyanja (if they are in Lusaka). And then, again, if you listen closely to the same group of people, you will hear Nyanja being spoken as well as

English in many Lusaka classrooms both by the teacher and by the children. And here, the topic of the conversation may be crucial. The teacher will give a lesson in English, but if somebody is making noise s/he may tell him off in Nyanja. And a pupil who answers the teacher's questions in English may ask in Nyanja for permission to leave the room. I am not suggesting that Nyanja is the language of mundane activities, but that in the school setting it is the language of extra-curricular topics.

This kind of situational analysis, however, takes you so far and no further. It obviously breaks down when you have a conversation amongst two or three people and the group does not change, the topic does not change, but the language keeps changing. And this is something we see quite often in Zambia. What is happening here cannot be called situational code-switching. It is not unique to Zambia. Gumperz has recorded this sort of thing in a community on the Yugoslavian-German border, amongst students in India, and amongst Hispanic students in the United States; and other people have observed it in the Phillipines. It is a very common phenomenon in multilingual societies. The first kind of theoretical account which Gumperz offered for this was what he called 'metaphorical code-switching'. The idea is that when you use a language which, on the face of it, does not seem quite appropriate to the situation, you use it as a metaphor for the situation in which it would have been appropriate. For example, when you use a bit of Nyanja in a formal lecture, you are introducing something about the context in which Nyanja is normally used (it is not normally used in formal lectures) into the lecture situation. This kind of example is, I think, quite illuminating. It tells us something about the meaning of a choice of code when the switching does not appear to be dependent on the social situation. But it is not the whole story and people trying to analyse the phenomenon are now tending to move away from 'code-switching' to other, more elaborate, theoretical devices to explain it. I will not go into the full range of these here. But I want to point out that the multilingual speech behaviour of urban Zambians shows a remarkable degree of creativity. You find very imaginative combinations of words often used in humorous situations. Indeed, this is a great source of quips and jokes in Lusaka society. And I would say that this is a part of the cultural context which we should take account of when trying to understand how English, Nyanja, Bemba and other languages are used in Zambia and how they are learned; that this phenomenon is not just an accidental feature of language usage but part of Zambian culture.

The language learning context of the Zambian pre-school child

After these preliminary remarks, let me try to take an illustrative child through his or her life sequence of language learning in order to point out some of the notable features of the cultural environment. The theoretical literature on first language learning by children from the age of six months to five years (which is usually the developing period in which people talk about first language acquisition taking place) is unfortunately based, mainly for methodological reasons, on a very small sample of little children. It is very, very difficult to follow the full range of linguistic behaviour of a young child. Think of the two-year old you know, and imagine running round after him with a microphone! And when you recall that the portable tape recorder is a recent invention, you will realize that it was very hard indeed, before the 1970s, to do that kind of work. Because we have data from so few children speaking, between them, so few languages, it is very difficult to say anything to which I would attach confidence about laws of language acquisition. The theoretical debate has been centred on the question of whether the child is copying what he or she hears, or is inventing new expressions like a sort of minitheorist working out what language is all about. I don't think that debate is over yet.

The notion that a child learns its first language from its mother (learns its 'mother tongue') is one that comes from middle-class Western European and North American societies. Traditionally, in these societies, the first child spends its early years at home with the mother (the father is out at work) and while it is young does not mix with other children. This is not what happens to most Zambian children. Zambian babies have very, very privileged physical access to their mothers during the first 12 to 18 months of life – this is true also of babies in other African countries – then, when the next baby comes along, that privileged access is abruptly cut off, and from the age of two years or so most Zambian babies spend more time in the company of other children than of their mother or father. We know that language acquisition generally gets into top gear around the end of the second year and that at this age children make dramatic progress in their first language. It is important to realize that brothers and sisters and other children, rather than the mother, may be the dominant linguistic influence.

I do not just want to make a semantic point about the term 'mother tongue'. What I am saying is that we should look at the actual corpus of language to which a child is exposed. Amongst his/her older brothers and sisters there are going to be children who are in Grade One learning the English medium. The few studies we have of first language acquisition in Africa bear out my description; they show that a major influence on the child's language acquisition is other young children. For instance, Sarah Harkness found that a young Kipsigis child from a rural Kenyan community addressed more utterances to other children than to its mother during a sample period of observation. As we go on to the three–five year age range the influence of other children becomes more pronounced. Dan Slobin, who has reviewed the few studies done outside Western industrialized cultural settings of first language acquisition, suggests that this may be a phenomenon which is very widespread in the world today. The Zambian child may, in fact, be a much more typical child of the world than the American child.

The entrance into school

When the child enters school, it encounters many changes: changes in the way language is presented, changes in the kind of language that is used. And this is the moment at which one might perhaps talk of culture conflict or of a difficult cultural transition. Studies from the USA and from the UK suggest that children from families whose cultural style mimics the style of the school start off at a remarkable advantage. Basil Bernstein uses the terms 'restricted' and 'elaborated codes'. He says that the so-called elaborated code that the middle-class English mother uses with her child is, in fact, a sort of imitation 'school-teacher talk' and that she is trying to be a pre-school 'teacher' to her child. The lower-class English child gets no such preparation for school.

What about the Zambian child? I think we will all agree, from our observations of grade-one classrooms in Zambia, that there is not an awful lot of English being spoken by one child to another. Thus, when considering the context in which English is being learned in Grade One, we must conclude that most of the traffic is one-way, from teacher to the children. Yet, the children are coming out of a cultural setting where previously they were receiving another language, predominantly from other children. Here, then, clearly there is quite a dramatic change of situation.

We did a little study a couple of years ago in which we asked a very talented member of the University staff, Ms Nguluwe, who is fluent in English, Nyanja and Bemba, to talk to Grade-One children using a pre-programmed mixture of all three languages. She had three bits of talk. One was about their homes, about where they lived and how many brothers and sisters they had and who washed their clothes and who cooked dinner. The second was a sort of playful conversation; she threw a ball across the room and asked a child to go and fetch it and to do a few exercises, to clap his hands and things like that. The third bit was a 'bookish' conversation; Ms Nguluwe played the standard 'teachers' role and had a textbook open in front of her. Children and teacher looked at a picture in the book and she asked a child a series of questions about the picture. Thus, there were three topics: home, play and a picture, and three languages: English, Nyanja and Bemba. Ms Nguluwe questioned the children on all three topics and used all three languages in all the possible language-topic combinations.

We were interested to see how well the children would respond to these questions, and also which languages they would use. One of the things we had expected, and found, was that the children did not mind switching at all. In fact, only two children out of the 40 or so that we put through this exercise ever commented on the switching. Both of these children, when she switched into Bemba, said 'Siniziwa Chibemba' ('I do not speak Bemba'). They said that in Nyanja, you understand. We had anticipated this eventuality and the rule was that she should pretend they had not said anything and just carry on in Bemba. One of these two characters then proceeded to answer all her Bemba questions perfectly in Nyanja! With the exception of these two, all the other children apparently thought it was perfectly normal to switch around amongst three languages. But they did operate with varying degrees of efficiency in the different languages.

In summary, first, as you may expect, the children were not very good at answering questions about home in English. What was interesting was that they were just as good at answering questions about home in Nyanja as in Bemba, irrespective of their home language, which for half the children was Bemba and for the other half Nyanja. A third result was that the topic which they dealt with best in English was, as you might expect, the textbook picture, reflecting the context in which they had been learning English, the context of the school curriculum. This study, then, illustrates the fact that in a period of transition – the second term of Grade One – Lusaka children are remarkably adept at handling the multicultural, multilinguistic situation in which they find themselves. They take it very calmly when somebody switches around amongst these languages. But they do, in their use of language, demonstrate that they have to some extent a context-specific (or situation-specific) knowledge of the language.

Coping strategies

The problem the child faces, that of mastering the school curriculum in English, seems to me to be difficult enough to justify our using the term 'coping strategies' to describe his behaviour. I shall describe five such coping strategies which we can detect from the small number of available studies of children in the primary schools in Zambia. The first strategy I would call 'ritualized performance'. It is something which we observed very clearly in the picture situation with Ms Nguluwe. In the grade-one textbooks pictures and text are printed opposite one another, on different pages. The book lay open on the table and quite often, before she could ask a question about the picture, the child would say, 'They are eating nshima and fish'. In other words, the behaviour was already prepared; they knew what they were supposed to do as soon as they sat down beside teacher. Sometimes they would say, 'Mulenga lives with his mother', which does not feature on the page of text at all! This is what I mean by ritualized performance, it is not just the quality of the articulation of the English but the whole attitude of: 'I have got to produce this bit of behaviour on demand when you press the button'. And these are children who could not answer a question like 'How many brothers and sisters do you have?' Yet, they could produce a long sentence in English in answer to a question about a picture.

The second coping strategy I shall call 'unstructured guessing'. All children, when they are learning to read, use a lot of guesswork. This is part of the game and as far as we know, a very good way of learning. Studies of children learning to read show that those who guess usually end up reading a lot faster than those who do not guess. It is definitely a good thing to do a bit of guessing and, of course, the designers of readers for young children make a point of putting in a fair number of clues. You can get it wrong: for instance, you can say 'foot' when the word is 'shoe', and so on. But it certainly helps to have a picture there to give you an idea what might be the topic of the strange printed word. The unstructured guessing, to which I am referring, fails to take full advantage of linguistic structure. When an unfamiliar word appears in a sentence, if you know the language, it is usually possible to guess which part of speech the word is. Thus, supposing the sentence reads 'They are eating nshima' and you don't know the word 'nshima' because you have not learnt it. You might say 'fish', 'biscuit', 'porridge' or maybe (if you are a bit imaginative) you might say 'They are eating 'table' or 'glass', but it would be very unusual indeed for an English-speaking child to say 'They are eating walk', or 'They are eating yes'. You would not use the wrong part of speech because you know that, every time you read, the text always makes sense in terms of the sequence of words. Maybe they sometimes say rather silly things in school readers but they do not say things which are impermissible according to the rules of English grammar. And this, of course, is where the child who does not know the English language is at a great disadvantage. Christina Hvitfeldt, in a short paper on the behaviour of young Zambian children learning to read, shows very clearly that the mistakes made by those who do not speak English at home when guessing a word are quite different (i.e. they are less fully structured linguistically) from the guesses made by young English-speaking children using the same books in Zambian schools.

Another strategy is 'language mixing'. This occurs less in relation to reading than to other aspects of language learning. Very often, a child who does not have all the English words s/he needs for a particular topic, will come out with some words in English and some words in another language. I will have a little more to say later about whether this is a good or a bad thing, but it is certainly a different form of behaviour from what teachers will encounter in a so-called monolingual group.

Yet another phenomenon which falls into the general area I have been discussing should perhaps not be called a coping strategy. This is 'pseudoretardation' which, in my view, is a very worrying phenomenon. Rama Sharma, the head of the Psychological Service in the Ministry of Education, did a survey a number of years ago in which he tried to test the level of success in mastering reading at the grade-three level in a variety of classes around Zambia. The study has been criticized by a number of people on the grounds that he may have set his expectations too high. He expected pupils to have mastered everything that ideally should be known in the second term of Grade Three, and maybe he should have set his expectations a little lower. Nevertheless, his finding that a very large proportion of the children in these classes were unable to read any of the words in his text is very alarming. If we were to take this as a measure of reading retardation, it would suggest that we have a very serious problem in Zambia indeed. Now I have termed this pseudoretardation, because I do not believe that all those children really were retarded. But I think that their behaviour in the test, their reluctance to deal with frightening and difficult test material suggested retardation. I am talking here intuitively without any statistics to back me up. But I have often found that individual children know very much more than they can demonstrate in the formal testing situation.

Sharma's results, incidentally, are very closely paralleled by those of an advocate of the English-medium programme, the man who is largely responsible for introducing it in Zambia, Bryson MacAdam. He did a doctoral dissertation in which he compared the performance level, on a variety of tests, of children who had gone through what was then the newly introduced, experimental English-Medium Scheme and children who had gone through the conventional scheme. The results which he emphasizes are, as you might expect, the ones which show superior performance by the children who had gone through the English-Medium Scheme. Not very surprisingly, these children on average knew a lot more English than those who had gone through the Zambian language scheme and been exposed to about one tenth as much English. Also, not very surprisingly, they dealt with the social studies test, in English, much better than the children who had gone through the Zambian system. They were significantly worse, on the other hand, in mathematics, a fact which I will not discuss today. Of special interest, however, is the fact that even though on average the children in the English-Medium Scheme showed a much better knowledge of English, the group included a large number who had gone through the English-Medium Scheme and seemed to have learnt nothing at all.

The statistics displayed in the thesis show us that the English-Medium Scheme produced two clearly demarcated groups, an average group who were well ahead of the Zambian language group, and another group who were well behind them on a test of English. I interpret this as meaning that there is a large minority of children in the English-Medium Scheme who could not read at all, which is just what Sharma found when he looked directly at reading. So there is a strategy (if that is the right word for it) which results in virtual failure to cope at all; it is a retreat into apparent retardation.

One more coping strategy I shall call 'narrow, non-generalized literacy'. I have no scientific evidence on which to base this one; it is based simply on a few observations. It seems to me peculiar that so often I meet highly educated Zambians who read fluently all the time in English and yet experience real difficulty in reading some of the Zambian languages they speak and understand. I usually encounter this phenomenon when I request technical assistance with translation. For instance, I present a draft in si-Lozi to a university graduate and ask him to translate it for me into English, and the reply I get is: 'I know a bit of Lozi but I do not know how to read it'. When I ask how much Lozi he knows, I find that he is very fluent in Lozi indeed, but that he did not learn at school how to read it. Lozi is just an example; I have encountered the same phenomenon with several different Zambian languages and people who are highly literate but only in English and in one Zambian language. And yet, for me, an amateur in Zambian languages, it is very easy to transpose the skill of reading aloud from one language to another. Of course, I will mispronounce because I do not have the articulation skills, but I can get words out of the text without any trouble. I suspect that there is something significant here, but I may be wrong. I think it is a possible coping strategy provoked by an inappropriately difficult introduction to the skill of reading and should be looked into. My hypothesis is that some people are taught reading as an activity which is too closely tied to one particular language.

English as a passport to success

It must be clear, from what I have been saying, that I think that for most Zambians the task of mastering English is an imposition. But it would be misleading if I implied that they stood to gain nothing from succeeding in this task. I will not dwell here on the literature to which a knowledge of English gives access or on the usefulness of English as a medium of international comunication. I have stated eleswhere that these benefits have been given undue weight in arguments about policy decisions on instruction media. The point I wish to make is that those who emphasize the importance of an early mastery of English are quite correct in believing that it plays a key role in an individual's progress through our present educational system.

National selection for secondary education is, of course, based on a wide range of tests but the principal selection criterion, we are told from Sharma's research, is the candidate's knowledge of English. A person's mastery of English at the primary level is what predicts better than any other test how well s/he will do in the secondary system. And, at the next level of education, when we look at the selection criteria applied to entrants to the University of Zambia (UNZA), we shall see that the ones which are most highly predictive of performance at the University are those which are heavily language-loaded. So, within the educational system, as in the world of employment, as Mr Mwanakatwe emphasized yesterday, English is a 'passport to success' in Zambia today. Now, if the benefits conferred by a knowledge of English are so evident and widely understood, why is it that the task of obtaining that knowledge is in practice such a daunting one? And why are many children driven to adopting one or more of the inadequate coping strategies which I have outlined?

The effects of being educated in a second language

This is a large topic which I cannot hope to review comprehensively in this brief presentation. But I should like to try and place in a Zambian perspective the rather widely publicized studies conducted by Walter Lambert and his colleagues in Canada which have been followed up in the USA with a number of replications.

The first thing to note about these studies is that they concern the effect of immersion in a non-dominant language curriculum of children from homes where the dominant language is the family language. Parents who chose this kind of schooling for their children evidently gave them full support and encouragement in learning the non-familial language. Perhaps more important, being predominantly middle-class families they also, no doubt, provided ample opportunity at home for practice in the family language. Lambert found that in Canada, under these circumstances, children who had been immersed right from Grade one in a language foreign to the home (namely French or Spanish) made progress throughout their school careers that was equal to the progress achieved by native speakers of the curriculum language and that these children showed no appreciable retardation in mastery of their home language. Subsequent studies made in various parts of the USA have produced similar findings.

Some writers have interpreted these remarkable findings as proving that 'where there's a will there's a way'. And that may be a good summary of their significance. But the collective will shown by the children, parents, teachers and school peers, involved in these experiments, may be a phenomenon hard if not impossible to replicate in other cultural settings. Studies of the educational progress of children from homes where a *non*-dominant language is spoken who are immersed willy-nilly in a dominant language curriculum have stressed time and again the importance of motivational factors. French-speaking Canadians and Hispanic Americans seem to suffer from feelings of inadequacy in English-medium schools. Their parents can do little to assist them in this respect, since they share the feeling that their home culture and language are marginal in the context of mainstream North American society. Furthermore, their parents often feel that the more thoroughly their children absorb and master the school language and culture, the more alienated they become from the family culture. Consequently, these children often achieve a very low level of competence in the family language.

What about Zambia? What cultural forces are at work in our society sustaining or impeding the learning of particular languages? We noted earlier two major features of the cultural patterning of language use: the superordinate status of English and the public–private dichotomy with Zambian languages playing a predominant role in the private domain. The influence of these two factors on the relations between family and school is a complex one. Most parents in Zambia want their children to master English at school. But, at the same time, most of them use a Zambian language as the principal medium of communication in the home. This results in a paradoxical ideal – the child who *can* speak English but doesn't do so in the presence of his or her parents. (To reply to one's parent in English when addressed in a Zambian language is surely a sign of rudeness, according to current norms of behaviour.)

Must English always carry a particular cultural load?

A second widely cited conclusion reached by Lambert from his Canadian immersion studies was that the best motivation for learning a new language is the 'integrative' approach of seeking to assimilate the culture associated with the language, rather than the 'instrumental' approach of learning the language as a tool with no regard to its cultural content. Now, as John Pride has pointed out, this contrast between instru-mental and integrative motives makes a number of assumptions which simply disregard the realities of how English and French are used outside the borders of their countries of origin. These languages have long ceased to be attached to a single culture. They serve as vehicles for numerous different cultures. When V.S. Naipaul or Alex La Guma use English they do so to express dimensions of a culture which has an intimate link with the English language but only a tenuous one with the culture of Great Britain. When Chinua Achebe, Ezekiel Mphahlele or Ckot p'Bitek use English they do so to express a culture which they themselves internalized through the medium of another language. The legitimacy and success of these (non-integrative) enterprises is amply demonstrated by the wide audience which these writers have managed to attract. Unlike Conrad, a non-native speaker of English no longer needs to become an Englishman before he can use the language creatively as a valid cultural medium.

And yet, despite these and many other shining examples of English used to express non-English cultural ideas, there remains in Zambia (as in a number of other countries) a deep ambivalence about the cultural load of English. Zambians see English both as a local, national resource and as an irredeemably foreign institution – one which we would like to own, but which could never quite be transplanted without absurd incongruity (like the London Transport, double-decker buses which an entrepreneur imported to Lusaka and labelled 'Picadilly Circus' rather than 'Chelston' or 'Chakunkula').

We see this ambivalence most clearly reflected in the standards of English set up in the school curriculum. The grade-one English readers produced by the Curriculum Development Centre set out to portray a Zambian lifestyle: Mulenga and Jelita eat nshima and fish at home and their environment is peopled with characters dressed in Zambian attire engaging in Zambian activities. Yet the language the readers teach is a far cry from the English that children are most likely to hear spoken in Zambia. 'Speechwork' activities and drills are prescribed which seek to impart phonemic distinctions and stress patterns which characterize the English spoken by middle-class Londoners but which are seldom observed by adult Zambian speakers of English. Perhaps fortunately, very few Zambian primary school teachers are likely to be able to produce the phonological patterns which these drills are designed to instil. If they were, we would soon witness a generation of Zambian school children speaking like Lord Jim, the house servant described by Mr Mwanakatwe yesterday. Nevertheless, the system does influence the kind of English spoken by our young children. This was brought home to me when we were 'piloting' the study with grade-one children, which I described earlier. Following Lusaka usage, I first posed one of our questions in the form 'Where do you stay?' But it soon became clear that those children who could understand any English form of this question preferred the Standard British English form 'Where do you live?'

At the secondary-school level, teachers tend, as Hugh Africa has pointed out, to emphasize two registers of written English – that of the academic essay and that of the letter. Until recently, the form-three examiners put a red pen through such lucid Zambianisms as 'far much better', 'cope up with' and 'he's coming just now'. (I believe an element of liberalism has been introduced in this area recently.) Yet, I would argue, that much of the stylistic impact of a well-written personal letter comes from the writer's use of colloquialisms. Many of the personal letters my Zambian friends have written me in English have a peculiar 'ring' to them which I can only describe as unreal. Perhaps the writers were only taught official letter-writing. But I suspect it goes deeper than this. Some of the most imaginative English writing I have read in Zambia is to be found in the pages of the 'student rags' which circulate on the UNZA campus. Thick with local idioms and topical references, the English of these papers is almost perversely non-standard. Articles are also frequently libellous or obscene and, above all, humorous. But what they demonstrate, unlike almost any other Zambian writing in English, is a sense of ownership of the language. For the freedom to play with a language in this way requires a sense of confidence. (Consider Malapropisms, Spoonerisms and puns.) I think the reason why this relaxed use of English is more possible in a campus magazine than in a personal letter is that English is a major vehicle of oral communication on the campus among students from widely scattered corners of Zambia, Zimbabwe and elsewhere in Africa. The campus columnist can draw for his writing style on the jargon of campus small talk, whereas the letter writer is often communicating ideas about which, with this correspondent, he would normally speak in a Zambian language.

Towards the appropriation of English by secondary school students

What can the secondary school teacher of English (be s/he Zambian, Indian, English or of any other national origin) do to help Zambian secondary school students acquire more of this confidence in the use of a language, which (rightly or wrongly) has such an important role in Zambian public life? It seems to me that the first thing to do is to stress the variegated nature of the language. This means acknowledging as legitimate some of the forms which traditionally were taboo. In a Zambian secondary school all the out-of-classroom activities (football games, field trips, assemblies, drama, etc.) in which English is used play a more important role in imparting knowledge of the language than they do in British, Canadian or North American Schools. The many informal uses of English, which teachers in those other countries might choose to ignore, deserve to be discussed and explored by Zambian school teachers of English.

To acknowledge that a form of the language is legitimate is not to endorse its indiscriminate use in every kind of context. Gumperz's concept of situational code-switching seems to me an interesting pedagogical starting point. The two categories 'spoken' and 'written' can be further broken down. Students can be given exercises in parody, e.g. 'write a letter to your friend in the style of your chemistry textbook', or 'compose a speech for the headmaster in the idiom of school slang'. The goal of such exercises would be to sensitize students to different styles and registers.

A third principle which I would advocate is, again, perhaps somewhat unorthodox, namely to encourage the use of other languages during English classes. Almost every Zambian student has a knowledge of two or three Zambian languages in addition to English and those with a knowledge of none are truly exceptional. The promotion of communicative competence in English must surely take account of these other codes in the students' repertoire. Cross-language comparison and translation are both highly illuminating exercises, even when the final conclusion is that an idea is untranslatable. Similarly, the analysis of what situations are appropriate for what languages is part of learning about the national culture. Finally, the mere fact of inviting students to generate discussion materials in Zambian languages may help to demystify English and place the question of linguistic competence in a more realistic perspective. The parallel between the teacher's imcompetence in one or more of the Zambian languages and the student's own incompetence in English is a social fact which should be acknowledged. Even if the student feels that proficiency in English is the more valuable asset, recognition of the fact that everyone is excluded from some kind of linguistic knowledge should help him or her realize that s/he is no less of a person by virtue of his present handicap.

In sum, then, I have argued that the cultural context of contemporary Zambian society poses special problems for students learning English and that a strategy for overcoming these problems should include:

(a) An emphasis on the variegated nature of English.
(b) Explicit recognition and discussion of the various forms of English appropriate for use in different situations.
(c) Comparisons between English and other Zambian languages in respect of their lexical codes and their patterns of social usage.

The goal of all these activities should, I submit, be to encourage Zambian students *to appropriate* the English language and use it with confidence, flexibility and creativity.

Notes

1. The conference at which this paper was presented was opened by J.M. Mwanakatwe with a paper entitled 'The future role of English in Zambia'.

Tasks

Task 1

Serpell's article highlights the relationship between the use of a language and the culture that language represents. This relationship has been investigated by a number of writers, notably Kaplan (1966), who believes there is evidence to show that different cultures organize their experience in different ways and that this organization of experience is reflected in the linguistic organization of texts.

(i) Look at the two texts below from Swales and Dudley-Evans (1980). Text (a) is a translation from Arabic of a newspaper report. Text (b) is an attempt to reproduce the same contents as they might have appeared in an English newspaper.

Text (a)

The Islamic revolution in Iran has recreated anxiety in the neighbouring countries in the area. And the Soviet Union is watching with anxiety the Islamic movement which has begun to spread on its southern borders. And the Kremlin is watching with obvious anxiety what is happening in Afghanistan where the Leftist government is fighting a war against dissidents in the Muslim tribes. And Farid Coleman the head of the Newsweek office in the Soviet Union observed when visiting some extreme tension and efforts to strengthen the armed forces in the areas of the southern borders.

Text (b)

The Islamic revolution in Iran has created anxiety in neighbouring countries in the area, in particular the Soviet Union. Evidence of this was given by Farid Coleman, the head of the Newsweek office in the Soviet Union, who has been travelling in some of the Muslim areas of the Soviet Union. He observed extreme tension in the area, and, in particular, that the armed forces seemed to have been strengthened in recent weeks. He noticed several signs of the recent and sudden arrival of one group of the army, this group being in a winter uniform totally inappropriate for the high temperature of Ashkabad,

Text (a) contd

The visitor to Ashkabad in the south of the Soviet Union can see two groups of soldiers parading in the streets in their uniform. The first group is wearing summer uniform which is suitable for the high temperature in Ashkabad. As for the second group, it is wearing a heavy uniform which is only suitable for the winter which is still prevalent in the northern part of the Soviet Union. And it is difficult to see members of these two groups mixing in the streets of Ashkabad which indicates that they belong to different groups which have not been together for long enough to establish friendships.

And it is worthy of mention that the changes of locality and movements of armies in the Soviet Union is surrounded by extreme secrecy and is considered a state secret but the inhabitants of Ashkabad will inform you that extra forces have arrived recently from Moscow to strengthen the forces situated on the borders.

And all the articles published in the Soviet Press in the week before last indicate the anxiety of the Kremlin about the new alliances opposed to communism in the area.

And the Soviet leadership fears that the Islamic movement will spread into the Soviet Union where there are thirty million Muslims.

Text (b) contd

and also evidently unacquainted with other army groups.

Evidence of the size of the build up in the Muslim areas is given by the fact that the arrival of reinforcements, normally kept very secret, is well known to the inhabitants.

The Soviet leadership seems to view with great anxiety the development in the area of new alliances opposed to communism, and seems to fear that the Islamic movement may spread to the Soviet Union itself where there are thirty million Muslims. The Kremlin is, therefore, watching with great anxiety events in Afghanistan where the leftist government is fighting a war, against dissidents in the Muslim tribes.

Try to compare how the two texts organize and present their content.

(ii) Do you have any evidence from your own teaching experience that your students' cultural background influences the way they structure their writing? If you do, give some examples.

(iii) Does a teacher have any right to assume that students should use the sort of organization represented in text (b) above as a model for their English writing? Give reasons for your answer.

(iv) If you answered yes to (iii) above, and you found your students tending to produce the model represented by text (a), how would you go about getting them to approximate to text (b)?

It could be argued that a number of writing problems arise because we are asking students to produce varieties or registers with which they are unfamiliar. If you would like to read more about registers, you could try Halliday and Hasan (1985) or Ure and Ellis (1984).

Task 2

Serpell refers to Fishman's (1980a) notions of diglossia and bilingualism. Diglossic societies use two languages: 'high' languages (H) and 'low' languages (L). The terms 'high' and 'low' refer primarily to the status and prestige of the languages. Fishman believes multilingual societies can be characterized in one of three ways:

(a) Both diglossic and bilingual.
(b) Diglossic without being bilingual.
(c) Bilingual with no diglossia.

Bilingualism here means a situation where all sectors of society have control of (H) and (L). Diglossia is a situation where (H) and (L) are separated according to function and access to either is restricted. Therefore (a) would occur in those societies where the (H) and (L) languages had different functions (e.g. (H) might be used in education (L) as a 'home language'), but where access to both (H) and (L) was relatively free for everyone. Diglossia without bilingualism – (b) – would occur where (H) and (L) had distinct functions and were used by different groups who did not communicate with each other except, perhaps, through interpreters or intermediaries. Bilingualism without diglossia – (c) – would occur where there was no (H) and (L) but all languages were used widely with no one language being used for a particular purpose which separated it from another language.

(i) It is unlikely you will find a country or society that fits exactly into one of the three categories, but can you think of any possible examples? If you have difficulty, try categorizing the language situations described in Part 3 of this book (see the table below). List the languages used in the countries concerned and whether they are (H) or (L).

Nation	(a, b, or c) Classification	Languages (H) or (L)
Namibia		
Nigeria		
Zambia		
Hong Kong		
Australia		
Malaysia		

(ii) Does your analysis reveal any generalization about the status of English and other languages internationally?

(iii) What use might the information in (i) above be to a teacher of English in any one of the countries listed who was trying to assess student attitudes and motivation to learn English?

A clear discussion of diglossia can be found in Fasold (1984: chapter 2).

Task 3

When you completed Task 2, you probably entered English as a 'high' language in most of the countries listed in the table. To do this, however, is to overlook the fact that different varieties of English (New Englishes) are emerging which reflect the social and cultural context within which they are used. Thus, in the last two articles, reference was made to Nigerian English and Zambian English and even these are very general categories. Such varieties of English reflect the functions of English as an additional language, but we can also see that English as an international language might also reflect the values of its context.

(i) Look at the following examples (from Brumfit 1980). They are all examples of English produced by Chinese speakers of English in China. (Note that all the examples were collected in 1976; some may therefore be the products of the political situation of that time and may in fact no longer be used.)

(1) I passed the translation to the polisher for revision. (A 'polisher' is one who produces the final version of a translation.)
(2) Those bad eggs will be punished for the wicked acts.
(3) That is the Japanese leader and with him is his running dog.
(4) The propaganda team (school dramatic society) will perform at the end of your visit.

(5) He is the chairman of our revolutionary committee.

(6) Tell me about the movements at your university.

(ii) List those items in the sentences above that you regard as strange in some way.

(iii) Why do you regard them as strange?

(iv) What aspects of the culture do they represent?

(v) Would you, as a teacher of English accept them, or would you want to 'correct' them? If the latter, what would you put in their place?

(vi) Give reasons for your decision in (v)

There are several books available on the subject of English and its role in the world, among them Quirk and Widdowson (eds 1986) and Kachru (1985).

Task 4

Serpell suggests that one way to solve the problems of Zambian students learning English would be to introduce the concept of varieties of English and to teach their appropriacy for different situations. (You may remember that in Judd Task 6 the notion of 'inappropriate' rather than 'incorrect' language was introduced. The issue will be discussed further in Abbott's article later in this collection.)

(i) Look at the short extracts below from two letters: (a) written by one friend to another in pidgin English (Todd 1982); (b) written by a solictor to a client in standard British English.

(1) How for your family? I think say all dem dey fine. Any time we you de write for them make you salute them fine for me...How for you sef? You trong fine?

(2) I refer to previous correspondence and would be grateful if you could arrange an appointment with my office in order that you can sign the Deed.

(ii) What linguistic differences do you notice between the two letters and why do you think they occur?

(iii) How might you use material like this in the classroom to demonstrate language variety and appropriacy?

Benson and Greaves (1984) discuss varieties and register. See also the further reading in Serpell Task 1.

Task 5

In English-medium institutions, the 'official' policy of teaching through English and not using the local language is often replaced in the classroom by a covert 'unofficial' policy of using a mix of local languages and English.

(i) Why do you think the 'covert' policy operates?

(ii) If you were an inspector of English and found a teacher using a 'mix' of languages in the classroom, contrary to official policy, would you:

(1) Enforce the 'official' policy.

(2) Take no action.

(3) Discuss the situation with the teacher without necessarily imposing policy? Give reasons for your choice of action.

(iii) Why do you think it is important for a materials designer to try to find out which policy (the official or unofficial one) is being used in the classroom?

(We shall be looking at some of these issues again in Gibbons Tasks 2 and 3 p. 135.)

Zughoul and Hussein (1985) give examples of official and 'unofficial' policies on language use operating in university classes in Jordan.

Task 6

Serpell comments on the ritualized performance of pupils in the English classroom. He says: 'these are children who could not answer a question like 'How many brothers and sisters do you have?' Yet, they could produce a...sentence in English on request in response to a picture'.

(i) Look at the following extract from a scene in a Malawian primary school English classroom (Thawe 1984).
    The class is looking at a text with accompanying pictures. The teacher has read the first paragraph of the text, and the pupils are reading it to themselves silently:

T	Have you finished?
P	(Chorus) Yes.
T	Finished?
P	(Chorus) Yes.
T	Who climbed a tree one day?
P	(NA) [No answer].
T	Who climbed a tree one day?
P	(Pupil puts up hand).
T	Malango.
P	(Inaudible answer).
T	Speak up. We can't hear you.
P	Dziko caliembed a tree one day.
T	Not caliembed. Climbed.
P	(NA).
T	Say it.
P	Dziko climbed.
T	Climbed. Say the whole sentence.
P	Dziko climbed a tree one day.
T	Yes. Dziko climbed a tree one day.
T	What flew out of the tree?
P	(NA).
T	What flew out of the tree?
P	A bird flew out.
T	Say it.
P	A bird flew out.
T	Say a bird flew out of the tree.
P	A bird flew out of the tree.
T	Again.
P	A bird flew out of the tree.
T	What flew out of the tree, class.
P	(Chorus) A bird flew out of the tree.
T	Again.
P	(Chorus) A bird flew out of the tree.

(ii) Why do you think this sort of teaching and learning might produce the 'ritualized performance' to which Serpell refers? (Your work on Tollefson Task 3 and Tollefson Task 5 (i) might help you here.)

(iii) What do you think are the reasons for the use of the method illustrated in the extract?

(iv) How would you go about trying to move the children away from ritualized performance towards one more focused on communication? (Look back to your replies to Rogers Task 6 for ideas.)

Allwright (1988); van Lier (1988) are useful for ideas on collecting data on teacher–pupil language in ELT classrooms and its relationship to methods and materials.

Chapter 10

What Should We Expect of Community Language Programmes?

T. J. QUINN

Editor's introduction

Quinn continues the discussion on the tension that can arise in multilingual societies over the use and role of English and other languages. He deals with the situation in Australia. English is the mother tongue of the majority and the dominant language; local languages, which Quinn refers to as community languages, are spoken by immigrants from other countries. English, at least for the first generation of immigrants is, in Judd's terms (this volume), a second language and the question in this situation is the extent to which the community languages should be introduced into the mainstream curriculum. Now it might well be asked why an article on Australia has been included in a collection which concentrates on the developing world, where English, as we have seen, performs very different roles. The main justification for including Quinn's article is that the English versus local language debate sometimes becomes unnecessarily narrowly-focused and, although it can be dangerous to draw general conclusions from dissimilar situations, it can be useful to do so, since a number of the underlying principles may be the same. For example, Quinn's general point, namely, that the reasons for the inclusion of any language in the curriculum should be clearly stated and realistically evaluated, can usefully be applied to many situations where language education is in question. Quinn suggests that local language programmes in Australia are initiated in order to achieve at least one of three major objectives. The first he terms the social justice perspective; the teaching of the local language is seen as a means of overcoming educational disadvantage. The second objective is to foster large numbers of bilinguals and multilinguals, who are seen as an important national resource. The third objective is to encourage linguistic–and hence social– interaction between different cultural groups. Quinn regards these objectives as laudable, but believes that as goals for community language teaching programmes they are unrealistic. He knows that such objectives cannot be achieved without major changes in society and that the school and the school curriculum are not powerful enough to bring about major social change. Teaching a community language will not, for example, change patterns of inter-group communication outside the classroom, nor will it improve the economic status of deprived groups. The criteria for including community languages in the curriculum should, Quinn believes, be the same as those for any language, including those European languages traditionally taught, and the decision which languages to teach should be made for intellectual and cultural, rather than social, reasons. This leads Quinn to the conclusion that community languages should, in fact, be taught as subjects on an equal footing with the other more traditional languages, though he is prepared to accept that, where resources permit, there is a case for using community languages in reception classes to ease the transition of immigrant pupils from the home to the school environment.

Course objectives

THE THRESHOLD-LEVEL movement in European language teaching circles has offered many new dimensions or perspectives to language curriculum planners. I believe that one of the most significant of these contributions is a healthy emphasis on the need to be very specific about objectives, about saying just what your language programme is for and what it is meant to achieve in the learner's life. Not so very long ago, defining levels and stating objectives was all about grammar and vocabulary: one listed words and patterns in more or less arbitrary blocks; one 'covered' certain tenses in the first stage of the course, leaving others till later, and so on. The threshold-level movement is changing all that: objectives and levels are now defined in terms of behaviour; the lists of words and structures are much less important that what the learner is expected to do with them in terms of real-life social interactions; course objective statements are now about people rather than grammar. Thus, one finds in one statement about threshold-level school courses (van Ek, 1976) an account of the learner population which tells us that they are expected to learn the behaviour of temporary visitors to the foreign country, or of people in temporary contact with foreigners in the learners' country, the encounters being of a superficial, non-professional type. Similarly, in the Introduction to *Waystage*, a great deal is said about the communication needs of the learner, and about the nature of the social interactions envisaged in the language course design.

This is the kind of thinking that I wish to apply to community language teaching in Australia: what sorts of objectives should we specify for school courses in languages like Greek, Spanish, Turkish and Arabic? What kind of social encounters are we aiming at? What do we want our students to be able to *do* with the language we teach them?

I have two reasons for believing that this kind of analysis of objectives is very appropriate, and indeed urgent, at the present time. In the first place, community language programmes in schools are still new enough not to have acquired an apparatus of 'hidden' or implicit objectives that resist change and rationalization; we still have the chance to get the basic principles clarified before established practice overtakes us and makes rethinking very difficult. Secondly, I am very much disturbed by some of the objectives that are being touted – often implicitly – for community language programmes in schools: such programmes are sometimes pushed as if they were panaceas for social ills, the basic ingredient in a formula for social reform and the key to a new kind of society. Such thinking is unrealistic, and having unrealistic objectives for language courses runs the risk of bringing the whole enterprise into disrepute. I believe it is urgent to specify realistic and achievable objectives for community language teaching, and this is the exercise I would like to engage in with you today.

What is a community language?

Before we begin this exercise in the clarification of objectives, I would like to say something about the terms 'community language' and 'community language programme'. I want to object to the former and define the latter.

The term 'community language' has become well and truly established as part of the popular rhetoric of multiculturalism, and I belive that this is very regrettable: the term is largely meaningless and absurd, and it is used to create divisions that are quite unnecessary. Every language – unless it is a dead language like Sanskrit – is a community language, in the sense that it is the living means of communication of some speech community. In this sense, the term 'community language' is tautological. Proponents of the term in Australia, however, would claim that they are not using a tautology, because they mean by community language a language spoken in Australia. Given the fact that so many languages are spoken in Australia, I wonder if that notion says anything non-trivial. In the context of Australian educational planning, does Albanian acquire a special status because there are, say 1,000 speakers of Albanian in a particular area of Sydney? In some sense, of course it does, but the implications of this linguistic numbers game can lead to absurdities. I have heard serious people argue earnestly about whether French is or is not a community language; I have been asked whether I believe that French is a community language or a foreign language; and I have been told triumphantly that 'French is now a community language'. One gets the impression that once a particular language passes a certain critical number of speakers in the Australian population, the nature of that language changes dramatically and it acquires a new status. I don't believe there is any such linguistic magic in numbers. Serious proponents of the term 'community language' would probably claim that it has two criterial components: to be classed as a community language, a language needs to have two characteristics:

(1) It must be spoken as a first language by a certain proportion of the population of Australia.
(2) It must not have a tradition of being taught as part of the Australian school curriculum.

In this sense, it would be claimed, French and German are not community languages, but Greek and Turkish are. What worries me about this is that the crucial difference is in the area of school status, not in the nature of the language itself, and our terms can blind us to this. To say that Greek is a community language but French is a foreign language suggests that there is something inherently different between the two languages in themselves, and I think that this obscures more important issues. The presence or absence of large numbers of speakers in the immediate community, or the presence or absence of community interaction as part of the school language programme are not, I believe, the essential determinants of high quality in a school language course; they are fairly marginal, as I hope to show you. The terminology of 'community' languages as opposed to 'foreign' languages suggests that the success of the school programme will somehow be determined by the choice of language: 'community' languages are good, and to be encouraged: 'foreign' languages are bad, and to be discouraged. I think that this is very misleading, and to the extent that the term 'community language' implies this kind of thinking, I believe it is a most infelicitous term. I would want to endorse the point of view expressed in a report of the Australian Ethnic Affairs Council (1979: p. 9):

> When considering the teaching of languages other than English in the context of the goals of multicultural education, there are no valid grounds for maintaining a boundary between 'foreign' languages and 'community' languages in future educational planning.

Having pointed out the unfortunate and misleading implications of the term 'community languages', I shall now go on using it. My dislike of the term will not alter the fact that it is very widely used in government and educational circles. I shall use the term to refer to languages spoken by Australian immigrant groups and not traditionally taught in school curricula.

What is a community language programme?

So much for the term 'community language'. Now a little about how people use the term 'community language programme'. This term seems to be used to cover three different sorts of programme:

(1) An arrangement where a community language is taught as a school subject, at either primary or secondary level, with a timetable allocation of one to three hours per week; this is a relatively common pattern.
(2) An adjustment to the primary school so that initial reception and induction into the school can be carried out in a non-English language; this reception arrangement may be accompanied by minimal teaching of one content area (say number skills) in the non-English language and perhaps even by attempts to achieve basic literacy in the non-English language; this 'reception' pattern is rather less common.
(3) A fully-fledged bilingual programme, where the non-English language is used as the medium of instruction for a significant proportion of the school day and curricular content; such bilingual patterns are quite rare.

From this point on, I want to use the terms 'community language programme' and 'community language teaching' to cover all or any of these. In the common rhetoric about community language teaching and the introduction of community language programmes, it is seldom clear which of these possibilities the proponents have in mind. So let us leave the term undifferentiated for a moment as we examine objectives, then return later, in an attempt to match realistic objectives to practical programmes.

If one peruses the abundant Australian literature on multicultural education and tries to extract the statements on language programmes, I believe that one can identify three types of objectives. Often, these are implied as general perspectives rather than stated in overt terms as specific objectives. I shall list these three areas or clusters of objectives, then discuss them in some detail. The three perspectives are:

(1) Social justice.
(2) Linguistic resources.
(3) Interactionist or multicultural.

Let me try to spell out the objectives for community language programmes that are stated or at least implied in each of these orientations.

The social justice perspective

This label covers a number of approaches to community language teaching. The thinking originates in a concern for the welfare of the non-English-speaking child, who is perceived as a member of a disadvantaged group, with a less than equal chance of success at school and hence of access to the good life in the form of satisfactory employment, upward social and professional mobility, and so on. The disadvantaged condition of the non-English-speaking child is seen as a serious instance of injustice and inequality of opportunity in Australian society and many educational critics and planners see the language factor as being at the heart of such injustice and inequality.

This being the case, community language programmes are seen as part of the remedy for disadvantage and inequality.

This language argument can take several forms, of which I shall mention three. Some proponents of community language programmes as a remedy for educational disadvantage would take the very straightforward view that a child must quickly and inevitably become educationally disadvantaged if the education he is offered is presented in a language he does not understand: the process of education must therefore be carried on in the child's home language if this is the only language he understands.

Some would take the social justice argument a little further. They would argue that the poor performance of minority language children in school is not due solely to the fact that the children don't understand the language of the school; it is due to their sense of alienation from a school system that ignores, perhaps even despises, their language and culture. In a multilingual society, so the argument goes, monolingual education represents a massive 'put-down' of minority language speakers. For critics who present this argument, the introduction of community language programmes is essentially a matter of status building and self-esteem: the child's self concept – and hence his or her school performance – will be improved if the home language is given a place in school.

Finally, a third form of the social justice orientation to community language teaching is the community rights approach; all groups in a multicultural society should have the right to remain distinct and to retain their language and culture; therefore the school, in its language programmes, should not only recognize and affirm the rights to linguistic diversity, but also assist each community in its attempts to exercise that right.

The sort of social justice perspective on community language teaching which I have just analysed is frequently encountered in government documents such as the Galbally Report (1978), the *Report of the Inquiry into Schools of High Migrant Density* (Australian Department of Education 1975), and various documents of the Poverty Commission (e.g. Fitzgerald 1976). It is also ably analysed in Horvath (1980).

The linguistic resources perspective

Whereas the social justice perspective is concerned principally with the fate of the individual, the resources approach considers the resource stock of the entire nation. Fluent bilinguals and multilinguals are seen as an important national resource. In the pithy phrase of Michael Clyne (Clyne 1980:7) – who is an able exponent of this perspective – 'multilingualism is . . . an asset for the entire nation'. The school system, through its language policies, is given several crucial roles (*ibid.*:8): to respond to social need by ensuring that future professionals will be at least bilingual; to ensure national economic advantage, for instance by providing the nation with 'its own reservoir of English-Arabic bilinguals'; and to provide the nation with a lofty internationalist vocation by enabling Australia to 'play an important role in the world as a mediator between nations and cultures'. From this point of view, community language programmes are thus seen as a means of safeguarding and developing the nation's language resources.

The interactionist or multicultural perspective

This third orientation towards community language teaching is probably the one we hear most about these days. Cultural diversity in a community is seen as an intrinsically desirable phenomenon, since it enriches the lives of all. The individual who lives out his life within the confines of one cultural group only is seen as, in some sense, culturally deprived. Thus, cultural interaction, interaction between members of different cultural groups, is an enriching experience for all concerned,

In terms of language programmes, I think this interactionist perspective takes two forms, which I shall call the popular or 'folk' form, and the academic form. The 'folk' view is the sort of vague feeling often articulated in school curriculum planning meetings by teachers or parents who make statements like: 'Surely Greek is more relevant than French these days', or 'With all these Italian children here, shouldn't we be teaching Italian?' The academic view makes the case for community language teaching in a much more explicit way, and is probably best articulated in the writings of J.J. Smolicz. Community language programmes are important precisely because cultural interaction is desirable and language is the essential key to successful interaction between different cultural groups. Cultural pluralism demands linguistic pluralism. Thus, Smolicz writes (1979a:128):

> In the absence of linguistic pluralism in Australia, not only can there be no true cultural pluralism, but even the policy of interactionism is a chimera or an ideal which, one knows in advance, can never be attained.

And again (1979b:1–2):

> A policy of cultural interaction or cultural pluralism will only be successful if the society as a whole accepts that there is a need to preserve and develop the ethnic languages in daily use in the community . . . Two-way cultural interaction is essential if the multicultural society is to be dynamic and not a static collection of linguistic enclaves.

Thus, within this multicultural perspective, community language teaching is all about interaction between different cultural groups.

Good programmes must have appropriate objectives

These, then, are the sorts of objectives for school programmes in community languages which I believe are floating around at the moment. I am now going to try to argue that all three sets of objectives are inappropriate, ill-conceived and unrealistic. Now, lest I be misunderstood, let me say at once that I believe that all three clusters of aims are eminently laudable and desirable: I am all for cultural interaction through language; I would be proud of a nation that cherished and fostered its linguistic resources; I respect and admire any ethnic community that chooses to preserve its language and culture; and I am appalled by the insensitivity with which minority language children are treated in many schools, and by the monstrous injustices of which they are victims. What I am going to argue is that community language teaching in schools is not an appropriate and effective way of achieving the eminently desirable goals that I have outlined. I believe that good community language programmes in schools have a very important role. But to be good, they have to have appropriate objectives. By setting up community language programmes with inappropriate objectives and unrealistic expectations, we run the risk of jeopardizing the whole enterprise. This is what concerns me, and this is why I want to demonstrate why the currently fashionable objectives are inappropriate, and what sorts of objectives might be more appropriate and realistic. Let me take each cluster of objectives and try to demonstrate why I regard them as ill-conceived. I will consider them in a different order, beginning with what I regard as the most ill-conceived, the multicultural perspective.

Misconceptions of the multicultural perspective

You will recall this orientation: community language teaching in schools is important, because language is seen as the key to social interaction between culturally different groups. I shall comment f rst on the academic version of this argument, then on the popular view. Much as I respect the work and good intentions of scholars exploring the language-interaction view of cultural pluralism, I cannot escape the conclusion that this is a singularly ill-conceived, and even pernicious approach. I say this because the approach embodies a paradox that will both hasten the death of community languages and imperil the long-term future of multiculturalism.

Let me try to explain this paradox, by means of a slightly technical socio-linguistic argument, which can be summarized in three propositions.

(1) Universal experience has shown that, to survive, a minority language must be part of a diglossic situation, i.e. a situation where the life of the speakers is rigidly compartmentalized, with clearly defined domains where only the minority language is functional.
(2) The whole thrust of multicultural interactionism is to *decompartmentalize* i.e. to break down the barriers, to penetrate cultural and linguistic ghettoes, to demolish the walls of social separation.
(3) To the extent that this multicultural thrust is successful, the diglossic situation is jeopardized, and the chances of survival of the minority language are diminished.

The major premise of this argument – the notion that language drift can be stemmed only by diglossia or functional separation – is a principle that has been amply documented, particularly in the vast research of Fishman (see Fishman, 1980a for a recent overview), as well as in other recent studies such as Gonzo and Saltarelli (1979). The principle explains the virtually universal phenomenon of the non-survival of immigrant languages beyond the third generation. Many people find this a bitter pill to swallow, but the facts are clear: the price you have to pay for cultural distinctiveness and linguistic survival is social separation; if you want a minority language to survive, then diglossic separatism is your only chance. If you are not willing to be separate from the mainstream, the language will go. As Fishman puts it:

Without compartmentalization of one kind or another – at times attained by ideological/philosophical and even by a degree of physical withdrawal from establishment society – the flow process from language spread to language shift is an inexorable one. (1980a:9)

If this analysis is correct – and I believe that the evidence is overwhelmingly strong – then the whole thrust of the language-interactionist view of multiculturalism, and community language teaching as part of this, will be to hasten the demise of minority languages in Australia, since it will undermine the diglossic compartmentalization essential for language survival. Barbara Horvath (1980:9) sums up the paradox thus:

> If all members of a speech community become true or balanced bilinguals (i.e. use both languages in all settings), there is no longer any need to be bilingual because no community needs two languages for the same set of circumstances.

This then, is the language-interactionist paradox: the more successfully it breaks down the barriers of social and linguistic separatism, the more surely it will hasten the disappearance of the minority languages.

I further claimed that this approach jeopardizes the possibility of a stable policy of long-term cultural pluralism. On socio-linguistic grounds, I have to state my conviction that the chances of our minority languages surviving more than two or three generations are very slight indeed. Now, if you pin all your multicultural policies and strategies on linguistic pluralism, where are you left when the minority languages have disappeared, as they sadly must? Thus, I find the scholarly approach to community language teaching as a part of the language-interactionist approach to multiculturalism very ill-conceived indeed.

All of this is pretty theoretical, so I want to turn to what I called the 'folk' view of the interactionist perspective on community language teaching, because it is more down-to-earth: no less ill-conceived, but more tangible. I believe that if you get proponents of the folk view of community language teaching to spell out what they mean, it goes something like this: we need school programmes in Greek so that non-Greek Australians will be able to talk in Greek to Greek Australians. I don't think I'm caricaturing unreasonably. I must confess that I find this kind of thinking – which appears quite common – unbelievably naive. For one thing, the amount of language that gets taught in school programmes is not all that great. But, even if it were adequate, there is a more important consideration: the folk argument assumes that knowing the language of another group readily promotes social interaction with that group. I don't believe that this is so. In fact, I believe that this view puts the cart before the horse: if you are already in a situation of social interaction with a group, then you are likely to learn the language of that group; it doesn't work the other way around. One could put it another way by saying that knowing the language is a necessary but not sufficient condition for cultural interaction.

To document this point of view, let me quote from a recent review of a very important and thorough study of the social patterns of use of the Irish language.

> Their most interesting finding...is that a positive attitude to Irish in itself is a relatively insignificant factor in explaining why a person used Irish. Much more important are two other factors, neither of which is surprising; ability to speak Irish, and...'group support'. In other words, however enthusiastic a person is about the virtues of using the Irish language, he will probably not use it himself unless he speaks it easily and belongs to a group which encourages him to do so by providing domains in which Irish is the normal choice of language. [Hudson, 1980b:610–11]

It is this question of natural and ready group support which is important. Even supposing that a non-Greek Australian manages to learn enough Greek at school to speak the language easily, does he thereby have ready access to Greek social situations? I doubt it. Sadly, but naturally enough, our society is culturally ghettoized, and just knowing the language of another ghetto doesn't give you free right of access to that ghetto. Nor should it. For many minority groups, the language is the symbol of territory, the wall around the sacred private world, and any idea that possession of the language gives you right of entry to that world leaves the way open to attitudes of insensitive condescension and impertinent intrusion.

Thus, I have the gravest reservations about the capacity of schools to create – by means of language programmes – situations of social interaction that don't already exist outside the school. Many observers have commented on the constant temptation for educators to endow schools with capacities for social reform which are simply not attested by experience. Taft (1980) speaks of 'proponents of social goals' who 'lay too heavy a responsibilty on the education system', and goes on to point out that 'it is very doubtful whether schools can have any fundamental effect on the outlook of the students unless the changes are consistent with those that are already occurring in the general Zeitgeist due to other causes'. Fishman (1977c:10) puts it thus: 'Schools are reflections of societal characteristics, societal needs, societal views and, above all, societal power constellations'. I therefore find it hard to take seriously the folk view that school programmes in community languages will create a situation where people will readily interact in the language of a minority group.

School programmes lack powers to change attitudes

Having set out my reasons for rejecting the multicultural or language-interactionist perspective on objectives of community language teaching at great length, I shall be briefer on the other two clusters of objectives. Basically, I reject them for the same fundamental reason: they attribute to school programmes powers that are very difficult to demonstrate. Thus, if the society at large cares little for bilingualism and multilingualism, school programmes are not going to create a radically new social climate that treasures and fosters the nation's linguistic resources, and we are deluding ourselves if we believe that this is what community language programmes are for.

Similarly, if we turn to the social justice perspective and the right of any community to maintain its language and culture, school programmes in community languages have got very little to do with this. Once again, I offer a bitter pill that many will find hard to swallow, but the facts have to be stated: the public school system will have little effect on the maintenance or demise of minority languages. Whether the community languages are taught in public school curricula or not, it will be other factors like marriage patterns and ethnic community attitudes that will determine the fate of the ethnic languages and cultures. As Taft (1980) puts it, if the languages and cultures are to survive, 'the second generation "ethnics" would need to be more competent than they are in their ethnic language, to be more closely bound to their families and their ethnic communities, to resist exogamy and to bring up their children to value their ethnic ideology and identity'. In other words, the choice is there for the ethnic communities to make, and community language programmes in schools are not going to do their job for them. By all means let us respect their choice and support them in obtaining every possible assistance to implement whatever choices they make, but don't let us mislead them by pretending that whatever we do about community language teaching in the public schools is going to ensure the maintenance of their language and culture. We owe it to them to be honest and tell them the bitter truth, despite what Fishman calls 'the touching belief of many . . . linguistic minorities that bilingual education will save their language'. He goes on:

> A decade and a half of language maintenance research has conclusively demonstrated – in the U.S., in Ireland, in Wales, in Israel, in Scotland, in Friesland, and elsewhere – that the school is a rather unreliable ally of language maintenance, leading appreciably and frequently in other directions. [1977c:47]

A realistic approach

Thus far, I have rejected as unrealistic and inappropriate the vaguely popular objectives being touted for community language teaching. Now it is time to be positive, and to suggest what might be an appropriate and realistic set of objectives for a community language programme. What objectives should we have for a school programme in a language like Modern Greek? Why should we choose to have such a language in our school curriculum? My short answer to that question is this: we should choose to have Modern Greek (or any other of the community languages) for the same reasons that we have any other language, or indeed any other subject, in the school curriculum. We should make this choice on intellectual and cultural grounds that are equally valid whether there happens to be a Greek community nearby or not.

Similarly, our objectives should be to ensure that our community language programme offers the same kind of demonstrably valuable intellectual and cultural experience as a good 'traditional' language programme. A community language programme – a programme in Greek or Turkish or Serbo-Croatian – will be a good, high-quality programme because of the same factors that make a successful traditional school language programme a good one. There, of course, is the rub. What makes a school language programme a good one? We have not been successful at articulating a convincing answer to this question, and the penalties we have paid for this failure are very evident: we haven't convinced the students, and we haven't convinced the planners, like the authors of the recent Curriculum Development Centre document on the core curriculum, who at least left the question of languages in the core partly open.

For what it is worth, let me offer my version of what makes a language programme a good one. I offer these remarks very tentatively, because I believe the main challenge for language teachers should be to stimulate many different answers to this question. If we can articulate from our experience those features that make *any* school language programme a good one, then we are in a position to build these into statements of objectives for community language programmes.

Language as a means of experiencing culture

I believe that traditional language programmes have come a long way in recent years, and that there are now many admirable features of good foreign language programmes that can show the way to planners of community language programmes. If I contrast the best present-day language with the sort of programme I went through at school, one thing stands out very clearly: the best school language programmes are now an authentic experience of a cultural reality, in a way that my boyhood French programme never was. In the exams of 25 years ago, there was translation of insipid inanities devoid of any cultural reality. In the exams and syllabuses of today, the cultural reality is present in such things as film study, French song, study of the contemporary press, the cultural tradition of cuisine, and so on. And in all of this, the language is the vehicle for the study of such content areas. Nor is it only in examinations that this presence of the cultural reality can be observed. What are called *documents authentiques* are the core of the best foreign language programmes: the press, radio, film and song of the other culture are present in the language class. This is very clear in the best modern source books, in such work as the Steele and Strong *Nouvelles Perspectives*, or Steele's work using the French press, or Ian Adams' course books (*Le Français*) using authentic cultural documents on virtually every page. What is important and essential in all this is that in the school programme the language becomes functional as a means of experiencing the foreign culture. This happens in the classroom, with modest but imaginative resources, and that is quite a remarkable fact. This is what I would hold up for emulation by the planners of community language programmes. If they can provide a school language programme which is in itself an authentic experience of a cultural reality in the way I have described, then I believe they will be providing an educational experience that is amply justified on strictly educational and cultural grounds.

Community language prgrammes must transcend the local community

Thus, I have obviously played down the 'community' part of a community language programme, and I have several reasons for this, some of which I have hinted at earlier. In principle, I would want to be cautious about the general notion of having the legitimacy and authenticity of any school programme defined by the character of the immediate local community, which may change at any time. I would want the essential basis of my language programme to remain equally valid whatever happens to the local community. More importantly , I believe that community language programmes must transcend the local community. The full riches of, say, Greek culture are in no way confined to nor defined by the community that happens to be in a certain place at a certain time.

Thus, to come back to the three styles of community language programme which I enumerated at the beginning, I have pushed for a quite traditional 'subject' approach. I believe that this is the most promising one, because it is realistic and modest in its expectations. Of the other two models, I would say this: the 'reception' model in the primary school should certainly be offered if the school has the resources to cope with large numbers of different languages; the full bilingual model needs to be tried in carefully-controlled experimental situations, but with a great deal of preliminary discussion about what it is for.

My conception of minimal, threshold objectives for community language programmes is thus very modest and quite traditional. I don't see social reform, the remediation of injustices or the maintenance of minority languages as feasible objectives for school programmes, and if we hold out such unreasonable objectives as the justification for community language programmes, we run the risk of creating disillusionment and leaving community language teaching in the pattern of stop-start confusion that is already fairly prevalent. I believe that modest objectives will serve us well. School programmes in Greek or Turkish or Serbo-Croatian are not going to achieve wonderful things that French and German programes have not been able to achieve. But if Greek, Turkish or Serbo-Croatian programmes manage to do what the best French and German programmes do, then Australian schools will be all the richer. I earnestly hope that there will be many schools that are so enriched.

Tasks

Task 1

   (i) How would Judd (see pp.35–41 this volume) classify the English language situation in Australia as described by Quinn (i.e. ESL, EAL, ELWC or EFL)?
   (ii) What differences are there between the language situations described by Emenyonu and Serpell and that described by Quinn?
  (iii) How might these differences affect language policy?

Task 2

Dorian (1981:47) has said that 'language loyalty persists as long as the economic and social circumstances are conducive to it, but if some other language proves to have greater value a shift to that other language begins'. Scotton (1972:89) makes a related point: 'People will add a language...that promotes their socio-economic advantage'.

   (i) If these comments are true, what are the long-term implications for the roles and functions of English and the community languages in Australia?
  (ii) Would your answer to (i) above affect the sort of community language programme you might offer? (For three types of programme see Quinn p.113.)

Task 3

   (i) Fill in the table below from the information given in Quinn's article.(Use note form.)

Justification for community language programmes	Objectives	Quinn's arguments	His solutions
1 Social justice	1		
	2		
	3		
2 Linguistic resource	1		
	2		
	3		
3 Multicultural aspects	1		
	2		

  (ii) Do you agree with Quinn's solutions? Give the reasons for your answer.
  (iii) Skutnabb-Kangas (1986) has tried to categorize the views of different groups on the subject of minority language education according to whether they wish to change:

     (1) Society.
     (2) The school, for majority children (e.g. minority language teaching for majority children).

(3) The school, for the benefit of both minority and majority children.

(4) The individual minority child (i.e. give individual help, e.g. to get qualifications to obtain jobs).

Which of these views do you think Quinn would agree with? Give evidence from the article.

(iv) Which do you agree with? Give the reasons for your choice.

Task 4

Community language learners and their needs may vary considerably.

(i) Look at the groups below.

(1) Children in their first year of infant school speaking a wide variety of languages and using the spoken, dialect form of their language rather than the written, standard form.

(2) Children in the primary school speaking a wide variety of dialects, but wanting to read and write the standard form of their language.

(3) Secondary school speakers of a community language wanting to take a formal examination in their language.

(4) Secondary school speakers of the majority language wanting to take a formal examination in a community language.

(5) Adults speaking a community language but unable to read or write it.

(6) Adults from the majority culture wanting to learn a community language for professional purposes (e.g. police, teachers, social workers).

Assume for the purposes of this task that the majority culture is English-speaking. (You could take Australia, New Zealand, or England as an example.) Try to isolate the language needs and wants of each group. See what sort of materials might satisfy these needs and wants, then consider whether there might be constraints on the teaching (e.g. financial, administrative, etc.).

Group	Needs/Wants	Materials	Constraints
1			
2			
3			
4			
5			
6			

(ii) Do the materials derived from this analysis differ from the sorts of materials that Quinn recommends?

Task 5

Cazden (1986) shows how ESL schoolchildren, especially those at secondary level, can be faced with a number of learning difficulties that result from their being taught by several different teachers, each teaching his/her own subject (history, geography, science, and so on). (Difficulties of this sort are faced by majority-language children as well, of course, though it could be argued that the problems will be accentuated if your home language is a different language from your school language.) Cazden talks of:

(a) Different demands for language use.
(b) Different patterns of teacher–pupil talk.
(c) The same concepts and skills being taught in different subjects.

Cazden suggests the learning difficulties created by (a), (b), (c), above, might be reduced if, within the same institution, teachers of English as a second language, teachers of English as a first language, and subject teachers worked together in some way.

(i) Have you any feasible suggestions as to how such co-operation might be fostered and what the result might be in terms of materials and methodologies for the minority language speakers?
(ii) What barriers to co-operation would need to be overcome, and how might this be done? (See the Horvath article for possible strategies.)

Task 6

Community language speakers may come from a culture which is very different from the majority language culture. An extreme example is reported in Christie (1985) who describes the situation of Aboriginal children in Australia being educated in Australian schools. Such children, Christie suggests, come from a tradition of informal education which is community-based and which does not involve the intervention of a figure like the teacher found in formal classroom learning.

Some of the differences between formal and informal learning environments are listed below.

Formal	**Informal**
(1) Learning based on verbal instruction	Learning based on observation and imitation. Personal trial and error important
(2) Classroom (i.e. contrived) situation	Based on real-life experience
(3) Process important, with teacher providing assessment	End product important, with completion of task proof of success
(4) Artificial motivation. Goals set by teacher	Activities provide the motivation. Goals explicit in the task

(i) Leaving the classroom aside for the moment, can you think of any ordinary, everyday skills you have acquired, or knowledge you have gained, through the informal mode: Did the informal mode have any advantages? Could you have acquired the skills/knowledge more efficiently through formal learning?
(ii) What sorts of problem might a teacher have to face when teaching children who are not used to learning in a formal environment?
(iii) Do you have any suggestions for ways of overcoming such problems?

Chapter 11

The Issue of the Language of Instruction in the Lower Forms of Hong Kong Secondary Schools

JOHN GIBBONS

Editor's introduction

Gibbons' article on Hong Kong provides an illustration of many aspects of Tollefson's LP model presented in Chapter 3. The author describes the language situation in Hong Kong, the formulation of language policy in education and its implementation in schools. He shows that a view of planning as a smooth sequence of events with each level implementing the policy decisions of the level above it is probably an ideal, and that the top-down variety of planning needs to take seriously the feelings and wishes of those most directly affected by policy implementation if it is to succeed (see Olshtain Chapter 5). Gibbons shows how the language situation and the economic opportunities it reflects, government language policy in education, and parental concerns combine to produce a complex situation of potential conflict between the various interested parties. English in Hong Kong can be characterized (using Judd's terms, see Chapter 4), both as an 'external' language of wider communication and an 'internal' additional language used between Chinese- and non-Chinese-speaking groups (the latter mainly Westerners working in Hong Kong) to a large extent in business and occupational contexts. English has high status and the main motivation to learn it is economic and social advancement. The government, concerned that English-medium education places too great a learning burden on pupils, has tried to promote the use of Chinese as a medium of instruction in schools. This policy appears to have succeeded at primary level, but plans to extend Chinese-medium education to the first three years of secondary school have met with resistance from parents who believe that such a move would adversely affect their children's career prospects. The government has been forced, therefore, to leave the decision to individual schools, in effect to market forces. The result has been an increase in the number of English-medium schools and a corresponding decrease in Chinese-medium schools. However, Gibbons goes on to demonstrate how necessary it is (see Serpell Chapter 9) to look at the effect that the implementation of such policies has in classrooms. He finds that the so-called English-medium schools do not, in fact, use English consistently but tend to switch from Chinese to English, depending on whether the children are doing oral or written work and on what skills are involved. Thus, though reading texts are in English, much explanation is conducted in Chinese and the texts are heavily annotated in Chinese by pupils, raising the question of whether the students are in fact improving their reading comprehension. In other words, teachers and pupils adopt their own covert language policy, which may conflict with the intentions of the official policy, to suit their own circumstances and needs. The article ends with a consideration of the policy options open to the government in these circumstances and with suggestions for strategies which could be adopted in order to ensure successful policy implementation, reminding us how necessary it is for planners to have some knowledge of innovation theory (see Horvath Chapter 6).

Introduction

SINCE HONG KONG is a small (approximately 1050 square-kilometre) territory on the coast of southern China, it is hardly surprising that its population is largely ethnic

Chinese, even though it is administered by Britain. The 1971 census revealed that in a population of around four million at that time (probably five million now) approximately 1 per cent consisted of Westerners, 0.5 per cent of non-Chinese Asians, and around 98 per cent were ethnic Chinese. Hence, Hong Kong is ethnically highly homogeneous, far more so than most British cities. It is the education of the Chinese majority that will be discussed here.

Over the period since the Second World War, Hong Kong has been transformed from a rather sleepy colonial backwater into a dynamic and economically successful centre for commerce and industry. This change has been mirrored in government attitudes and in the education system. From condescending, colonialist and essentially racist assumptions in the provision of education and in government policy in general in the pre-war era (see Fu (1979) for a well documented description) there has been a move to more power sharing with the local Chinese elite, and a steady growth in educational provision. The fiercely competitive nature of Hong Kong's capitalist society is also mirrored in an education system that lays great emphasis on success in examinations.

This paper will attempt to give an overview of an issue which is currently much debated in Hong Kong, namely the language through which education should take place. This is, in fact, an issue which has been controversial on numerous occasions since the turn of the century (Fu 1979) when two separate education streams became established, comprising English-medium and Chinese-medium schools. These two types of school are referred to by the government Education Department in Hong Kong as 'Anglo-Chinese Secondary Schools' (English medium apart from the subjects Chinese and Chinese History) and 'Chinese middle schools' (Chinese medium apart from lessons in the subject English). This separation by language of instruction is defined in the 1973-74 Hong Kong Education Department's Annual Survey (pp. 3-4) as follows:

> *Anglo-Chinese secondary schools.* Instruction is in the medium of English and a wide range of academic subjects is taught in the five-year course from Form 1 to Form 5.
> The study of Chinese as an academic subject is also important in these schools, a few of which also offer the study of a second European or Asian language...
> *Chinese middle schools.* These schools offer their pupils the same kind of general academic education as the Anglo-Chinese, and English is taught as a second language.

Students from the two types of school take their Certificate of Education examinations in English and Chinese respectively. Many secondary schools also have Chinese names that reflect a commitment to English or Chinese as a medium of instruction, indeed the Chinese translation of 'Anglo-Chinese' refers specifically to the English language. Simplifying slightly, in practice 'Chinese' consists of Cantonese speech (Cantonese is the indigenous spoken variety of Chinese) and written Chinese (using characters: variants of these are found in nearly all Chinese communities). The terms 'Chinese', 'Cantonese', and 'written Chinese' will be used in these senses in the rest of this paper.

Language in Hong Kong society

Chinese recently joined English as the other official language of Hong Kong. Within the Chinese community the spoken language is usually Cantonese or a semi-systematic mixture of English and Cantonese in which Cantonese is dominant (see Gibbons 1979).

However, for many official purposes, and also for reasons of prestige or familiarity, a substantial proportion of written communication takes place in English; a recent British Council survey of the use of English in Hong Kong gave a (possibly exaggerated) figure of 30 per cent of written communication at work in English, for example. Communication with Westerners is normally, of necessity, in English, since few are willing or able to expend the large amount of time and effort necessary to master Chinese.

English is the main international language of the following activities, which are the principal ways in which Hong Kong makes a living; the export and re-export of manufactured goods; commerce; banking and insurance; aviation; shipping (Hong Kong is a major port, and ranks third in the world for ownership of vessels); tourism (many visitors speak English as a first or second language). Furthermore, English is the internal language of official communication in the civil service and in many companies. The importance of English to Hong Kong's economy is continually referred to in government statements about the medium of instruction and there appears to be some justification for this.

In this situation, it is hardly surprising that a good command of the English language is regarded as crucial to personal economic and social advancement, even though Chinese rarely speak the language among themselves. Moreover, Hong Kong's colonial past and present, and the desire of the Chinese community to retain its identity combine to make the learning of English a demanding requirement for a successful career rather than a pleasurable exploration of another culture for most young Chinese – Lyczak, Fu and Ho (1976) give evidence of this from a matched guise experiment.

Government policy

Although not entirely consistent, there has been a distinct trend in government policy in the post-war years towards the promotion of Chinese as the language of instruction in the first three years of secondary education. (This would provide continuity from the primary level, where more than 90 per cent of children receive their education through the medium of Chinese.) In the sixties the government established the Marsh Sampson Education Commission, which in 1963 reported:

> English as a medium of instruction imposes a great burden on pupils. With the establishment of a Chinese University of Hong Kong consideration should be given to the proportion of children placed in schools where the medium of instruction is English with a view to increasing the number of Chinese schools where English is taught as a second language.

In other words, the Commission wished to see a growth in the proportion of Chinese-medium schools. I also saw the decision as a clear cut one between supporting an English-medium sector and a Chinese-medium sector, rather than suggesting any compromise mixing of media in schools.

These recommendations were rejected in the 1965 Education White Paper, owing in large part to parental pressure, which derived in turn from the economic value of English; as the White Paper (p.83) expresses this:

> in face of marked parental preference for Anglo-Chinese education, the fact is that English language is an important medium of international communication and that a knowledge of it has undoubted commercial value in Hong Kong.

This scenario was repeated ten years later, when the Education Green Paper of 1973, *Report of the Board of Education on the proposed expansion of secondary education over the next decade*, made proposals concerning the provision for the first time of universal secondary education in forms 1–3 (up to 15 years of age approximately). Among the proposals was the adoption of Chinese as the medium of instruction in the lower forms of secondary schools:

> The medium of instruction bears significantly upon the quality of education offered at post-primary level. Pupils coming from primary schools where they have been taught in the medium of Cantonese have a grievous burden put on them when required to absorb new subjects through the medium of English. We recommend that Chinese become the usual language of instruction in the lower forms of secondary schools, and that English should be studied as the second language. [p.6 para.16.]

The proposal once more met with strong opposition, and again the government backed down. The Education White Paper of 1974, *Secondary education in Hong Kong over the next decade,* again cited the commercial value of English and parental wishes as reasons for not imposing Chinese medium instruction:

Language of instruction
2.16 In the past secondary education has been conducted mainly through the medium of English. Now that it is intended to make secondary education in Forms 1–3 available to all, it is appropriate to review this practice. On educational grounds there are strong arguments for maintaining that the medium of instruction for children aged 12–14 should be Chinese. However, there are other considerations. Hong Kong is a commercial and industrial centre which has reached a high level of technical and professional sophistication and has established close contacts all over the world. It is undeniable that Hong Kong, if it is to maintain its progress, will continue to need people at all levels in commerce, industry and the professions who are at home in English as well as in Chinese. For these practical reasons, the standards of Chinese and English must be maintained, and indeed, if possible, improved, and parents are likely to demand that they should be. These considerations suggest the need for a balanced approach.
    2.17 It is the Government's intention that individual school authorities should themselves decide whether the medium of instruction should be English or Chinese for any particular subject in junior secondary forms.

Schools were, therefore, left free to select their language of instruction, and the rolls of Chinese language schools continued to decline. Parents were voting for English-medium education by not sending their children to Chinese-medium schools. To remain viable some Chinese-medium schools changed to English-medium, and many schools opening in Hong Kong new towns were officially English-medium schools. The trend away from Chinese-medium instruction can be seen clearly in the figures from Education Department sources (Table 11.1).
    Why have parents acted in this way, and what attitudes and beliefs underlie this pressure for English medium instruction?

Attitudes in the community

The British Council *Survey of Use of English in Hong Kong* provides some valuable pointers to the reasons for parental preference for English language education. In a fairly representative sample of 3784 subjects, the relationship, shown in Table 11.2, was

TABLE 11.1

Percentage of day pupils in two types of school expressed as a percentage of joint total enrolment

Year	Chinese middle schools Chinese medium	Anglo-Chinese schools English medium
1960	42.1	57.9
1965	29.0	71.0
1970	23.3	76.7
1975	21.3	78.7
1980	12.3	87.7

TABLE 11.2

Proficiency in English expressed as percentages of income band total

Monthly income	Proficiency in English				
	None	Poor	Adequate	Good	Excellent
below HK$500	53.3	22.4	17.3	6.8	0.8
HK$501–1000	52.0	24.7	17.7	5.8	0.6
HK$1001–2000	30.6	22.0	24.0	22.2	1.8
HK$20011–3000	5.4	8.5	31.0	47.3	10.0
HK$3001–4000	2.9	2.8	14.0	54.3	25.7
HK$4001–5000	10.5	5.3	15.8	31.6	36.8
HK$5000 plus	9.4	6.2	9.4	31.2	46.9

Note: 63% of those respondents in the 'below HK$500' band indicating adequate or above levels of English were full-time students.

found between proficiency in English and income.

The correlation between income and proficiency in English is clear. People in the Hong Kong community are well aware of this. In the survey, the 42.8 per cent of the sample who wished to improve their English gave the following reasons:

55.7 per cent more money better prospects
14.7 per cent to be better informed
 9.0 per cent to be enabled to study work abroad
21.1 per cent other reasons.

The following figures represent the degree of importance given by parents to the learning of English by their children:

26.6 per cent essential
37.1 per cent very important
24.5 per cent relatively important
 4.3 per cent slightly important
 2.1 per cent irrelevant
 5.4 per cent don't know

English is, therefore, considered (probably correctly) by the great majority of parents to be economically important, and most wish their children to learn it.

It is widely accepted in Hong Kong that an important factor in parental demand for English-medium education is the better standard of English that this sector is assumed to provide. For example, the *Fourth report* of the Chinese Language Committee (p.6) states:

graduates from Anglo-Chinese (English-medium) schools have a standard of English which is generally higher than that of their Chinese Middle school counterparts, while the reverse is true of standards in Chinese.

Recent Education Department figures show that it is the parental demand for English-medium education for their children that has led to the decline in the provision of Chinese-language instruction; parental demand has been below the actual provision of places in Chinese-medium schools (Table 11.3).

TABLE 11.3
Percentage of primary school leavers with Chinese-medium schools as first choice

Year	Percentage
1978	8.1
1979	6.7
1980	6.1

This situation is not recent. Among the population sampled by Etherton, Ong and Lee in 1974, 46 per cent of the parents who had children in Chinese-medium schools would have perferred English-medium schools.

There are, however, two important but unproven premises in the parents' reasons for preferring English-medium instruction. Namely, that their children are capable of receiving instruction through the medium of English (see following section), and that there is a necessary link between English-medium education and acquisition of English. It is an unfortunate fact that the English of many Hong Kong secondary school teachers is not of native-speaker standard; it is questionable whether regular contact with imperfect spoken and written English will improve pupils' English.

To summarize therefore, we have a somewhat paradoxical situation in which the British colonial government presses for the use of Chinese as the language of instruction, but is strongly resisted by the local Chinese community, which insists on English! Although this is the reverse of conventional expectations the situation is far from unprecedented (Pride 1978).

Problems in the use of English as the medium of instruction

There have been a number of studies of the comparative effectiveness of English and Chinese as languages of instruction in Hong Kong (Siu et al. 1979, Poon 1978, Cheung 1974). Although all have imperfections, their cumulative evidence is that Chinese (or predominantly Chinese) is the more effective medium of instruction, for the simple reason that, by and large, Chinese children understand it better (see also Tam 1980, fig 5). In fact, in many cases the English of children entering secondary school is grossly inadequate for receiving instruction in that language: 'after about 800 hours given over to English in the primary school curriculum, most pupils enter secondary school with no more than the most rudimentary competence in English, and many without even this' (Tongue and Gibbons, 1982:61). The cumulative evidence from the three studies mentioned above (see particularly Siu et al. 1979:131) also indicates that the lower a child's academic ability, the more problems are caused by use of the English medium – hardly a surprising finding. In the past, when entry to secondary school was selective, the difficulties resulting from English-medium instruction were less severe: with the recent introduction of universal secondary education in forms 1–3 of secondary schools, the English medium is virtually unusable with many children.

Kvan (1969:334) also presents evidence that the switch to second language instruction just before the onset of puberty may adversely affect creativity; describing research findings, he writes:

> it seems clear that the students who had used Chinese as a medium of instruction but had studied English as a subject, were showing greater originality of thought and greater maturity in general than those who had used English as a medium.

He also comments even more tellingly:

> it does seem likely that this sudden reduction of the possibilities for expression would cause a neurosis fully as severe as the one we find in children backward in reading and writing.

So the use of English as the language of instruction appears to be both educationally and psychologically undesirable for most pupils, even though their parents favour it so strongly for pragmatic reasons.

Realities in the school system

Although the Hong Kong school system is divided into streams which theoretically use either English or Chinese as a medium of instruction, the reality is of course, far more complex. At one pole there are traditional Chinese-language schools where all materials and classes are in Chinese. At the other pole there is a small number of elite English-medium schools (taking many of their students from elite feeder schools) where English genuinely is the medium of instruction. Between these poles lie the great majority of Hong Kong secondary schools. Looking first at ostensibly Chinese-medium schools, we find that in some nowadays a significant proportion of the reading material is in English, since English language textbooks are often regarded as superior to the counterparts available in Chinese. Furthermore, in the speech of some teachers certain technical terms of the subject area will be in English, partly because the teacher is often more familiar with English technical terms, having himself been educated in English, and partly because the textbook is in English. The spoken language, therefore, can be predominantly Cantonese with some English admixture (I have observed lessons of this type in Chinese-medium schools). So, in some Chinese-medium schools *speech* is a mixture, *reading* can be in both English and Chinese, and *student writing* will normally be in Chinese.

The English-medium schools are having to cope with a difficult situation. Parents are insisting on English-medium schooling, while at the same time it is virtually impossible for their children to understand English-medium instruction. Faced with the fact that the education of the children must proceed, many schools call themselves 'Anglo-Chinese', but teachers in fact mix Chinese and English instruction: Tam's (1980) survey into the medium of instruction actually used in these schools makes it clear that various types of mixture of English and Chinese are the most common media. In the writer's experience, while there exists a confusing variety of mixtures, there is, typically, a steady progression through the school towards the increased use of English. For example, in the early forms the normal spoken language is the predominantly Cantonese mixture mentioned in the second section of this chapter. Later on, there is code-switching between this mixture and pure English. To some extent then, Chinese as a spoken medium of instruction is already dominant at lower form level. By upper form level there is far less Chinese, and English is in most schools the major spoken language of instruction. Writing in most English-medium schools is done in a form of pidginised English which slowly approximates towards standard English. As far as reading material is concerned, this is nearly all in English (apart from Chinese and Chinese History lessons) – however, in forms 1 and 2 it is often heavily annotated by students in Chinese, to the point of being virtually bilingual; teachers also often interpret the textbook into Cantonese during the lesson Siu et al (1975:5). The reasons for the dominance of English-language textbooks, even in some Chinese-medium schools, are complex. Schools which accept the title 'Anglo-Chinese' may possibly feel under an obligation to use English-language textbooks, especially since their students sit examinations set in English. As such schools comprise nearly 90 per cent of the textbook market, there is more investment by publishers in English-language books, and a consequent improvement in both the quality and range of textbooks available in English to the detriment of those written in Chinese; thus the situation perpetuates and reinforces itself.

It can thus be seen that excessively polarised stances on the medium of instruction issue are misleading. Although not identical, many English-medium and Chinese-medium schools are at fairly close points along a continuum in their medium of instruction. While student writing is in English and Chinese respectively, reading and speech may use both languages in both types of school.

Principles and possibilities

To recapitulate briefly, therefore, the Hong Kong school system has, in principle, two alternative media of instruction, English or Chinese. Schools join one sector or the other, and thereby make public which of the media they have opted for (this is often also given in the Chinese name of the school). Nevertheless, in practice, as we have seen, most schools mix the languages of instruction in some way. Parental pressure often forces schools to become part of the English-medium sector, while the realities of the teaching situation compel teachers to use some Chinese. This compromise is clearly unprincipled, in that many schools are not using their ostensible medium of instruction. It is, however, a practical solution to an anomaly left by the 1974 White Paper: schools were left divided into Chinese-medium and English-medium types (and in the minds of many members of the community probably remain so); but the wording of the Paper made it clear that schools could adopt whatever medium they felt was appropriate to the circumstances.

The most obvious way out of this dilemma is for the government to impose Chinese as the medium of instruction in forms 1–3 of all secondary schools. Although this might lead to a fall in the standard of English in some schools, it would have the following advantages:

(1) It would remove the almost insurmountable obstacle to education that a second-language medium places in the path of low ability children.
(2) It would make education more efficient for the great majority of pupils, as on the available evidence Chinese is the more effective medium of instruction.

(3) It would avoid the shock of a transition to a language of instruction that many children poorly understand.

(4) It would leave open the option of a switch at fourth form level to *genuine* English-medium instruction with a selected group that had been adequately prepared within the school, possibly by a transition stage; by the end of the fifth form, given reasonable help, the English standard of this group might not be much inferior to that of many present students who have studied ostensibly through the medium of English since the first form.

(5) It might help to establish more firmly both the Chinese identity of Hong Kong children (see Luk 1979) and their Chinese language (possibly adversely affected by English-medium instruction – (Siu et al. 1979:131)).

(6) It would probably lead to improvements in learning materials written in Chinese (particularly textbooks) because of a greatly expanded market, and also because a most influential sector of the community would have a stake in them.

There is, in fact, a considerable consensus within the Schools of Education of the two universities in Hong Kong, and in the upper echelons of the government Education Department, that the Chinese language should play a much larger role as a medium of instruction. There are, however, certain very important practical and political difficulties in the introduction of universal Chinese-medium instruction in the lower forms of secondary schools.

Earlier parts of this paper document both the strong parental preference for English-medium schools and possible reasons for this. Any government would obviously be reluctant to override the wishes of the majority of its citizens on an issue of such immediate relevance to so many of them. In the second place, there are a few elite schools which make successful use of English as a true medium of instruction. Their success derives in part from the nature of their intake, which includes many children of above average academic ability, and children from the exceptional middle-class homes where English is found (e.g. parents watch English language television). These schools have educated many of Hong Kong's powerful and prestigious Chinese elite. Any attempts to impose Chinese-medium instruction in the early forms of these schools would run into three problems. First, the government may not have the authority to impose policy on all these schools, since some of them are independent in varying degrees; second , it would be trading proven success in one sector for possible but unverified improvement in other sectors, and governments are traditionally very reluctant to tamper with proven success in such circumstances; finally, the powerful group who have graduated from these schools and normally wish to send their children to them would be outraged at this interference in their children's education, and would probably be able to block any such change, as they helped to do in 1964 and 1974.

A second alternative is to leave this small number of elite-schools alone and impose the Chinese-medium on the remainder. This would be undesirable for two reasons. It would create, in the public mind at least, a system of first class schools and second class schools. Second, as a consequence there would almost certainly be even more ferocious competition for admission to such schools and their feeder schools (two hours of homework every night and private classes after school and at week-ends are already the experience of many ten-year-olds).

The most principled and educationally desirable alternative in the medium of instruction therefore appears to be closed for practical and political reasons. What possibilities exist, therefore? One is to attempt to change the attitudes of parents (and employers) towards Chinese-medium education. They will need to be convinced that children attending Chinese-medium schools can attain a good standard of English, and that other subjects can be learnt better through Chinese than through English. This will require a determined positive effort to foster and improve existing Chinese-medium schools, and in particular upgrade the standard of English teaching in them.

A second alternative is to acknowledge the current reality that much education takes place in both languages and attempt to improve the effectiveness with which this is done. This may require making it publicly known that many Anglo-Chinese schools cannot and do not use English as the sole language of instruction, so that parents are prepared for any changes in the curriculum. As we have noted, it is common to find in Anglo-Chinese schools a disjunction between the (English) written materials and (predominantly Cantonese) speech; this is probably to some extent a pragmatic compromise between parental demands for English and effective classroom communication – there is little evidence that it is sound educational practice. There will be a need for further work along the lines of Tam's (1980) pioneering investigations into the effectiveness of various mixes of languages of instruction. A possible outcome may be the development of genuinely bilingual learning material, and bilingual learning and teaching strategies. There will certainly have to be a frank dialogue with parents, and careful evaluation before we can say with any certainty that the current blend of languages in much of Hong Kong's secondary education is the best available in the circumstances.

Tasks

Task 1

Kwo (1987) has suggested a number of possible models for secondary level bilingual education in Hong Kong. They are listed below.

Model (1)

(a) From secondary 1–3, all subjects other than English would be taught in Chinese.
(b) From secondary 4 onwards, all subjects other than Chinese and Chinese history would be taught in English.

Model (2)

(a) Different streams among and within individual schools.

 (i) Chinese-medium education: all subjects except English would be taught in Chinese.
(ii) English-medium: all subjects except Chinese would be taught in English.

(b) English language tests used to allocate students to either stream.
(c) A bridging English language programme is offered at secondary 1 to prepare students who are likely to reach adequate levels to enter the English stream.

Model (3)

   (a) In secondary 1 all subjects other than English would be taught in Chinese. From secondary 2 onwards there would be a gradual shift to English.

   (b) The school principal would decide which subjects should move to English first, taking into account the demands of the subject and competence of teachers' and students' English.

Model (4)

   (a) The majority of subjects would be taught in Chinese from secondary 1–3. A few would be taught in English.

   (b) Schools deciding which subjects should be in English to take account of nature of subject and level of English of students and teachers.

Model (5)

   (a) Continued existence of three types of education; English-medium, Chinese-medium, and mixing approach in Anglo-Chinese schools.

   (b) All subjects for university entrance (other than language-specific ones) to be examined in both English and Chinese.

   (c) Entrants to English-medium schools would have to pass test in English.

   (d) Those not wishing to enter Chinese-medium schools, but who are not ready for English-medium, to be offered a bilingual programme from secondary 1–3, preparing students for a switch to English-medium at secondary 4 (subject to a test pass in English.) Accordingly:

      (i) Bilingual textbooks would be developed.

      (ii) Teachers would be trained in bilingual education.

   (i) Using the information about Hong Kong supplied in the Gibbons article, your own knowledge of different situations and the information from other articles in this collection, fill in on the table below:

      (1) The disadvantages of each model.

      (2) The advantages of each.

      (3) The resources (physical and human) required to implement each.

Model	Disadvantages	Advantages	Resources
1			
2			
3			
4			
5			

   (ii) In the light of your notes, which model would you choose as the one to implement? (You may of course design an additional model of your own.)

Task 2

Anglo-Chinese schools in Hong Kong are supposed to be English-medium. However, Tam's research (1980), based on questionnaires given to students, showed that in practice a mix of Chinese and English was used. Tam's survey into student preferences in the lower forms of Anglo-Chinese secondary schools showed that with reference to all subjects not just English:

(a) Students would like to see more Chinese used in teaching and in the textbooks.
(b) They did not favour an entirely English-medium or entirely Chinese-medium classroom.
(c) There were differences in attitudes between groups (boys and girls for example) and between schools.

 (i) One decision that could be taken as a result of Tam's survey might be to use bilingual (Chinese/English) subject textbooks in the classroom, rather than monolingual (English) ones. Can you think of different ways in which the two languages might be used in new bilingual textbooks? What might you need to investigate further before designing them?
(ii) The students also wanted more Chinese used in the classroom. Again, what might you need to find out about the classroom before you decided how to do this? What sorts of strategies could you use you use to encourage the use of Chinese? Would you leave it to the teacher or try to lay down a rigorous policy?
(iii) What might have led to the differences Tam found between schools and between individuals? Do these differences have any implications for language policy in the schools?

For more information on the complex linguistic situation in Hong Kong see Gibbons (1987).

Task 3

Williams and Dallas (1984), analysing English-medium social studies textbooks designed for use in Hong Kong secondary schools, found they presented considerable comprehension problems for pupils who had to read them. Some of the problems identified were as follows:

(a) Unknown vocabulary contained in definitions, making the definition as difficult to understand as the word it was attempting to explain.
(b) Idiomatic expressions in reading texts (e.g. 'working off steam'; 'cut across country').
(c) Words in reading passages having the same form but several potential meanings (homonyms) (e.g. 'if the staircases are *blocked* with *goods*, the owners must put the matter *right*').
(d) Difficult vocabulary contained in quoted or source material (e.g. from newspapers: items such as 'unique', 'upsurge').

 (i) Have learners you have taught experienced similar problems with vocabulary? Can you give any examples either from the four categories of problems above or from further categories that you would like to suggest?
(ii) Such vocabulary problems can be tackled in a number of ways, either by the textbook writer or by the teacher who has to teach from such difficult texts. Bearing in mind the problems listed in (a)–(d) above, and your answer to (i), what advice would you give to:

  (1) A textbook writer who was about to write a secondary-level subject textbook (say, social studies, history) in English for learners for whom English was a second language, but who had little knowledge of the problems of learning a subject through the medium of English as a second/foreign language:

    (2) An English-medium subject teacher (whose second language was English) who had no knowledge of the techniques of ESL/EFL teaching but who had to teach learners for whom English was their second language?

Ways of trying to improve the readability of subject texts for ESL learners are discussed in Williams and Dallas (1984).

Task 4

Elley (1984) in a different situation (Fiji), but also talking of problems in English-medium education, suggested that a greater emphasis should be given to reading skills in the English classroom. Do you think this might be a possible course of action in Hong Kong? Give your reasons.

Task 5

Gibbons indicates that the attitude of the community towards English, (especially parental attitude) has been an important factor in the government's lack of success in promoting Chinese-medium education. What strategies might the government adopt if it wished to convince parents of its reasons for encouraging Chinese-medium education? (See Horvath Chapter 6 for different types of strategy.)

Task 6

Sometimes, in English-medium institutions, the demands made on pupils in an English language lesson are very different from those made on them when other subjects are being taught through the medium of English.

    (i) Look at the two sets of questions below. The first set are comprehension questions on a text about the life of Mohammed to be taught in an English language class. The second set is taken from a social studies textbook and refers to a text about the history of Fiji. Both sets are for the same group of pupils learning English and other subjects in an English-medium secondary school. English is a second language to the learners and all use a different local language at home.

        (1) English language textbook questions.

> *What two things are we told about Mohammed's wife?*
> *What didn't Mohammed like about his people?*
> *What happened when Mohammed began to talk to the people about the new religion?*

        (2) Social studies textbook questions.

> Fill in the details in Table 11.4
> Which group of Europeans had the greatest effect at the time of their coming?
> Which group do you think had the greatest long-term effect?

To answer the two sets of questions, pupils have to read the text about Mohammed and the text about the history of Fiji. When we read in real life we often have a purpose, and we have an objective or outcome in view. To achieve our objective, it may be sufficient to extract different bits of information from a text, but we will often need to relate the different bits to one another, and then we may need to evaluate the information and perhaps match it with other knowledge we already possess. Go back to the sets of

TABLE 11.4
Early European contact

Europeans	Dates	Names, ships, etc.	Why they came	Influence on Fijian life
SANDALWOOD TRADERS				
BEACHCOMBERS				
MISSIONARIES				
PLANTERS				

questions (a) and (b) and try to work out which set appears to offer a better training for 'real-life' reading outside the classroom, as described above. This is a little difficult to do without the texts to which the questions refer, but it should be possible. Try to provide evidence for your decision.

(ii) The two different sets of questions, (1) and (2), are fairly representative of the general content of the books. You probably discovered when you answered (i) that the questions from the English language textbook and those from the social studies textbook demanded different types of reading skills from the pupil, and that the social studies questions provided a better training for 'real-life' reading. What implications might this information have for English language textbook writers and English language teachers in this situation?

(iii) Try to obtain copies of books designed to teach English language and other subjects, like social studies and science, in an English-medium situation. See if you can find further examples of mismatches between the two sorts of textbooks (e.g. you could look at types of texts, topics, vocabulary, grammar, cognitive level of the texts).

A good source of ideas for integrating language work and content subjects like science and history is Morris and Stewart-Dore (1984). See also Davies and Greene (1984).

Chapter 12

Understanding One Another's Englishes

GERRY ABBOTT

Editor's introduction

In the previous article we saw that what actually happens in the classroom may be rather different from the formally planned policy. Many different parties are involved – planners, teachers, pupils, pupils' parents and employers – each with their own view of the problems and their own interests. A compromise has to be reached that takes into account what is feasible and what is in the pupil's interest. Tension between interested parties often arises when the subject of New Englishes is discussed and in particular the question of their use and role in education. As Abbott points out, New Englishes are often advocated by those not directly involved in the classroom, while the teachers themselves may take a more cautious view. Previous articles (Emenyonu on Nigeria; Serpell on Zambia) have shown how, when English is used as an additional language for national inter-group communication, varieties emerge specific to the nations concerned. Known collectively as New Englishes, these varieties are different phonologically, grammatically and lexically from the original external model of Standard British English introduced during colonial times, and now serve as markers of national identity for the users. We know that all speakers will vary their manner of speaking and writing to fit the circumstances of any particular speech event and Abbott makes the point that the users of the New Englishes are no exception. We should not, therefore, imagine that these varieties are uniform, but recognize that they comprise a wide range of styles, registers, forms and sounds. The question addressed in the article is whether the formal end of this continuum or an external British or American standard should be the target for educational use. Abbott believes the tendency is for the New Englishes to draw further apart both from the external standard and from each other, that this process may be accelerated if the standard form of a New English is officially sanctioned as a target, and that mutual intelligibility between and within countries using English as a lingua franca may well be lost as a consequence. On the other hand he recognizes that an external standard is far removed from pupils' needs, that it is perhaps not a feasible objective and that local teachers, themselves users of New Englishes, cannot be expected to imitate models based on external norms. Abbott's solution is similar to that of Serpell and Emenyonu, namely, to use both national and international varieties in the classroom according to the different purposes and circumstances of classroom communication and pedagogy. Thus, the formal mode of the New English would be the accepted standard for classroom interaction between teacher and pupil, but in the course of an English language lesson, pupils would be introduced to different varieties and styles and shown which forms of English were appropriate for both intra- and inter-national communication. These proposals are some way from implementation – much more descriptive work needs to be done on the New Englishes and decisions taken as to what an appropriate standard might be – but they should be useful in sensitizing examining boards (and others) to the issues which need to be considered before an educational policy can be devised.

COMPLEX PROBLEMS ARISE in multilingual countries where English is a second language used as the medium of all or some national education and often for other national purposes too. Each territory of this sort has developed its own variety of English; these varieties have been called 'New Englishes' (for brevity below, NE). The teacher is usually well aware of the differences between his NE and the sort of English that he hears when listening to the BBC World Service or expatriate Britons. He himself is usually unable to produce anything other than the local NE, which will comprise a formal mode, suitable for cross-cultural use, and an informal 'off-duty' dialect, often with its own phonology, vocabulary, grammar, and discourse features. Probably everyone draws on such a dialect range when using the mother tongue (MT), and a similar range usually exists in the NE. The segment of the range chosen for use will depend on who is talking to whom, on what occasion, and for what purpose.

Go to a classroom in an English-medium school, listen to science and social science teachers, for example, talking to their students during a lesson for the purpose of explaining a point, or questioning the class, or maintaining discipline: they are operating fairly near the formal end of their NE. The English teacher performing the same functions is using the same NE – except when quoting from the textbook or other lesson material! There are lexical and grammatical discrepancies between the two Englishes. Educational policy makers are confronted with a choice: should the target language be an external model, such as standard British English, or should it be the educated, fairly formal range of the NE? The decisions of the politicians will, of course, have an impact on the work of the syllabus makers, the textbook writers, the examiners . . . and the teachers and learners.

In countries where English is a second language most teachers of English do not claim to speak anything other than local NE; one would, therefore, expect them unhesitatingly to favour the NE as the target language. Yet, although socio-linguists, educators and other non-teachers press for the adoption of the NE, many teachers remain uneasy. It may be that they share my misgivings, the first of which is the apparent lack of historical perspective shown by many of the non-teachers referred to above.

In areas where English has been, and still is being, used as a medium of instruction in schools and tertiary education, there were until quite recently numerous expatriates working as teachers, headmasters, inspectors, and so on. Working alongside them was a much larger corps of 'locals', who in their turn had been educated largely by expatriates working to the standard British English model. That sort of situation existed in the Anglophone regions of Africa and SE Asia, for example, up to the sixties, since when national independence has brought with it the need to recognize the existence of various African and Asian Englishes. It is well known that the features of an NE, especially its phonology, are influenced by the MT. We can therefore regard the NE as a sort of communal 'interlanguage' somewhere between the target language (TL) and the MT. For example:

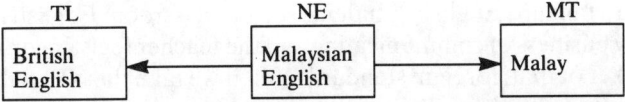

Furthermore, we know that in the historical context outlined above the difference between the TL and NE did not preclude communication between two parties, one of whom was using the TL and the other the NE (British English and Malaysian English, taking the example above). It may well be precisely because of the recency of such contacts that the NE is intelligible beyond the national boundary. Perhaps it was the tension – the striving towards an internationally intelligible dialect – which established the working approximations which have gained status as new Englishes. Take the tension away, by making the NE the TL, and the pull exerted by the MT may well increase, drawing the NE further and further away from the parent English and thereby restricting its range of intelligibility.

Some may argue that this will not necessarily happen and that command of a standard NE is a more attainable goal; and that if one is aiming at something reasonably easy one does not fall short of one's goal. Gross examples can be put forward to support this argument: a marksman six feet from a six-foot bull's eye is going to be on target every time he shoots. But, given the delicate 'dialect range' available to both teacher and student, I believe there will be an inevitable tendency to accept whatever communicates in the classroom and that, since the communication is between locals, the tendency will be to use an ever more localized dialect. After all, teachers of all subjects know the difference between expectations and results: no student is *expected* to get 100 per cent in *any* subject; just as we do not *expect* to be morally *perfect,* however hard we may try.

Still, the next question must be: Does it *matter* if these Englishes draw further and further apart from British English and (perhaps more seriously) from each other? This is for the politicians to decide. It is they who decree whether English is to be studied and, if so, for what purposes. If they want English taught solely for national purposes, then the national English can be so different from any other English as to be unintelligible outside the national borders, yet still fulfil its purpose. However, most national syllabuses state, or imply, that the English learnt should have a wider currency than this.

Even assuming that an English is only for national rather than international use, there is a further doubt in my mind. The NE I have used above as an example was Malaysian English; but I rather doubt the existence of a homogeneous entity that can be so labelled. Only about 47 per cent of Malaysians are Malays and because of the influence of various MT phonologies, there are definitely a number of distinct (spoken) Malaysian Englishes. While their use of lexical and syntactic features seems to be fairly homogeneous, the sound patterns produced by Tamil, Chinese, Malay, Iban and other speakers of Malaysian English (to name but a few) do differ, in some cases very noticeably. On the other hand, it seems to me that speakers of Bantu languages produce a fairly uniform kind of pronunciation when speaking their Englishes, but use somewhat different lexical sets from region to region. Still, I think it possible that some multilingual nations may find even newer Englishes springing up within their borders and that these may hamper internal as well as international intelligibility.

But let us get back to the classroom. What tends to happen if an attempt is made to teach an 'outside' standard English? Students see the classroom English as remote from the real everyday business of communicating and the teacher feels uncomfortable trying to pose as a speaker of that 'foreign' standard. Yet, if we take the NE as the TL, we have to answer questions such as 'If you're going to teach (in secondary schools, for example) the local standard that everyone already speaks, what exactly are you going to teach that is new? Will some international standard English be needed for work and/or further education? If so, will it be easy to switch over from the NE? Are we to ignore totally the *cultural* benefit normally derived from learning a foreign language?'

I would suggest that – even in primary schools, once the initial concerns of literacy teaching are past – both local and international Englishes could be deliberately and overtly used. The NE would, of course, be the language of all classroom business, but the material for study would largely comprise samples of English (especially on tape) being used as an intercultural language (e.g. a Kenyan greeting an Arab visitor, a Malaysian introducing an Australian to a Filipino, etc.). The nationalities and situations most likely to be encountered would be the ones used initially, and texts would be short and simple – almost certainly scripted in the first few years. This would be, I am sure, a welcome change from the boys and girls pictured in textbooks who look local and have local names but who speak British English. Occasionally, exchanges in NE between local people could be contrasted with an equivalent exchange in an international version, a British version, or a North American or Antipodean one for example:

Malaysian version	*British version*
A Where Frankie go now?	A Where's Frankie going?
B He send his wife home, lah	B He's taking his wife home.
A You got your car now, isn't it?	A You've got your car now, haven't you?
B Aah, I just repair it.	B Yes, I've just had it repaired.
A You don't have one, is it?	A You haven't got one, have you?
B Yes.	B No.

We will have to wait for some years, no doubt, before syllabuses and materials incorporating such ideas are provided. But such an approach would, I think, do much to take the resentment out of many an English lesson; to show children from the start, that the way we speak depends on various features of our situation; and to inculcate a sensitivity to a range of Englishes, some of which may sound very funny at first. Realizing that we must 'sound funny' to some people is one prelude to tolerance, and the earlier the realization dawns the better. Finally, the tension between the NE and the internationally acceptable Englishes should help to ensure that the NE does not become unintelligible abroad.

Tasks

Task 1

Look at the examples of Malaysian English quoted by Abbott above. There are only a few and you would not want to draw definite conclusions from them, but you could begin to make some hypotheses about possible differences between Malaysian English and standard British English which you could later test if you were able to collect more examples.

From the evidence of the examples, in what ways (looking at grammar, lexis and discourse), does Malaysian English (ME) seem to differ from standard British English (BE)? Use the layout below if it helps.

	ME	BE
Grammar		
Lexis		
Discourse		

Task 2

Serpell (1982) gives some examples of Zambian English. Ten of those examples are listed below with their British English equivalents. Serpell claims that five of the examples would present no problems in communication between a Zambian and a non-Zambian, but that five other examples would.

(i) Try to decide which five might present problems and which would not.

Zambian English	British English	Potential problem Yes/No
(1) far much better	far better	
(2) cope up with	cope with	
(3) I am from town	I've just come from town	
(4) is it?	did you?	
(5) just now	in a moment	
(6) these people are strangers	these people are visitors	
(7) I hope the police are coming	I think the police are coming	
(8) too much	very much	
(9) I'm enjoying	I'm enjoying myself	
(10) he refused	he denied it	

(ii) How did you reach your decision?

(iii) Does the separation into the two categories ('problematic/non-problematic') have any implications for the English teacher in Zambia?

Task 3

Look at the following examples of 'New Englishes' (all taken from Platt, Weber and Ho 1984).

(1) That film was very gbeye (beyond description) (Ghanaian English).
(2) cracko (a crazy fellow) (colloquial Singapore English)
(3) kempt (opposite of unkempt i.e. neat and tidy) (East African English)
(4) brown-out (short interruption to the electricity supply,) (Phillipine English)
(5) to be aftering someone (to follow someone,) (Papua New Guinea)
(6) to friend (to be friends with,) (Singapore English)
(7) to prepone (opposite of postpone) (Indian English)
(8) dry coffee (coffee without milk and sugar) (East African English)
(9) the gift of the gap (gab) (Singapore English)
(10) I can hear (understand) five different languages. (African English)
(11) open (turn on) the radio. (Phillipine English)
(12) mud-mud (a lot of mud) (Jamaican English)

These examples show different processes at work in the formation of the New Englishes (many the result of the interantion between the 'indigenous' languages and the 'imported' English language). Such processes include:

(a) changes in pronunciation
(b) direct loan words from the local languages
(c) extension of meaning, creating new collocations
(d) prefix/suffix addition/deletion sometimes by incorrect analogy with existing forms
(e) repetition
(f) grammatical shift (e.g. from preposition to verb)
(g) joining words to create new collocations

(i) Try to match the examples given in 1–12 with one of the processes listed in (a)–(g).

Process	Example nos
a	
b	
c	
d	
e	
f	
g	

(ii) Turn back to Task 2 and look at the ten examples of Zambian English. Try to match the examples with the processes (a)–(g) above.

You may find that some of the ten examples of Zambian English represent additional processes that are not covered in (a)–(g). If that is the case, then note down the processes which you would like to add to the list.

(iii) You may have further examples of 'New Englishes'. If so, add them to the table of examples and processes you have completed above.

Task 4

Shaw (1981) in a survey of students from Singapore, India, and Thailand, asked which variety of English was spoken by educated speakers in the country concerned. The results are set out in Table 12.1.

TABLE 12.1
Variety of English presently spoken by educated speakers

	Singaporeans %	Indians %	Thais %
(1) British	40.5	27.4	6.5
(2) American	6.0	3.2	28.1
(3) Australian	0.6	0.0	0.0
(4) Unique	42.3	50.6	40.3
(5) Others	10.6	18.8	25.1

(4) = unique to my country, i.e. a new form of English.
(5) = like educated non-native speakers from other countries.

He then asked what variety should be learnt in the future. The results are given in Table 12.2.

TABLE 12.2
The variety that should be learnt

	Singaporeans %	Indians %	Thais %
(1) British	38.3	28.5	49.1
(2) American	14.4	12.0	31.6
(3) Australian	0.6	0.3	0.3
(4) Own way	38.9	47.4	3.5
(5) Others	7.8	11.8	15.5

(i) How can you account for the differences and similarities both within each table and between the two tables?
(ii) What conclusions can you draw about the future of 'native' and 'non-native' varieties of English in the three countries concerned?

Task 5

Look at quotations (A) and (B) from Platt, Weber and Ho (1984).

(A) The heretical tenet I feel I must take exception to is the idea that it is best, in a country where English is not spoken natively but is widely used as a medium of instruction, to set up the local variety of English as the ultimate model to be imitated by those learning the language.

(B) It is obvious that in the Third World Countries the choice of functions and models of English has to be determined on a pragmatic basis, keeping in view the local conditions and needs. It will, therefore, be appropriate that the native speakers of English abandon the attitude of linguistic chauvinism and replace it with an attitude of linguistic tolerance. The strength of the English language is in presenting the Americanness in its American variety, and the Englishness in its British variety. Let us therefore appreciate and encourage the Third World varieties of English too.

(i) Which view, (A) or (B), do you think Abbott would agree with?

(ii) Looking back at the article by Serpell (p.92), which view do you think he would be likely to support?

(iii) Which view do you support yourself? Give reasons for each of your answers.

Task 6

Some believe that the world may soon need a single language for international communication. At the moment, the English language is the strongest contender for such a role for a wide range of social, political and economic reasons. If English is to be the international language (and you may like to spend some time discussing whether there is the need for a single language for international communication and whether English would be an internationally acceptable choice) there will be the problem of what sort of model should be chosen. There are a number of views on this, four of which are summarized below:

(a) Choose an existing native-speaker variety of English and promote it as the international model.

(b) Quirk (1981) thought that it would be possible to create an international language (Nuclear English) from a simplified form of native-speaker English (his examples are drawn from standard British English), which everyone including native speakers would have to learn as a new variety. For example, 'isn't that right', or 'is that so' could be used as a universal question tag instead of the present variations (e.g. 'aren't I'; 'was it'; 'didn't she'). Nuclear English would not be an artificial language since it would draw on existing vocabulary and structures, it would not create new ones.

(c) Wong (1982) puts forward a proposal for Utilitarian English, a language which would not be based on a simplified standard variety of native-speaker English, like Quirk's Nuclear English, but on the common linguistic features of the emerging New Englishes (some examples of which we met in the first three tasks of this chapter). The element of simplification would, therefore, not have to be planned (as it would have to be in the case of Nuclear English), but would be a natural process which is already taking place as the New Englishes develop. Utilitarian English would be particularly suitable for use in communications involving Third World Countries.

(d) Widdowson (1982:12–13) is sceptical of interventionist policies.

> One is bound to be involved in serious difficulties, both practical and ethical, when one contrives to promote English as an international language...The best service we can offer...is to support the use of English...by developing more effective ways of teaching it as it is...Any refashioning of the language...can be left...to...the users themselves as they adjust it quite naturally to meet changing needs and circumstances.

(i) What arguments can you bring both for and against each of the four proposals above?

Bibliography

Abbott, G. and Wingard P., (1981): *Teaching English as an International Language*. Glasgow: Collins.

Achebe, C., (1975): *Morning yet on creation day*. London: Heinemann.

Abduhamdia, Z.A., (1984): 'English departments at Arab universities: towards a "planning-based model",' *LPLP* vol. 8, 1, pp. 21–34.

Adekunle, M., (1972): 'Sociolinguistic problems in English language instruction in Nigeria', in Smith, D.M. and Shuy, R.W. (eds), *Sociolinguistics in cross-cultural analysis*. Washington, D.C.: Georgetown University Press, pp. 83–101.

Afendras, E.A. (ed.), (1980): *Patterns of bilingualism*. Singapore: Singapore University Press.

Afendras, E.A. and Kuo, E. (eds),(1980): *Language and society in Singapore*. Singapore: Singapore University Press.

Afolayan, A., (1976): 'The six year primary project in Nigeria', in A. Bamgbose (ed.), pp. 113–134.

Afolayan, A., (1977): 'The new language policy and effective instruction in schools', *Language in Education in Nigeria*, vol. 7.

Afolayan, A., (1984): 'The English language in Nigerian education as an agent of proper multilingual and multicultural development', *JMMD*, vol. 5, 1, pp. 1–22.

Africa, H.P., (1978): 'Selection of language modes', in L. Omondi and Y.T. Simukoko (eds), *Language and education in Zambia*, Communication no. 14. Lusaka: Institute for African Studies.

Alatis, J.E. (ed.), (1978): *International dimensions of bilingual education*. Washington D.C.: Georgetown University Press.

Alatis, J.E. and Tucker, G.R. (eds), (1979): *Language and public life*. Washington D.C.: Georgetown University Press.

Alderson, J.C. (ed.), (1985): *Evaluation* London: Prentice Hall. Lancaster Practical Papers in English Language Education, vol. 6.

Alisjahbana, S.T., (1971): 'Some planning processes in the development of the Indonesian-Malay language', in Rubin, J and Jernudd, B.H. (eds), pp. 179–87.

Allwright, R., (1988): *Classroom language learning*. London: Longman.

Angogo, R. and Hancock I., (1980): English in Africa: emerging standards or diverging regionalisms?' *EWW*, vol. 1, 1, pp. 67–96.

Annamalai, E. and Rubin J., (1980): 'Planning for language code and language use: some considerations in policy-formation and implementation', *Language planning newsletter*, vol. 6, 3, pp. 1–4.

Apter, A. H., (1982): 'National language planning in plural societies: the search for a framework', *LPLP*, vol. 6, 3, pp. 219–40.

Asmah, H.O., (1979): *Language planning for unity and efficiency*. Kuala Lumpur: University of Malaya Press.

Australian Department of Education, (1975): *Report of the inquiry into schools of high migrant density*. Canberra: Australian Government Publishing Services.

Australian Ethnic Affairs Council Committee on Multicultural Education, (1979): *Perspectives on multicultural education*. Canberra: Department of Immigration and Ethnic Affairs.

Ayodele, S., (1983). 'A description of the varieties of Nigerian English for pedagogic purposes', *BJLT*, vol. 21, 2, pp. 101–08.

Bailey, R.W. and Robinson, J.L. (eds), (1973): *Varieties of present day English*.London: Macmillan.

Bailey, R.W. and Görlach, M. (eds), (1982): *English as a world language*. Ann Arbor: University of Michigan.

Bamgbose, A. (ed.), (1976): *Mother tongue education – the West African experience*. London: Hodder and Stoughton.

Bamgbose, A., (1977): 'Towards an implementation of Nigeria's language policy in education', *Language in Education in Nigeria*, vol. 1.

Banjo, A., (1977): 'On the goals of language education in Nigeria', *Language in Education in Nigeria*, vol. 1.

Barnes, D., (1976): *Communication and the curriculum*. London: Penguin.

Basso, K., (1974): 'The ethnography of writing', in Baumann, R. and Sherzer, J. (eds), *Explorations in the ethnography of speaking*. Cambridge: Cambridge University Press.

Bautista, L.S., (1975): 'A model of bilingual competence based on an analysis of Tagalog-English code-switching', *Philippine Journal of Linguistics*, vol. 6, (1), pp. 51–89.

BBC TV, (1980): 'San Giorgio's bitter fruits', *The world about us*. London: BBC.

Beardsmore, H.B., (1981): *Bilingualism: basic principles*. Clevedon, Avon: Tieto.

Bell, A., (1982): 'This isn't the BBC: colonialism in New Zealand English', in *Applied Linguistics,* vol. 3, 3, pp. 246–58.

Bell, J., (ed.), (1982): *Aboriginal languages and the question of a national language policy*. Papers presented at second meeting of Aboriginal Languages Association, Batchelor, N.T., Australia, April 1982

Bell, R.T., (1976): *Sociolinguistics*. London: Batsford.

Bell, R.T., (1981): *An introduction to applied linguistics*. London: Batsford.

Bennis, W.S., Benne, K.B. and Chin, R. (eds), (1970): *The planning of change*. London: Holt, Rinehart and Winston.

Benson, J. and Greaves W., (1984): *You and your language*. Oxford: Pergamon.

Bentahila, A., (1983): *Language attitudes among Arabic-French bilinguals in Morocco*. Multilingual Matters, no. 4. Clevedon, Avon: Multilingual Matters.

Benton, R.A., (1981): *The flight of the Amokura*. Wellington: New Zealand Council for Educational Research.

Berman, P., (1978): *The study of macro and micro implementation of social policy*. Santa Monica: The Rand Corporation.

Bernstein, B., (1960): 'Language and social class', *British Journal of Sociology,* vol. 2, pp. 217–76.

Bhatia, T.K., (1982): 'English and the vernaculars of India: contact and change', *Applied Linguistics*, vol. 3, 3, pp. 235–45.

Boey, L.M. (ed.), (1980): *Bilingual education*. Singapore: Singapore University Press.

Bokamba, E.G., (1981): 'Language and national development in sub-Saharan Africa: a progress report', *Studies in the Linguistic Sciences*, vol. 11, 1, pp. 1–25.

Bourhis, R.Y. (ed.), (1983): *Conflict and language planning in Quebec*. Clevedon, Avon: Multilingual Matters.

Bowen, J.D., (1971): 'Trends in English abroad', *ERIC Document*. E 052 651. Paper presented at the 5th Annual TESOL Convention, New Orleans.

Bowen, J.D., Cooper, R.L. and Ferguson, C., (1976): *Language in Ethiopia*. London: Oxford University Press.

Boys, O., (1981): 'What newspaper advertisements have to say about English language needs', *EST/ESP Chile*, vol. 10, pp. 7–13.

Brann, C.M.B., (1979): 'Multilingualism in Nigerian education', in Mackey and Orstein (eds), pp. 379–92.

Brann, C.M.B., (1981): *Trilingualism in language – planning for education in sub-Saharan Africa*. Paris: UNESCO.

Brickner, W.H. and Cope, D.M., (1977): *The planning process*. Amherst: University of Massachusetts Press.

Bright, J.A. and McGregor, G.P., (1970): *Teaching English as a Second Language*. London: Longman.

Bright, W. (ed.), (1966): *Sociolinguistics*. The Hague: Mouton.

British Council, (1978): *English as an international language*. London: ETIC, British Council. ELT documents 102.

British Council, (1980): *Study modes and academic development of overseas students*. London: ETIC, British Council. ELT documents 109.

British Council, (1983): *Language teaching projects for the Third World*. London: ETIC, British Council and Oxford: Pergamon. ELT documents 116.

British Council, (1986): *Evaluation of Educational Projects* (seminar papers). Birmingham: University of Birmingham.

British Council, *Profiles* [of different countries]. London ETIC, British Council.

British Council, *Survey of use of English in Hong Kong*. British Council (unpublished).

Britten, D. and O'Dwyer, J., (1987): *Self-evaluation in in-service teacher training*, (mimeo). London: Centre for British Teachers.

Brown, R., (1970): *A first language*. Cambridge, Mass: Harvard University Press.

Brumfit, C., (1980): *Problems and principles in ELT*. London: Prentice Hall.

Brumfit, C. (ed.), (1982): *English for international communication*. London: Prentice Hall.

Brumfit, C. and Carter, R. (eds), (1986): *Literature and language teaching*. Oxford: Oxford University Press.

Burstall, C., (1975): *Primary French in the balance*. Windsor: NFER.

Campbell, R.N., El-Ezaby. Y, and Harrison, W., (1972): *English language teaching in Jordan: a preliminary study*, (mimeo.). Cairo: Ford Foundation.

Candlin, C. and Murphy, D. (eds), (1987): *Language learning tasks*. Lancaster Practical Papers in English Language Education, vol. 7. London: Prentice-Hall.

Carter, R. and Long, M. (1988): *The web of words*. Cambridge: Cambridge University Press.

Cazden, C., (1986): 'ESL teachers as language advocates for children', in Rigg, P. and Enright, D. (eds), *Children and ESL*. *TESOL*.Washington.

Chai, H.C., (1971): *Planning education for a plural society*. Paris: UNESCO, International Institute for Educational Planning.

Cheung, M.W., (1974): The relative effectiveness of teaching comprehension through the use of Cantonese and English as medium of instruction. Unpublished Masters' thesis. Chinese University of Hong Kong (in Chinese).

Chin, R. and Benne, D., (1970): 'General strategies for effecting changes in human systems', in Bennis, W.S., Benne, K.B. and Chin R. (eds), pp. 32–59.

Chomsky, N., (1957): *Syntactic structures*. The Hague: Mouton.

Christie, M., (1985): *Aboriginal perspectives on experience and learning*. Victoria: Deakin University Press.

Clyne, M. (ed.), (1976): *Australia talks: essays on the sociology of Australian, immigrant, and aboriginal languages*. Canberra Pacific Linguistics. Series D, No. 23.

Clyne, M., (1980): *Communication in a multicultural society*, (mimeo.). Address given at the National Conference on Australian society in the multicultural 80s. Canberra.

Cobarrubias, J and Fishman, J.A. (eds), (1983): *Progress in language planning*. The Hague: Mouton.

Cohen, G. and Aronson, R., (1964): *The teaching of English in Israel*. Jerusalem: Hebrew University, School of Education.

Conrad, W. and Fishman, J.A., (1977): 'English as a world language: the evidence', in Fishman, J.A., Cooper R.L. and Conrad, W. (eds), pp. 3–76.

Cooper, R.L., (1980): 'Sociolinguistic surveys: the state of the art'. *Applied linguistics*, vol. 1, 2, 113–28.

Cooper, R.L., (1981): 'Language spread as a perspective for the study of second-language acquisition', in Andersen, R.W. (ed.), *New dimensions in second language acquisition research*. Rowley, Mass: Newbury House.

Cooper, R.L. (ed.), (1982): *Language spread: studies in diffusion and social change*. Washington, D.C.: Centre for Applied Linguistics, and Bloomington, USA: Indiana University Press.

Crewe, W. (ed.), (1977): *The English language in Singapore*. Singapore: Eastern Universities Press.

Croft, K., (1980): *Readings on English as a Second Language*. Cambridge, Mass: Winthrop Publishers, 2nd edition.

Crystal, D. and Davy, D. (1973): *Investigating English style*. London: Longman.

Curle, A., (1966): *Planning for education in Pakistan*. London: Tavistock.

Cziko, G.A., (1982): 'Vernacular education in the Southern Sudan: a test case for literacy', *JMMD*, vol. 3, 4, pp. 293–314.

Dasen, P.R., (1978): *Naissance de l'intelligence chez l'enfant Baoule de Côte-d'Ivoire*. Berne: Huber.

Davies, F. and Greene, (1984): *Reading for learning in the sciences*. Edinburgh: Oliver and Boyd.

de Bono, E., (1967): *The use of lateral thinking*. London: Jonathan Cape.

Deuchar, M., (1976): What are language attitudes and how can they be measured? Unpublished Manuscript.

Dil, A.S. (ed.), (1981): *Language diversity and language contact: essays by S. Lieberson*. Stanford, California: Stanford University Press.

Dil, A.S. (ed.), (1982): *Language, society and paleoculture: essays by E.C. Polomé*. Stanford, California: Stanford University Press.

Dorian, N., (1981): *Language death: the life cycle of a Scottish Gaelic dialect*. Philadelphia: University of Pennsylvania Press.

Douglass, E.F., (1976): 'The discovery of commonness essential for cross-cultural dialogue – based on anthropological studies in Sierra Leone', *Ideas and Action*, vol. 112. Rome: FAO.

Eastman, C.M., (1981): 'Language planning, identity planning and world view', *IJSL*, vol. 32, pp. 45–53.

Eastman, C.M., (1983): *Language planning: an introduction*. San Francisco: Chandler and Sharp.

Edwards, J.R., (1981): 'The context of bilingual education', *JMMD*, vol. 2, 1, pp. 25–44.

Ekang, P., (1982): 'On the use of an indigenous model for testing English in Nigeria', *World language English*, vol. 1, 2, pp. 87–92.

Elley, W., (1980): Recent studies of English reading levels in Fiji, (mimeo.). Suva, Fiji: University of the South Pacific.

Elley, W., (1984): 'Exploring the reading difficulties of second-language learners in Fiji', in Alderson, J. and Urquhart, A. (eds), *Reading in a foreign language*. London: Longman. pp. 281–97.

Ellis, R., (1984): *Classroom second language development*. London: Prentice Hall.

Engle, P.L., (1975): 'The use of vernacular languages in education', *Papers in applied linguistics. Bilingual education series no. 3*. Arlington, Va: Center for Applied Linguistics.

Essien, O.E., (1981): 'The case against English', in *Calabar Studies in Languages*, vol. 2, 4. Calabar, Nigeria: University of Calabar.

Etherton, A.R., Ong, J. and Lee, J. (1974): Parental motivation in the choice of secondary schools. Hong Kong: Chinese University of Hong Kong (unpublished).

Fasold, R., (1984): *The sociolinguistics of society*. Oxford: Blackwell.

Ferguson, C.A., (1959): 'Diglossia', *Word*, vol. 15, pp. 325–40. Reprinted in Giglioli (ed.), (1972): 232–51.

Ferguson, C.A., (1966a): 'National sociolinguistic profile formulas', in Bright, W. (ed.), pp. 309–24.

Ferguson, C.A., (1966b): 'Sociolinguistically oriented language surveys', *Linguistic Reporter*, vol. 8, 4, pp. 2–6.

Ferguson, C.A., (1971a): 'Contrasting patterns and literacy acquisition in a multilingual nation', in Whiteley (ed.), *Language use and social change*. Oxford: Oxford University Press, pp. 234–52.

Ferguson, C.A., (1971b): *Language Structure and Language Use*. Essays by Ferguson, selected by A.S. Dil, Stanford: Stanford University Press.

Fillmore, C.J., (1968): 'The case for case', in Bach, E. and Harms, R.T. (eds), *Universals in linguistic theory*. New York: Holt, Rinehart and Winston, pp. 1–87.

Findley, C.A. and Nathan, C.A., (1980): 'Functional language objectives in a competency based ESL curriculum', *TESOL Quarterly*, vol. 14, 2, pp. 221–31.

Finocchiaro, M., (1964): *English as a Second Language: From Theory to Practice*. New York: Regents.

Fishman, J.A., (1967): 'Bilingualism with and without diglossia; diglossia with and without bilingualism', *Journal of Social Issues*, vol. 23, 2, pp. 39–48.

Fishman, J.A., (1968a): 'Some contrasts between linguistically homogeneous and linguistically hetero-geneous polities', in Fishman, J.A., Ferguson, C.A. and Das Gupta, J. (eds), pp. 53–68.

Fishman, J.A., (1968b): 'Nationality-nationalism and nation-nationism', in Fishman *et al.* (eds). pp. 39–51.

Fishman, J.A., (1970): 'Sociolinguistic perspectives on internal linguistic tensions and their impact on external relations', in *Transactions of the Sixth World Congress of Sociology*, vol. 3, pp. 281–89. Milan: International Sociological Association.

Fishman, J.A., (1971a): 'National languages and languages of wider communication in the developing nations', in Whiteley (ed.), pp. 27–56.

Fishman, J.A., (1971c): 'The impact of nationalism on language planning'. in Rubin and Jernudd (eds), pp. 3–20.

Fishman, J.A. (ed.), (1971/72): *Advances in the sociology of language*. The Hague: Mouton. vols. 1 and 2.

Fishman, J.A., (1972a): *Language and nationalism: two integrative essays*. Rowley, Mass.: Newbury House.

Fishman, J.A., (1972b): *National languages and languages of wider communication in developing nations*. Stanford: Stanford University Press.

Fishman, J.A., (1972c): *The sociology of language: an interdisciplinary social science approach to language in society*. Rowley, Mass: Newbury House.

Fishman, J.A., (1977a): *Bilingual education*. Rowley, Mass.: Newbury House.

Fishman, J.A., (1977b): 'The sociology of language', in Cole, R. (ed.), *Current issues in linguistic theory*. (London: Harvester Press), pp. 51–75.

Fishman, J.A. (ed.), (1977c): *Advances in the creation and revision of writing systems*. The Hague: Mouton.

Fishman, J.A. (ed.), (1978): *Advances in the study of societal multilingualism*. The Hague: Mouton.

Fishman, J.A., (1980a): 'Bilingualism and biculturalism as individual and as societal phenomena'. *JMMD*, vol. 1, pp. 3–15.

Fishman, J.A., (1980b): 'Bilingual education, language planning, and English', *EWW*, vol. 1, 1, pp. 11–24.

Fishman, J.A., Ferguson, C, and Das Gupta, J. (eds), (1968): *Language problems of developing nations*. New York: Wiley and Sons.

Fishman, J.A., Cooper, R. and Conrad, A. (eds), (1977): *The spread of English*. Rowley, Mass: Newbury House.

Fishman J.A., Cooper, R.L. & Rosenbaum, Y. (1977). 'English Around the World' in Fishman, Cooper & Conrad (eds.), 77–108.

Fitzgerald, R.T., (1976): *Poverty and education in Australia*. (Fifth Main Report in the Australian Government Commission of Inquiry into Poverty). Canberra: Australian Government Publishing Service.

Freire, P. (1972). *Pedagogy of the oppressed*. New York: Herder.

Fries, C.C., (1966): *The teaching of English*. Ann Arbor, Michigan: George Wahr.

Fu, G.S., (1979): 'Bilingual Education in Hong Kong: a Historical Perspective', in *Working papers in Language and Language Teaching* 1. Hong Kong: University of Hong Kong, Language Centre, pp. 1–19.

Gair, J.W., (1983): 'Sinhala and English: the effects of a language act', *LPLP*, vol. 7, 1, pp. 43–59.

Galbally, (1978): 'Review of post-arrival programms and services for imigrants', *Immigrant Services and Programms*, Canberra: Australian Government Publishing Service. (The Galbally Report).

Gallagher, C.F., (1971): 'Language reform and social modernization in Turkey', in Rubin, J, and Jernudd, B.H. (eds), pp. 159–78.

Gardner, R.C. and Lambert, (1972): *Attitudes and motivation in second language learning*. Rowley, Mass: Newbury House.

Gibbons, J., (1979): 'Code-Mixing and koineising in the speech of students at the University of Hong Kong', *Anthropological Linguistics*, vol. 21, 3, pp. 113–23.

Gibbons, J., (1987): *Code-mixing and code choice – a Hong Kong case study*. Multilingual Matters, 27. Clevedon, Avon: Multilingual Matters.

Giglioli, P. (ed.), (1972): *Language and social context.* Harmondsworth: Penguin.

Giles, H. and Edwards, J. (eds), (1983): *Language attitudes in multilingual settings.* Special issues of *JMMD* vol 4, 2 and 3.

Glasser, R., (1977): *The net and quest: patterns of community and how they can survive progress.* London: Temple Smith.

Goldberg, S., (1970a): Infant development in Zambia: measuring maternal behaviour, (mimeo.). *Human Development Research Unit Reports 13.* Lusaka: University of Zambia.

Goldberg, S., (1970b): Infant care, stimulation and sensory-motor development in a high density urban area of Lusaka, (mimeo.). *Human Development Research Unit Reports 15.* Lusaka: University of Zambia.

Gonzo, S. and Saltarelli, M., (1979): 'Monitoring, pidginization and immigrant languages', In Andersen, R.W. (ed.), *The acquisition and use of Spanish and English as first and second languages.* Washington, D.C.: TESOL, pp. 153–163.

Gonzalez, A., (1980): *Language and nationalism: the Philippine experience thus far.* Manila: Ateneo de Manila University Press.

Gorman, T., (1973): 'Language allocation and language planning', in Rubin and Shuy (eds), pp. 72–82.

Gorman, T.P. (ed.), (1971): *Language in education in Eastern Africa.* London: Oxford University Press.

Grant, N., (1983): 'Materials design for Nigerian secondary schools', in British Council ELT Docs. 116, pp. 69–84.

Greenbaum, S., (1984): *The English Language Today.* London: Prentice Hall.

Grenier, G. and Vaillancourt, F., (1983): 'An economic perspective on learning a second language', *JMMD,* vol. 4, 6, pp. 471–84.

Grieve, D.W., (1964): *English language examining.* Lagos: African Universities Press.

Gumperz, J.J., (1971): *Languages in social groups,* (selected and introduced by A.S. Dil). Stanford : Stanford University Press.

Gumperz, J.J., (1972): 'Types of linguistic communities', In Fishman, J.A. (ed.), *Readings in the sociology of language.* The Hague: Mouton, pp. 460–72.

Gumperz, J.J., and Blom, J.P., (1971): 'Social meaning in linguistic structures: code-switching in Norway'. In Gumperz 1971, 274–310.

Halliday, M.A.K., (1970): 'Language structure and language function', in Lyons, J. (ed.), *New horizons in Linguistics* Harmondsworth: Penguin, pp. 140–165.

Halliday, M.A.K., McIntosh, A. and Strevens, P., (1970): 'The users and uses of language', in Fishman, J.A. (ed.), *Readings in the Sociology of Language.* The Hague: Mouton, pp. 139–169.

Halliday, M. and Hasan, R., (1985): *Language, context and text.* Victoria: Deakin University Press.

Hansford, K., Bendor-Samuel, J. and Stanford, R., (1976): *Studies in Nigerian languages* No. 5. Ghana: Summer Institute of Linguistics.

Harkness, S., (1976): 'Modernization and child language development in rural Africa'. Paper presented by the 2nd Pan-African Conference on Psychology, Nairobi, Kenya.

Harrison, D.S. and Trabasso, T., (eds), (1976): *Black English: a seminar.* Hillsdale NJ: Erlbaum.

Harrison, W., Prator, C. and Tucker G., (eds), (1975): *English language policy survey of Jordan.* Washington D.C.: Center for Applied Linguistics.

Haugen, E., (1966a): 'Dialect, language, nation', in Pride and Holmes (eds), pp. 97–111.

Haugen, E., (1966b): 'Linguistics and language planning'. in Bright (ed.), pp. 50–71.

Haugen. E., (1972): *The ecology of language.* Stanford: Stanford University Press.

Hildebrand, N. and Giles, H., (1980): 'The English language in Japan: a social psychological perspective', *JALT Journal* vol. 2, pp. 63–87.

Hill, L.A., (1978): 'Learning a language at the tertiary level through a reading approach', *ELTJ* vol. 32/4, pp. 318–22.

Hill, J. and Coombs, D., (1982): 'The vernacular remodelling of national and international languages', *Applied Linguistics* vol. 3, 3, pp. 224–34.

Hofman, J.E. and Fisherman, H., (1971): 'Language shift and maintenance in Israel', *International Migration Review,* vol. 5, pp. 204–226.

Holliday, A., (1984): 'Research into classroom culture as necessary input into syllabus design', in Swales, A. and Mustafa, H. (eds), pp. 29–51.

Holliday, A. and Cooke, T., (1982): 'An ecological approach to ESP', in Waters (ed), pp. 123–43.

Horvath, B. (1980). *Community languages in the schools.* Sydney: Department of Linguistics. Report submitted to the Schools Commission.

Hudson, R.A., (1980): Review of W.F. MacKay and J. Ornstein (eds.) Sociolinguistic Studies in Language Contact Methods and Bases. In Polyglot, vol. 2, fiche 2, G7–G14.

Hudson, R.A., (1980a): *Sociolinguistics.* Cambridge: Cambridge University Press.

Hurst, P., (1981): 'Some issues in improving the quality of education', *Comparative education,* vol. 17, 2, pp. 185–93.

Hvitfeldt, C., (1978): 'Initial reading instruction in an unfamiliar language: some psycholinguistic implications'. Lusaka: University of Zambia, (unpublished seminar paper).

Hymes, D., (1972): 'On communicative competence', in Giglioli (ed.), pp. 269–293.

Jernudd, B., (1971): 'Notes on economic analysis and language planning', in Rubin and Jernudd (eds), pp. 263–276.

Jernudd, B., (1973): 'Language planning as a type of language treatment', in Rubin and Shuy (eds), pp. 11–23.

Jernudd, B., (1981): 'Planning language treatment: linguistics for the third world', *Language in society,* vol. 10, 1, pp. 43–52.

Jernudd, B. and Das Gupta, J., (1971): 'Towards a theory of language planning', in Rubin and Jernudd (eds), pp. 195–215.

Johns, T., (1981): 'Some problems of a world-wide profession', in ELT documents 112, *The ESP Teacher,* pp. 16–22. London: British Council.

Judd, E.L., (1978): 'Language policy and TESOL: Socio-political factors and their influence on the profession', in Blatchford, C.H. and Schachter, J. (eds), *On TESOL '78 EFL policies,programs, practices.* Washington, D.C.: TESOL, pp. 75–82.

Kachru, B., (1976): 'Models of English for the Third World: white man's linguistic burden or language pragmatics?' *TESOL Quarterly,* vol. 10, 2, pp. 221–39.

Kachru, B., (1981): 'The pragmatics of non-native varieties of English', in Smith, L.E. (ed.), pp. 15–39.

Kachru, B. (ed.), (1983): *The other tongue: English across cultures.* London: Prentice Hall.

Kachru, B., (1985): *The alchemy of English.* London: Prentice Hall.

Kaplan, R., (1966): 'Cultural thought patterns in inter-cultural education', *Language Learning,* vol. 16, 3/4.

Kaplan, R. (ed.), (1982): *Annual review of applied linguistics.* (Issue on language planning and language in education). Rowley, Mass: Newbury House.

Kashoki, M., (1979): 'Communication at Annual General Meeting of Zambian Language Group', *Zambia Daily Mail,* 19 June, 1979.

Kelman, H.C., (1971): 'Language as an aid and barrier to involvement in the national system', in Rubin and Jernudd (eds), pp. 21–51.

Kennedy, C.J. (ed.), (1984): *Language planning and language education.* London: Allen and Unwin.

Kennedy, C.J. (1985a) 'Language planning', in Kinsella, V. (ed.), *Language Teaching Surveys,* vol. 3, pp. 19–41, Cambridge: Cambridge University Press.

Kennedy, C.J., (1985b): 'Formative evaluation as an indicator of student needs and wants', *ESP Journal* vol. 4, 2, pp. 93–100.

Kennedy, C.J., (1985c): *Survey of ESP teachers in Tunisia.* Tunis: Ministry of Education.

Kennedy, C.J., (1986a): 'Language planning, and channel management', in *Language in education in Africa* (qv), pp. 69–100.

Kennedy, C.J., (1986b): 'The future of English language teaching', *System,* vol. 14, 3 pp. 307–14.

Kennedy, C.J., (1987): Innovating for a change', in *ELTJ* vol. 41, 3, pp. 163–70.

Kennedy, C.J., (1988): 'Evaluation of the management of change in ELT projects', *Applied Linguistics,* vol. 9, 4, pp. 330–42.

Kingsley, P.R., (1977): The measurement of intelligence in Africa: some conceptual issues and related research, (mimeo.). *Human Development Research Unit Reports, 28.* Lusaka: University of Zambia.

Kloss, H., (1967): 'Bilingualism and nationalism', *Journal of Social Issues,* vol. 23, 2, pp. 39–47.

Krashen, S., (1976): 'Formal and informal linguistic environments in language acquisition and language learning', *TESOL Quarterly,* vol. 10, pp. 157–168.

Krashen, S., (1978): 'Individual variation in the use of the monitor', in Ritchie, W.C. (ed.), *Second language acquisition research.* New York: Academic Press, pp. 175–183.

Kvan, E., (1969): 'Problems of bilingual milieu in Hong Kong: strain of the two language system' in Jarvie, I.C. and Agassi, J., *Hong Kong: a society in transition.* London: Routledge and Kegan Paul, pp. 327–43.

Kwo, O., (1987): 'Bilingual secondary education in Hong Kong', in *Working papers in linguistics and language teaching,* no 10. pp. 1–10. Hong Kong: University of Hong Kong.

Labov, W., (1972): *Sociolinguistic patterns.* Philadelphia: Pennsylvania University Press.

Lambert, W.E. and Tucker, G.R., (1972): *Bilingual education of children: the St. Lambert experiment.* Rowley, Mass: Newbury House.

Lambright, W. and Flynn, P.L., (1980): 'The role of local bureaucracy-centered coalitions in technology transfer to the city', in Agnew, J.A. (ed.), *Innovation Research and Public Policy,* Syracuse: Department of Geography, Syracuse University.

Language in education in Africa. (1986). Seminar proceedings 26. Edinburgh: Centre of African Studies, University of Edinburgh.

Larsen-Freeman, D., (1976): 'An explanation for the morpheme acquisition order of second language learners', *Language Learning,* vol. 26, pp. 125–34.

Lewis, G.E., (1971): Migration and language in the USSR. International Migration Review 5, 147–79.
Lewis, G.E., (1981): *Bilingualism and bilingual education.* Oxford: Pergamon Press.
Lieberson, S., (1980): 'Procedures for improving sociolinguistic surveys of language maintenance and language shift', *IJSL,* vol. 25, pp. 11–27.
Lieberson, S., (1982): 'Forces affecting language spread', in Cooper, R. (ed.), pp. 37–62.
van Lier, B., (1988): *Second language classroom research.* Longman.
Lorwin, V.R., (1972): Linguistic pluralism and political tension in modern Belgium. In Fishman, J.A. (ed.) Advances in the Sociology of Language, vol. 2, pp. 386–412. The Hague: Mouton.
Luk, B., (1979): 'Schooling through the Mother Tongue', in Cheung, N.L. (ed.), *Issues in language of instruction in Hong Kong.* Hong Kong: Cosmos.
Luk, K.K. and Richards, J.C., (1982): 'English in Hong Kong: functions and status', *EWW* vol. 3, 1, pp. 47–58.
Lyczak, R., Fu, G.S. and Ho, A., (1976): 'Attitudes of Hong Kong Bilinguals toward English and Chinese Speakers', *Journal of Cross-Cultural Psychology,* vol. 7, 4, pp. 425–38.
MacAdam, B.H.G., (1973): The effectiveness of the new English-medium primary school curriculum in Zambia. Manchester: University of Manchester, unpublished PhD dissertation.
Mackey, W.F. and Ornstein, J. (eds), (1979): *Sociolinguistic studies in language contact.* The Hague: Mouton.
Maley, A., (1985): 'On chalk and cheese, babies and bathwater and squared circles', in *On TESOL 84.* Washington DC: TESOL. pp. 159–70.
Markee, N., (1986a): 'The relevance of sociopolitical factors to communicative course design', *ESP Journal,* vol. 5, 1, pp. 3–16.
Markee, N., (1986b): 'Towards an appropriate technology model of communicative course design', *ESP Journal,* vol. 5, 2, pp. 161–72.
Mazrui, A., (1975): *The political sociology of the English language.* The Hague: Mouton.
McGroarty, M., (1980): Language policy, immigration and education in three English-speaking countries. Paper presented at TESOL conference. San Francisco.
Mkanganwi. K.G., (1980): *Zimbabwe: sociolinguistically speaking.* Issues in development, 15. Harare: University of Zimbabwe, Centre for Applied Social Sciences.
Miller, J.R., (1981): 'The politics of Philippine national language policy', *LPLP,* vol. 5, 2, pp. 137–52.
Moag, R., (1982a): 'The life cycle of non-native Englishes', in Kachru, B. (ed.), *The other tongue.* Oxford: Pergamon.
Moag, R. (1982b): 'English as a foreign, second, native, and basal language', in Pride, J. (ed.), *New Englishes.* Rowley, Mass: Newbury House. pp. 11–50.
Molde, B. and Sharp, D. (eds). (1984): *Second international conference on minority languages.* Special issues of *JMMD,* vol. 5, 3, and 4.
Morris, A. and Stewart-Dore, N., (1984): *Learning to learn from text.* Workingham: Addison-Wesley.
Munby, J., (1978): *Communicative syllabus design.* Cambridge: Cambridge University Press.
Mwanakatwe, J.M., (1976): 'Reflections on the use of English as medium of instruction in schools', *Bulletin of the Zambia Language Group,* vol. 2, 2, pp 1–21.
Neustupny, J.V., (1968): 'Some General Aspects of "Language" Problems and "Language" Policy in Developing Societies', in Fishman, Ferguson, Das Gupta, (eds.), 285–294.
Neustupny, J.V. (1970): Basic types of treatment of language problems. *Linguistic communications,* 1, 77–98.
Neustupny, J. (1974): 'The modernisation of the Japanese system of communication', *Language in society,* vol. 3, 1, pp. 33–50.
Neustupny, J.V., (1978): *Post-structural approaches to language.* University of Tokyo Press.
New Internationalist No. 76, June 1979. 'Children's Voices', Melbourne: New Internationalist Publications.
Nicholls, A., (1983): *Managing educational innovations.* London: Allen and Unwin.
Nigeria (1977): *National policy on education.* Lagos.
Nigeria (1979): *The Constitution of the Federal Republic of Nigeria.* Lagos.
Noss, R.B., (1971): Politics and language policy in Southeast Asia. *Language Sciences,* pp. 16, 25–32.
Okoh, N., (1979): 'Survey of the language situation in Nigeria', *Polyglot.* vol. 1, 2, B3-C11.
Olshtain, E., (1985): 'Language policy and the language teacher', in Celce-Murcia, M. (ed.), *Essays for language teachers,* Rowley, Mass: Newbury House.
Ohannessian, S., Ferguson, C, and Palome, E, (eds), (1975): *Language surveys in developing nations.* Arlington, Va: Center for Applied Linguistics.
Papers of 16th regional seminar on new varieties of English, (1981). Singapore: RELC.
Parasher, S.V., (1981): 'Indian English: a sociolinguistic perspective', *ITL,* vol. 51, pp. 59–70.
Pattanayak, D., (1981): *Multilingualism and mother-tongue education.* Delhi: Oxford University Press.
Pattanayak, D., (1986): 'Educational use of the mother tongue', in Spolsky (ed.), pp. 5–15.
Payne, R.M. (ed.), (1983): *Language in Tunisia.* Language and Linguistics Series for Education. Tunis: Bourguiba Institute of Modern Languages.

Perkins, K. and Larsen-Freeman, D., (1975): 'The effect of formal language instruction on the order of morpheme acquisition', *Language Learning* vol. 25, pp. 237–43.

Perren, G.E., (1969): 'Education Through a Second Language' in Jolly, (ed.), *Education in Africa,* Nairobi,: East African Publishing House, pp. 197–208.

Perren, G.E. (ed.), (1979): *The mother tongue and other languages in education.* London: CILT.

Paulston, B., (1986): 'Linguistic consequences of ethnicity and nationalism in multilingual settings', in Spolsky (ed.), pp. 177–52.

Phillipson, R., Skutnabb-Kangas, T. and Africa, H., (1986): 'Namibian Educational language planning: English for liberation or neo-colonialism? in Spolsky, B. (ed.), pp. 77–95.

Platt, J.T., (1977): 'The sub-varieties of Singapore English', in Crewe (ed.), pp. 83–93.

Platt, J.T., (1980): 'Varieties and functions of English in Singapore and Malaysia', *EWW* vol. 1, 1, pp. 97–121.

Platt, J., Weber, H. and Ho, M. (1984): *The new Englishes. RKP.*

Polomé, E.C., (1982): 'Sociolinguistically oriented language surveys: reflections on the survey of language use and language teaching in Eastern Africa', *Language in Society* vol. 2, 2, pp. 265–83.

Poon, S.K., (1978): An Investigation of the Language Difficulties Experienced in Hong Kong Primary School Leavers in Learning Mathematics through the medium of English. Unpublished M. Phil thesis, University of Hong Kong.

Povey, J. (ed.), (1980): *Language policy and language teaching. Essays in honour of Clifford Prator.* Culver City, C.A.: English Language Services.

Prator, C., (1968): 'The British heresy in TESL', in Fishman *et al.* (eds), pp. 459–76.

Pride, J.B., (1978): 'Communicative Needs in the Use and Learning of English', *Indian Journal of Applied Linguistics,* vol. 4, 2, pp. 1–36.

Pride, J.B. (ed.), (1979a): *Sociolinguistic aspects of language learning and teaching.* London: Oxford University Press.

Pride, J.B., (1979b): 'Communicative needs in the use and learning of English', in Richards, J. (ed.), *New Varieties of English.* RELC Singapore pp. 33–72.

Pride, J.B. (ed.), (1982a): *New Englishes.* Rowley, Mass: Newbury House.

Pride, J.B. (ed.), (1982b): 'Language for the Third World universities.' *Indian Journal of Applied Linguistics,* August 1982.

Pride, J.B. and Holmes, J. (eds), (1972): *Sociolinguistics.* Harmondsworth: Penguin.

Quinn, T.J., (1980a): 'New directions for school language study', in Christie, F. and Rothery, J. (eds), *Varieties of language and language teaching,* Melbourne: Horwood Language Centre, University of Melbourne, ALAA Occasional Papers, 4, pp. 59–71.

Quinn, T.J., (1980b): Establishing a threshold-level concept for community language teaching in Australia. Paper presented at National Congress of Modern Language Teaching Associations, Sydney.

Quirk, R., Greenbaum, S, Leech, G. and Svartvik, J., (1972): *A Grammar of Contemporary English.* London: Longman.

Quirk, R., (1981): 'International communication and the concept of Nuclear English', in Smith, L.E. (ed.), pp. 151–65.

Quirk, R. and Widdowson, H. (eds), (1986): *English in the world.* Cambridge, Cambridge University Press.

Rabin, C., (1971): 'A tentative classification of language planning aims', in Rubin and Jernudd (eds.), pp. 277–79.

Rhodes, J., (1977): *Linguistic diversity and language belief in Kenya: the general position of Swahili.* Syracuse: Maxwell school of citizenship and public affairs, foreign and comparative studies. African Series 26.

Rice, F.A. (ed.), (1962). *Study of the role of second languages.* Washington, D.C.: Center for Applied Linguistics.

Richards, J.C., (1979a): 'The Dynamics of English as an international foreign, second and auxiliary language', in Richards, J.C. (ed.) *Form and function in second language learning.* Singapore: RELC. RELC Occasional Papers, 7, pp. 18–38.

Richards, J.C. (ed.), (1979): *New varieties of English: issues and approaches.* Singapore: RELC. RELC Occasional Papers, 8.

Ridler, N. and Pons-Ridler, S., (1984): 'Language economics: a case study of French', *JMMD,* vol. 5, 1, pp. 57–63.

Roe, P., (1977): *Scientific text.* Birmingham University of Birmingham. ELR Monographs 4.

Rogers, E.M. and Shoemaker, F.F., (1971): *Communication of innovations: a cross-cultural approach.* New York: Free Press of Glencoe.

Rogers, E.M., Eveland, J.D. and Klepper, C., (1977): *The innovation process in public organisations, a report to the National Science Foundation.* Ann Arbor: University of Michigan.

Rogers, J., (1969): 'Why not abandon English teaching in the elementary school?' *Ethiopian Journal of Education,* Addis Ababa: Faculty of Education, Haile Sellassie I University. vol. 3, 1, pp. 24–31.

Rosen, H. and Burgess, T., (1980): *Language and dialects of London school children.* London: Ward Lock Educational.

Rubin, J., (1971): 'Evaluation and language planning', in Rubin and Jernudd (eds), pp. 217–52.

Rubin, J., (1977): 'Language planning: discussion of some current issues', in Rubin and Shuy (eds), pp. 1–10.

Rubin, J., (1977): 'Bilingual education and language planning', in Kennedy C.J. (ed.), (1984).

Rubin, J., and Jernudd, B.H. (eds), (1971): *Can language be planned?* Honolulu: University of Hawaii, East–West Center.

Rubin, J., Jernudd, B.H., Das Gupta, J., Fishman, J.A. and Ferguson, C. (eds), (1977): *Language planning processes*. The Hague: Mouton.

Rubin, J. and Shuy, R. (eds), (1973): *Language planning: current issues and research*. Washington D.C.: Georgetown University Press.

Sandell, L., (1982): *English language in Sudan: a history of its teaching and politics*. New York: Ithaca Press.

Schmied, J., (1985): 'Attitudes towards English in Tanzania', *EWW*, vol. 6, 2, pp. 237–70.

Schumann, J.H., (1976): 'Second language acquisition research: getting a more global look at the learner', in Brown, H.D. (ed.), *Papers in Second Language Acquisition*. Ann Arbor: Language Learning, pp. 15–28.

Schumann, J.H., (1978): 'The relationship of pidginization, creolization and decreolization in second language acquisition', *Language Learning* vol. 28, pp. 367–79.

Scotton, C., (1972): *Choosing a lingua franca in an African capital*. Edmonton, Canada, and Champaign, IL: Linguistic Research Associates.

Scotton, C., (1978): 'Language in East Africa: linguistic patterns and political ideologies', in Fishman (ed.). pp. 719–59.

Serpell, R., (1980): 'Linguistic flexibility in urban Zambian school children', in Teller, V. and White, S.J. (eds), *Studies in child languages and bilingualism*. Annals of the New York Academy of Sciences, vol. 345, pp. 97–119.

Serpell, R., (1982): 'Learning to say it better', in Pride (ed.), pp. 100–118.

Sharma, R., (1973): The reading skills of grade-three children. Lusaka: Ministry of Education and Culture. Psychological Service Report 2/1973, (mimeo.).

Sharma, R., (1974): The grade-seven composite examination: a critique. Lusaka: Ministry of Education and Culture. Psychological Service Reports 2/1974, (mimeo.).

Shaw, W., (1981): 'Asian student attitudes towards English', in Smith, L.E. (ed.).

Siu, P.K., Cheng, S.C., Hinton, A., Cheng, Y.N., Lo, L.F., Luk, H.K., Chung, Y.P. and Hsai, Y.S., (1979): *The Effects of the medium of instruction on student cognitive development and academic achievement*. Hong Kong: School of Education, Chinese University of Hong Kong.

Skutnabb-Kanagas, T., (1986): 'Who wants to change what and why', in Spolsky (ed.), pp. 153–81.

Slobin, D.I., (1972): 'Seven questions about language development', in Dodwell, P.C. (ed.), *New horizons in psychology 2*. Harmondsworth: Penguin, pp. 185–208.

Smith, A.H. and Quirk, R., (1959): *The Teaching of English*. London: Secker and Warburg.

Smith, L.E., (1976): 'English as an international auxiliary language', *RELC Journal* Vol. 7, 2, pp. 38–53.

Smith, L.E. (ed.), (1981): *English for cross-cultural communication*. Hong Kong: Macmillan.

Smith, L.E. (ed.), (1983). *Readings in English as an international language*. London: Prentice Hall.

Smolicz, J.J., (1979a): *Culture and education in a plural society*. Canberra: The Curriculum Development Center.

Smolicz, J.J., (1979b): Review of education for a multicultural society. Report of the Committee on Multicultural Education to The Schools Commission (mimeo.).

Soni, D.C., (1977): 'The spoken and unspoken word in rural communication: a view-point from India' *Ideas and Action* vol. 115. Rome: FAO.

Spencer, J. (ed.), (1963): *Language in Africa*. Cambridge: Cambridge University Press.

Spencer, J., (1971): *The English language in West Africa*. London: Longman.

Spencer, J., (1980): Economic and technological implications for language planning. Paper presented at English strategies for Namibia seminar, Lusaka.

Spolsky, B., (1978): *Educational linguistics*. Rowley, Mass.: Newbury House.

Spolsky, B.(ed.), (1986): *Language and education in multilingual settings*. Clevedon, Avon: Multilingual Matters 25.

Spolsky, B. and Cooper, R. (eds), (1977): *Frontiers of bilingual education*. Rowley, Mass.: Newbury House.

Spolsky, B. and Cooper, R. (eds), (1978): *Case studies in bilingual education*. Rowley, Mass.: Newbury House.

Spolsky, B., Engelbrecht, G. and Ortez, L., (1983): 'Religious, political and educational factors in the development of biliteracy in the Kingdom of Tonga', *JMMD*, vol. 4, 6, pp. 459–70.

Stern, H., (1981): 'Unity and diversity in L2 teaching', in Smith, L.E. (ed.), pp. 57–73.

St. Clair, R. and Eiseman, J., (1981): 'The politics of teaching English as a foreign language', *ITL*, vol. 51, pp. 21–36.

Strevens, P., (1969): 'Where has all the money gone? The Need for Cost-Effectiveness Studies in the Teaching of Foreign Languages', in Strevens, P., (1978): *New orientations in the teaching of English*. Oxford: Oxford University Press, 166–71.

Strevens, P., (1981): 'What is "structure English"?' *RELC Journal,* vol. 12, 2, pp. 1–9.

Stubbs, M., (1980): *Language and literacy.* London: Routledge and Kegan Paul. *Survey of language use and language teaching in Eastern Africa,* various eds), 5 vol. series. (1972–1980). London: Oxford University Press.

Swain, M., (1979): Future directions in second language research. Manuscript discussed at TESOL Institute, Los Angeles.

Swales, J, and Dudley-Evans T. (1980): Study modes and students from the middle East. London: British Council. ELT documents 109. pp. 91–103.

Swales, A. and Mustafa, H. (eds) (1984): *English for specific purposes in the Arab world.* Birmingham: University of Aston.

Tadadjeu, M., (1980): *A model for functional trilingual education planning in Africa.* Paris: UNESCO, Division of structures, content, methods and techniques of education.

Taft, R., (1980): 'Review of J.J. Smolicz *Culture and Education in a Plural Society', The Australian,* April 30th, 1980, p18.

Taiwo, O., (1979): 'The problems of beginning and developmental reading in Nigerian primary schools', in Feitelson, D. (ed.), *Mother tongue or second language?* Newark, Delaware: International Reading Association.

Tam, P.T.K. (1980): 'A survey of the language mode used in teaching junior forms in Anglo-Chinese secondary schools in Hong Kong' *RELC Journal,* vol. 2, 1, pp. 43–60.

Taylor, A., (1981): 'Language policy in Papua New Guinea', *Linguistic Reporter,* vol. 24, 1, pp. 1 and 8–9.

Thawe, L., (1984): Improving the teaching of communicative skills in the Malawi primary school. Birmingham: University of Birmingham. B Phil dissertation.

Theroux, P., (1977): 'The flower of Malaya', in *The Consul's File.* London: Hamish Hamilton.

Thorburn, T., (1971): 'Cost benefit analysis in language planning', in Rubin and Jernudd (eds), pp. 253–62.

Thornton, E., (1980): A needs analysis for a degree programme in Tunisia. Los Angeles: UCLA. MA thesis.

Tickoo, M, (ed.), (1986): Language in learning. Singapore: RELC. RELC anthology series 16.

Todd, L., (1974): *Pidgins and creoles.* London: Routledge and Kegan Paul.

Todd, L., (1982): 'English in Cameroon', in Pride, J. (ed.), *New Englishes.* pp. 119–37.

Tollefson, J.W., (1980): 'Types of language contact and the acquisition of language', *Language Sciences,* vol. 2, pp. 231–45.

Tollefson, J.W., (1981): 'Centralised and decentralised language planning', *LPLP,* vol. 5, 2, pp. 175–88.

Tongue, R.K., (1974): *The English of Singapore and Malaysia.* Singapore: Eastern Universities Press.

Tongue, R. and Gibbons, J., (1982): 'Structural syllabuses and the young beginners', *Applied Linguistics,* vol 3, pp. 60–69.

Tosi, A., (1979): 'Mother-tongue teaching for the children of migrants', *Language Teaching,* vol. 12, 4, pp. 213–31.

Tosi, A., (1983): *Immigration and bilingual education.* Oxford: Pergamon Press.

Toukamaa, P., (1982): Semilingualism and the education of immigrant children: the Scandinavan research and debate. Paper presented at the 17th Regional Seminar, RELC, Singapore.

Trappes-Lomax, H., Basha, R. and Moha, Y. (eds), (1982): *Changing language media.* Tanzania: University of Dar-es-Salaam.

Treffgarne, C., (1981): 'The World Bank on language education: a lot more could be done', *Comparative Education,* vol. 17, 2, pp. 163–171.

Trudgill, P. and Hannah, J., (1982): *International English.* London: Arnold.

Tucker, G.R., (1977): 'Can a second language be taught?' in Douglas-Brown, H., Yorio, C.A. and Crymes, R.H. (eds), *On TESOL '77: Teaching and learning English as a second language.* Washington, D.C.: TESOL, pp. 14–30.

Ubahakwe, E., (1973): *Language education in Nigeria.* Nsukka: GUDIMAC Series, No. 2.

Ubahakwe, E., (1979): *Varieties and functions of English in Nigeria.* Ibadan: African Universities Press.

Underhill, N., (1981): 'Your needs are different from my needs' *World Language English.* vol. 1, 1, pp. 15–24.

UNESCO (1953). *The use of vernacular languages in education.* Paris: UNESCO. Monographs on fundamental education 8.

Ure, J., (1981): 'Mother-tongue education and minority languages: a question of values and costs', *JMMD,* vol. 2, 4, pp. 303–08.

Ure, J. and Ellis, J., (1984): *Patterns and meanings.* London: Allen and Unwin.

Vaillancourt, F., (1983): 'The economics of language and language planning', *LPLP,* vol. 7, 2, pp. 162–78.

van Ek, J.A., (1976): *The threshold level for modern language learning in schools.* London: Longman.

van Ek, J.A., and Alexander, L.G., (1977): *Waystage.* Strasbourg: Council of Europe.

Wafer, J., (1981): *Planning for Australian Aboriginal languages: a preliminary guide to resources and concepts.* Alice Springs: Institute for Aboriginal Development.

Waters, A., (ed.), (1982): *Issues in ESP*. London: Prentice Hall. Lancaster practical papers in English language education, vol 5.

Weinreich, B. (1953). *Language in Contact: Findings and Problems*. The Hague: Mouton.

Weinstein, B., (1980): 'Language planning in francophone Africa', *LPLP*, vol. 4, 1, pp. 55–77.

Weinstein, B., (1983): *The civil tongue: political consequences of language choices*. London: Longman.

Whiteley, W.H., (1971): 'Some factors influencing language policies in Eastern Africa', in Rubin, J. and Jernudd, B.H. (eds), pp. 141–158.

Whiteley, W.H. (ed.), (1971): *Language use and social change*. London: Oxford University Press.

Whiteley, W., (1973): Sociolinguistic surveys at the national level. In Kennedy (ed.), (1984), pp. 68–79.

Whiteley, W.H. (ed.), (1974): *Language in Kenya*. London: Oxford University Press.

Widdowson, H.G., (1968): 'The teaching of English through science', in Dakin, J., Tiffen, B., and Widdowson, H. (eds), *Language in education*. London: Oxford University Press, pp. 115–175.

Widdowson, H., (1982): 'What do we mean by International language?' in Brumfit, C.(ed.), pp. 9–14.

Widdowson, H., (1983): *Learning purpose and language use*. Oxford: Oxford University Press.

Wigzell, R., (1983): 'The role and status of English as a subject in the Zambian English-medium context', London: British Council ELT documents 116, pp. 1–14.

Wilkins, D.A., (1976): *Notional syllabuses*. London: Oxford University Press.

Williams, R. and Dallas, D., (1984): 'Aspects of vocabulary', in Alderson, C. and Urquhart, S, (eds), *Reading in a foreign language*, pp. 199–212.

Williamson, K., (1976): 'The Rivers readers project', in Bamgbose, A. (ed.), pp. 135–53.

Wober, M., (1975): *Psychology in Africa*. London: International African Institute.

Wong, I., (1982): Native-speaker English for the Third World today? in Pride J.B. (ed.), New Englishes, pp. 259–86.

Wood, R. (ed.), (1979): 'National language planning and treatment'. *Word*, vol. 30, 1 and 2, (special issue).

Wurm, S.A., (1968): 'Papua New Guinea nationhood: the problem of a national language. Language problems of developing nations', in Fishman, J.A., Ferguson, C.A. and Das Gupta, J. (eds), pp. 345–63.

Yap, A. (ed.), (1978): *Language education in multilingual societies*. Singapore: Singapore University Press. RELC Anthology series 4.

Young, R, and Lee, S., (1985): 'EFL curriculum innovation and teachers' attitudes', *On TESOL '84*, Washington, TESOL.

Zughoul, M. and Hussein, R., (1985): 'English for higher education in the Arab World', *ESP Journal*, vol. 4, 2, pp. 133–53.